The Heroic Battle of Aintab

Kevork Baboian

originally edited and prepared for publication by
Kevork. A. Sarafian

translated with a new introduction by
Ümit Kurt

Gomidas Institute
London

Photo credits: A. Gesar, Այնթապի Քոյամարդը, [Ayntabi Koyamardu or The Self-Defense of Aintab] (Boston: Hairenik, 1945).

The Near East Relief Collection photographs Courtesy of Special Collections, Fine Arts Library, Harvard University

"The Heroic Battle of Aintab" [Այնթապի Հերոսամարտը or Ayntabi Herosamardu] by Kevork Baboian originally appeared in Պատմութիւն Անթէպի Հայոց [Badmoutiun Antebi Hayots - *History of Anteb Armenians*], Kevork A. Sarafian (comp. and ed.), Vol. II (LA: Union of Aintab Armenians, 1953).

This publication has been made possible with the generous support of the Armenian Aintabtzy Cultural Association (Los Angeles) and the M. Victoria Karagozian Kazan and Henry S. Khanzadian Endowment, Armenian Studies Program, California State University, Fresno.

For more information about this book and related documentation, please visit *www.gomidas.org*

ISBN 978-1-909382-41-1

For further details please contact:
Gomidas Institute
42 Blythe Rd.
London, W14 0HA
England
Email: *info@gomidas.org*
Web: *www.gomidas.org*

To my two mothers: Ayyuş and Hanım

CONTENTS

Appendix

Maps

Photographs

Acknowledgements

This project depended upon many kinds of support. I am very appreciative of the all the individuals and institutions that helped me make this work possible.

First and foremost, I offer my gratitude to Union of Armenians of Aintab in Los Angeles; Barlow Der Mugrdechian (Armenian Studies Program, Fresno); Calouste Gulbenkian Foundation and the Gomidas Institute for their support. Simply put, this book would not have been possible without them. It has been an honor to complete this project with their generous support.

Mark Chenian has strongly supported this project from the very beginning and encouraged me a lot to publish it. I truly appreciate his adamant push.

Varak Ketsamanian deserves here a special note of gratitude who gave his precious time for reading my translation line by line, correcting and editing it meticulously. Without his priceless support, knowledge and help, this book would never have been accomplished. Along with Emre Can Dağlıoğlu and Yektan Türkyılmaz, Varak has given me incredible countenance and intellectual stimulation.

There are a few people who deserve special thanks here. This book would not have been possible without Murad Uçaner's unprecedented help and support. As a local historian and novelist from Aintab, his deep knowledge made an enormous contribution to this work.

I am also grateful to Nazar Nazarian Family in New Jersey. Another special thanks goes out to my family (Hasan, Hanım, Hamit, Dilek, Figen, Ergün and my little princes Deniz Çağan and Ali Aras).

I am thankful for a number of archivists, institutions, scholars, and librarians: Megerditch Basma, Boris Adjemian from *Nubarian Library* (La Bibliothèque Nubarian); officers of Armenian National Archives, British National Archives, Armenian National Library, Prime Ministry Ottoman and Republic Archives; Marc A. Mamigonian from the National Association for Armenian Studies and Research (NAASR); Antranig Dakessian from Haigazian University Library.

Last but not least, I would like to thank Ara Sarafian, the director of the Gomidas Institute in London. He spared his valuable time to read various drafts of my translation and shared his considerations and critiques with me that greatly enriched this work. His particular interest and constant support made this book come into existence.

As a native son of Aintab and having spent four years for this translation, I do not know how to express my happiness to be an intermediary for conveying the critic history of my compatriots, Armenians of Aintab, who really constituted the major actor of this city's history. And this reality will never be erased from the memory of Aintab and his people. If this book helps keep this memory alive, lucky me!

Ümit Kurt
29 November 2017

Introduction

The Ottoman Empire entered World War I (WWI) on the side of the Central Powers in October 1914. It remained in the world conflict until 30 October 1918, when it signed the Armistice of Mudros with the Allied Powers. This pact marked the defeat of the Ottoman Empire in WWI. Under the terms of the armistice, the Ottoman government surrendered its remaining garrisons in Hejaz, Yemen, Syria, Mesopotamia, Tripolitania and Cyrenaica, and the Allies were allowed to occupy the Dardanelles and Bosporus Straits, Batumi, and the Taurus tunnel system. In case of disorder, the Allied powers also reserved the right to occupy the six Armenian provinces in the east and seize "any strategic points" that might be threatening them. The Ottoman army was entirely demobilized, and Turkish ports, railways, and other strategic points were made available for the use of the Allies – mostly the British and the French.

After the disastrous conclusion of WWI, the Union and Progress Party government (CUP) resigned and its members fled on 8 October 1918. The rest of the party, meeting at its final congress, dissolved the CUP a month later on 4 November 1918.[1] The first new cabinet was established by Ahmet İzzet Pasha on 11 October 1918, and from then until 4 November 1922 eleven governments in all held office.[2] Among the first actions of these governments were the initiation of legal proceedings against the members of the CUP,[3] and the granting of permission for surviving Armenians to return to their towns and villages. The return of Armenians also led to new issues, such as the return of Armenian women, children in Muslim households, and the restitution of Armenian properties to their rightful owners.

The CUP had already granted limited permission for the return of surviving Armenian deportees at the beginning of 1918. However, a few weeks before the Armistice of Mudros, on 21 October 1918, orders were sent to the relevant provinces allowing the return of all deported Armenians and Greeks.[4] On the same date, the Ministry of Interior took an important decision concerning converts and instructed that individuals who had been converted to Islam by force, oppression or fear should be free to return to their religion of choice.[5] On the following day,

22 October, the authorities considered removing travel restrictions and asked whether any harm might come of it.[6] The following day, they requested that the necessary steps were taken to allow Armenian and Greek deportees to return to their homes safely.[7] On that same date, according to a telegraphic circular sent by the İskan-ı Aşair ve Muhacirin Müdüriyeti (Directorate for the Settlement of Tribes and Immigrants; IAMM), people who had been deported during WWI and wanted to return to their hometowns were allowed to do so. The provincial authorities were ordered to provide the necessary means for their return in a secure way.[8]

British Occupation (December 1918 to October 1919)

In the Treaty of Mudros, the district of Aintab, modern day Gaziantep (fifty-five kilometers to the west of the Euphrates and forty-five kilometers to the north of the modern Turkish-Syrian border), was not listed as an area of Allied occupation. However, according to the seventh article of the Treaty, the Allies reserved the right to control certain territories in case their armies were threatened. For that reason, British forces occupied Kilis and Aintab in December 1918. Already in the Sykes-Picot agreement, concluded secretly on 19 May 1916, France and Britain had carved the Arab territories of the former Ottoman Empire into spheres of influence. Under this agreement, the Syrian coast and modern-day Lebanon went to France, and Britain assumed direct control over central and southern Mesopotamia.

To better understand the British occupation of Aintab, it is crucial to consider district governor Celal Kadri (Barlas) Bey's coded telegram to the Ministry of Interior on 28 December 1918. In his telegram, Celal Kadri reported that Aintab-Armenians in Aleppo had appealed to the British commander for their safety, as they feared Muslim attacks upon their return to Aintab.[9] Armenians informed the British commander that unless British forces occupied Aintab, they would not return.[10] Heeding this request, the British commander sent cavalry units stationed in Kilis to Aintab.

Even though Celal Kadri had informed Major Mills, the liaison officer and commander appointed by Sir Mark Sykes (military commander), that public order was assured in the city and that there was no reason for the involvement of British soldiers—which would have been against the terms of the armistice—the general told him that British soldiers would

Aintab - panorama postcard

not interfere in any matters and that their sole intention was to ensure public order in cooperation with the local government.[11] On 18 December 1918, the British entered Aintab to supposedly procure food for their horses and ensure the security of their forces in Aleppo.[12] Central Turkey College (American College) was used as the headquarters for the British troops.[13]

On the next day, Sir Mark Sykes visited the Protestant chapel, the main Armenian Apostolic church, and the Vartanian and Atenagan school buildings, along with Prof. Lutfi Hodja Levonian.[14] On the way, they noticed half-ruined buildings festooned with graffiti such as, "We have desecrated this Protestant Chapel and turned it into a wasteland, we turned this Catholic Church into a stable and we turned that Armenian Church into a barrack and a wasteland."[15] Sykes reported this situation to General Clayton, stating that "Turks systematically demolished empty Armenian houses."[16] On 25 December, regiments of the Indian Cavalry entered Aintab.[17] They encamped around the college. Afterwards, *Antep Kalesi* (Aintab Fortress) and the *Belediye Hanı* (the Municipality Inn) were occupied by the British forces.[18]

The British occupation enraged the Muslim community, who claimed that not a single event endangering the safety of the returning Armenians had occurred in Aintab, and that the occupation was therefore illegal. However, the well-organized British forces quelled this dissent. Aside from restoring peace, Sir Mark Sykes dealt with five main issues: 1) the collection of documents regarding deportations; 2) disarming Muslims in Aintab and its surroundings; 3) the arrest of the ex-CUP members who took part in the deportation and plunder; 4) the return of Armenians; 5) restitution of seized Armenian goods, commodities, and properties.[19]

Collection of Documents Regarding Deportations

As soon as the British arrived in Aintab, they demanded all documents related to the deportations of Armenians.[20] In February 1919, a British officer visited Celal Kadri Bey to "ask him to turn over all the telegrams and letters exchanged between the *vilayet* [province] and the Imperial Ministry on the one hand and the *mutesarifat* [district governorship] on the other in the period running from 1330 [1914] to 1334 [1918]."[21] Confronted with mayor Sheikh Mustafa Effendi's refusal to comply, the British had the building surrounded and seized the relevant documents. According to official Turkish historiography, the British troops in Aintab sent those records to Egypt.[22] This procedure was implemented after the dispatch of "a circular telegram from the head of the telegraph office in Diyarbekir instructing the agencies under his jurisdiction to destroy the originals of obsolete documents."[23]

The British occupation forces seized control of all official correspondence in January 1919. Major Mills confiscated the records at the governorate, raided the post office, and appointed Haykazun Levonian as censor.[24]

The Disarming Muslims in Aintab and its Surroundings

In late January 1919, Turks from Adana, İçel, Marash, Aintab, İskenderun, Beylan, Rithanin and Antakya who resided in Istanbul decided to form a committee in order to provide support for resistance organizations composed of former CUP members in their hometowns.[25] Given what they considered to amount to British and French invasions, they felt that the creation of such a committee was an urgent matter. The aim of this committee was to make every effort, before the public at home and abroad, and insist on their absolute right to retain the above-mentioned towns and their surroundings under Turkish authority. Delegates were sent to the above districts from Istanbul, but the committee thought it first advisable to prepare public opinion in these regions and undertake the necessary steps to open new regional branches.[26] Therefore, Aintab, as well as Marash and Urfa became centers of petty conspiracies organized by former local CUP members who

British captain in doorway beside stockpile of firearms and ammunition as a result of disarming Muslims in the city.

received support from this committee. At the same time, in order to prevent this organization from gaining public support and arming itself in Aintab, Major Mills ordered the disarmament of the Muslim population in late February 1919.[27]

General MacAndrew, commander of the British occupation forces, announced that the notables of Aintab would be held responsible for even the slightest disturbances and took extraordinary measures against the conspiratorial activities of former CUP members in the city.[28] He was also convinced that newspapers published in Aintab had collaborated with such conspirators.[29] He therefore summoned prominent local figures—including Daizâde Ahmed Hurşid Effendi,[30] Doctor Hamid Bey, reputable young literati, Muslim judges, accountants, and the mayor of Aintab— to Central Turkey College, where he conveyed his message that threats to public order in and outside of the city should not be tolerated.[31] Following a British decision, Celal Kadri ordered the newspaper *Antep Haberleri* (Aintab News) published by Hüseyin Cemil Bey and Ali Kemal Göğüş (two former members of Aintab's CUP club) to be shut down in February 1919 for spreading anti-British sentiments.[32]

The Arrest of Former CUP Members

After the British occupation, prominent members of Aintab's CUP club, such as Taşçızâde Abdullah, Mennanzâde Mustafa Effendi, Kethüdazâde

Hüseyin Cemil Bey, Hafız Şahin Effendi, Kurd Hacı Osman Agha, and Mamat Ağazâde Ali Effendi—all of whom played an active role in the deportation and dispossession of Armenians—founded *Müdafaa-i Hukuk Cemiyeti* (Society for the Defense of Rights) as a resistance front to foment discontent within the Muslim populace.[33] Thereupon, Major Mills began arresting members of Müdafaa-i Hukuk Cemiyeti and other masterminds of the deportation.[34] Accordingly, Besim Bey, the aforementioned provincial treasurer; Hakkı Bey, clerk of *Evkaf*; Eyüp Sabri Bey, title deed officer and influential CUP member; Mennanzâde Mustafa Effendi; Kurd Hadji Halil Bey; *Kasap* (Butcher) İncozâde; Taşçızâde Abdullah Effendi; and Hüseyin Cemil Bey were taken into custody by orders of General MacAndrew and Major Mills, with the cooperation of Celal Bey, in January 1919.[35] These people were held at the college and interrogated by Major Mills. They were charged with "vandalizing Armenian houses while they were sent away, committing murder and prospering on Armenian wealth."[36] For instance, Major Mills openly explained to Eyüp Sabri Bey the reasons for his arrest:

> You were present here during the deportation of Armenians and you sent them away. The lives and goods of those helpless people were under attack on the roads. You caused all of this and you are still involved in certain activities that would violate order and peace in this place. That is why you are a villain. You will be kept far away until a peace treaty is signed.[37]

Ultimately, General MacAndrews transferred these arrested men to Aleppo on 23 January 1919.[38] Later, Dişikırıkzâde Halil Agha, Sedat Bey,[39] Patpatzâde Nuri Bey, Abdülvehhab Bey, Celil Bey, Sabri Bey, Hadji Mehmet Agha, Hadji Süleyman Effendi, Sergeant Yusuf, and Hüseyin Bey[40]—all active members of the dismantled local CUP club—were also sent to Aleppo.[41] On 2 March, they were exiled to Egypt.[42] In the meantime, British forces continued to search for Ali Cenani Bey, another perpetrator and a former deputy from Aintab. At the time, he was one of the most influential figures of the Kemalist movement in Aintab and had formed a secret militia corps after the armistice.[43] Ali Cenani Bey was later exiled to Malta in 1919 along with other leading CUP members.

Return of Armenians to Aintab

After disarming the Muslim population and arresting individuals responsible for deportations and looting, the most urgent task of the

Armenian homes destroyed in Aintab after the 1915 deportations.

British forces was to facilitate the return of Armenians who survived the genocide and to find and deliver Armenian women and children who had been abducted and enslaved in Muslim households to their families or relatives. When British forces assumed military control of Aleppo, this matter was specifically addressed in a twelve-article memorandum issued by General Edmund Allenby, commander of the Allied forces in the Near East, to the Sixth Army Command of the Ottoman Empire. In fact, Article 6 stipulated that Allenby reserved the right to send Armenian refugees home and that their houses, lands, and other possessions should be "immediately restored" to them.[44]

Despite the anticipation and pleas, two major obstacles prevented immediate repatriation: the unstable political-military situation in the hinterlands and the lack of adequate transportation. Significantly, by its Circular No. 69-9 of 18 December 1918, the Ottoman government agreed to defray the repatriation expenses but subsequently failed to fulfill its obligation.[45] In early January 1919, the Ottoman government "issued a decree of repatriation" amounting to "a permission for the Armenians to return to their homes," but as reported by the special correspondent of the London *Times*,

> Many of them find their property occupied. Before and even for some time after the armistice, a Commission was appointed by the [Ottoman] Ministry of the Interior providing for the settlement of Mohamedans [Muslims] from Thrace and

> Macedonia on the land of the expatriated Armenians. These Moslem emigrants will presumably be evicted, but the authority of the Central Government is a dead letter in the provinces. The local officials are obstructive, and the process will not be easy until we have troops on the spot. Some time must pass before there is any security for Armenians in the outlying districts.[46]

Sir Mark Sykes expressed a similar view as he underscored the urgency of repatriation: "Indications show that unless steps are taken by the Entente to supervise repatriation, Turks will grow more obstructive, as they know that while Armenians remain exiled, birth rate is diminished and death rate has increased."[47] He accordingly offered a plan "to organize, cover and protect the repatriation of deported Armenians."[48] Notwithstanding these difficulties, some Armenians, including Aintab-Armenians, elected to return to Cilicia in late 1918. The Kilis refugees were the first to return.[49] In January 1919, other convoys of Armenians from Dörtyol, Mersin, Tarsus, Alexandretta, Kırık Han, Hacin, and Toprakkalı began returning by train with the help and organization of the Armenian National Union (hereafter ANU) in Aleppo.[50] Moreover, the Ministry of Interior requested the Ministry of War to send 2,000 liras as *Seferberlik Tahsisatı* (Mobilization Allowance) for Aintab-Armenians in order to compensate their return expenses.[51]

In January 1919, the Allied High Command decided to repatriate all Armenian deportees from camps in Syria and Palestine to their hometowns. The majority of these survivors were natives of Cilicia. Among the deportees concentrated in Aleppo, some 6,000 came from Aintab and 3,000 from Kilis.[52] In early February, the process of repatriation intensified in Aintab.[53] According to statistics provided by the Ecumenical and Armenian Patriarchates early in 1919, there were 430 Armenians who had returned to Aintab.[54] On 12 May 1919, Clouscard, Director of the Central Service of Armenian Repatriation, issued another order for the repatriation of Marash and Aintab refugees.[55] By 31 May 1919, 4,221 Armenians had returned to Aintab.[56] Between 1 January and 20 July 1919, a total of 5,607 Armenian refugees repatriated to Aintab.[57]

However, the exact number of Aintab-Armenians who returned to their homeland is unknown. There are various contradictory figures regarding the number who returned, from both Armenian and Turkish sources. In 1914 Aintab had an Armenian population that probably numbered somewhere between 36,000 and 40,000 people.[58] It is estimated that the number of Armenians deported from Aintab was approximately 32,000. Based on Armenian sources, overall, 18,000 Armenian survivors managed to return to Aintab by the end of 1919.[59] Of these, 1,500 were Armenians from Sivas, Gürün, and Kayseri, as well as 600–700 Armenian orphans from various places who returned to Aintab.[60] In 1920, these estimations were very important for the ANU Committee of Aintab, as it used the numbers to calculate the distribution of food rations as equally and economically as possible.[61]

From the British to the French: Occupation in Aintab

As of July 1919, the British military authorities decelerated the restitution process and arrests of those who perpetrated and profited from the Armenian massacres.[62] Jagadamard (Ճակատամարտ), an Armenian daily published in Istanbul, reported that the Armenian populations in Aintab and Kilis were in a desperate situation. Letters of complaint from Armenians addressed to local authorities were left unanswered.[63] Conversely, the Muslim population of Aintab, particularly local elites, was rather content with this situation. Turks were redistributing arms in Aintab and Kilis, and armed bands were created throughout the territory to resist the occupation.[64]

British military forces no longer searched Muslim houses and mostly focused on Armenian homes. If anyone was caught with a gun, they would be sentenced to prison.[65] Around the same time, a new nationalist resistance movement under the leadership of Mustafa Kemal began to emerge in various cities of the interior provinces, gathering all opposition forces to unite against foreign occupation. Mustafa Kemal organized a conference in Sivas on 4 September 1919, which resulted in the formation of *Anadolu ve Rumeli Müdafaai Hukuk Cemiyeti* (Society for the Defense of the Rights of Anatolia and Thrace). Afterwards, various defense fronts, resistance organizations, and irregular forces, known as *Kuvayı Milliye* (National Forces), emerged in Anatolia and Thrace. Although the British were aware of this movement in Aintab, they chose to overlook it.[66]

This new attitude resulted from a shift in British imperial policy. In order to attain oil resources in Mosul, the British reversed the Sykes-Picot Agreement and ceded Aintab, Marash, and Urfa to the French by signing the *Syrian Agreement* with the French government on 15 September

1919.[67] Thereafter, the British adopted a more lenient policy towards the Muslim population. For instance, Major Mills' first act after the Syrian Agreement was to stop the censorship of the telegrams of Mustafa Kemal, thus facilitating Kemal's communication with the nationalist movement and resistance forces.[68] The British began withdrawing from Aintab on 29 October, leaving the fate of Armenians in the hands of the French.[69] They also returned confiscated weapons to Muslims.[70] By 29 October 1919, two mounted French troops and a battalion of volunteers from the Armenian Legion, a special corps—formerly a *Légion d'Orient* (Eastern Legion)—in the French Army of the Levant, arrived in Aintab and were welcomed by Armenians.[71]

Sabri Bey, deputy to the district governor of Aintab, officially protested the French occupation on 1 November.[72] The reoccupation of the Cilicia region by French forces had indeed caused deep resentment among local Muslims.[73] The Muslim population, especially local elites, was extremely distraught with the presence of Armenian soldiers within the French forces, as well as the large number of Armenians who had returned. Muslims expressed their reaction to the occupation and the support of Armenians for it with the following menacing words: "İngiliz ve Fransız babalı deyyuslar, başınızdan onca şey geçti, hala akıllanmadınız (You, the progeny of the British and French, despite everything you have experienced, you have still not become wiser)."[74] The possibility that the French would restore Armenian properties to their rightful owners more systematically and thoroughly, and hold local notables involved in the genocide responsible for their actions led many frightened Muslim notables and inhabitants to support the nationalist movement, something they had been reluctant to do until the arrival of French and Armenian soldiers.[75] As historian Sabahattin Selek describes,

> A nouveau riche had emerged based on the purchase of Armenian properties for a song; the fortunes of the already established rich had become even larger. When the Great War ended with the defeat of the Ottoman Empire, the Turkish people from eastern and southeastern regions, which had been densely populated by Armenians, were faced with a terrifying threat. The common people were afraid of what Armenians would do in revenge,

> whereas local notables were not only concerned for their lives but also for their fortunes.[76]

Therefore, in the eyes of Aintab's Muslim population, the real force behind the French occupation were the Armenians, and the evidence for this was the French determination to expedite the restitution process.[77] Realizing that they would soon lose their fortunes, these elites agreed upon armed resistance with the foundation of the *Antep Heyet-i Merkeziye* (Aintab Central Committee) on 23 November 1919 and, more importantly, decided to provide economic and logistical support to Kemalist forces.[78] The president of the committee was Hocazâde Ferit Bey, and most of its members were local notables, civil and military bureaucratic elites who were former members of Aintab's CUP club.[79] These elites began working closely with the underground CUP movement, which somewhat cooperated with the Kemalist movement. Additionally, local elites and civil-military bureaucrats, who had been arrested and sent to Egypt during the British occupation, were either released or escaped from prison during the French siege. Most of these arrested men returned to Aintab and joined the national forces.[80]

Although the French military occupation was initially viewed as generally sympathetic to Aintab-Armenians, this became less so as the occupation progressed. Some reinforcements were sent to the city, but the High Command was unable or unwilling to undertake adequate offensive measures against the Turkish nationalists. As a result of the local Kemalist resistance, the French army was forced to retreat from Marash in early February and from Urfa in April 1920. After their withdrawal from Marash and Urfa, the French occupation forces started disarming the Armenian volunteers as part of a new (partial) appeasement policy, which would lead to an eventual rapprochement with Kemalist forces.

In the face of French occupation, local Kemalist forces instigated an armed struggle against French forces. The Turkish/Kemalist-French war in Aintab began on 1 April 1920, with Aintab-Armenians siding with the French. Until April the 1st, the situation in the city and its vicinity was volatile. The volatility had reached such an extent that a small spark would have ignited the gunpowder and start a war. French Colonel Andrea's battalion, which entered Aintab on 28 March 1920, had to deal with skirmishes against Turkish regular and irregular forces, and it halted for four days on the road to Kilis, around Adjar, Munedir, Sineb Sou, Kazukluh, Tcheorten, Baluk Sou, Misirdjik, Besh Geoz, Bostandjek, and

Elmaluh. Colonel Andrea's battalion, after delivering the necessary provisions to the battalion of Aintab, headed to Kilis, on 1 April 1920. Lieutenant Colonel Flye Saint Marie, military commander of French troops, remained in Aintab with a small force. According to Sarafian's account:

> The Turks had already finished their preparations weeks earlier. The Armenians did not yet suspect an imminent attack. Thus, a group of women and craftsmen went to the market in order to buy provisions. There was no sound at all. At 7:30 [in the morning], they began a surprise attack, and assaulted the Armenians of the market like wild tigers. A gun had gone off from the direction of the governorate and many gunshots had followed it. The terror had begun.[81]

In Armenian historiography, this war is depicted as an "Armenian struggle for existence" or the "Armenians' war of self-defense", whereas Turkish historiography defines it as the "Aintab War" or "Resistance and Defense of Aintab."[82] On 9 February 1921, the French defeated the nationalist forces in Aintab, and the city was ceded to them. Yet, despite this victory, the French eventually decided to retreat from the city and the entire Cilicia region. Cilicia was left to the Kemalists for the sake of ensuring a long-term French presence in Syria and Lebanon to counterbalance British gains in the Levant. The French retreat was officially completed by signing the Ankara Treaty on 20 October 1921. In the end, not only did the French fail to return Cilician Armenians' properties, but they also proved to be reluctant to leave them with any means to protect themselves.[83] In the words of Henri Franklin-Bouillon, the former president of the French Senate's Foreign Relations Committee and a former minister of propaganda in the war cabinet, who negotiated and signed the Ankara Agreement for France:

> In Cilicia, France was expending 5 million francs a year and had buried some 5,000 of its sons... France had incurred these losses in defense of the Armenians... France could make such sacrifices no longer and that there was no need, in view of these facts, to defend the decision to arrange a peace with the government of the Grand National Assembly of Turkey.[84]

The official declaration of the French evacuation from Aintab on 4 November 1921 led to panic among Armenians, as they believed that the French wanted to deliver them to the Kemalists, and this would have ultimately led to their destruction.[85] Despite French efforts to persuade the population to stay, virtually all Armenians chose to depart, leaving their properties to French protection and settling in Aleppo and Beirut, which were under a French mandate at the time.[86] In the beginning, the French granted passports and allowed the departure of Armenians, but this policy was changed in March 1921.[87] In early December 1921, 8,000 Armenians managed to leave Aintab by their own means, as the French authorities now prohibited migration and declined to issue them passports.[88] The French ceded complete control of Aintab to the Kemalist forces on 25 December 1921. The last French contingents left on 4 January 1922.[89] The following day, great ceremonies and popular demonstrations took place as Turkish forces and government officials entered the evacuated cities and towns.[90] A year later, on 4 January 1923, the Armenian population of Aintab was estimated at a mere eighty persons.[91]

***

Entire period of 1918-22 was characterized by an increasing lack of security in Aintab, which eventually led to the flight of much of the Armenian population from the city. In fact, the return of Armenians caused significant problems between those who returned, local Muslims, and other immigrants and refugees. Houses, which became vacant as a consequence of the deportation of Armenians, had been seized or rented by local officials and prominent Muslims, or given to Turkish-Muslim refugees from other places. In some cases, the local government had sold these assets. Occasionally, houses were returned to Armenians, but in most cases the local authorities refused to evict the existing occupants.[92] Furthermore, the Ottoman authorities were only returning Armenian houses to those whose names were written on their title deeds. Thus, if the father of a family had died during the deportation, it was impossible for the other members of that family to take back their properties. The Ottoman authorities were completely aware that most Armenian families had lost their male heads of households. Therefore, their chosen policy was simply a pretext for the government not to return Armenian properties to their owners.[93]

On 15 February 1919, the Ministry of Interior informed various provinces that a new law was being prepared for the restitution of abandoned properties, compensation for losses, and other related matters.

In order to prevent any further problems, provinces were warned not to give permission for the sale or pledging of abandoned properties, since such transfers among individuals could interfere with the restitution process.[94] However, there was a certain ambiguity as to which authority was actually in control. The legislative regulations of the Istanbul government were not fully abided, and local actors and officials, who were reluctant to restore Armenian properties despite the Ministry of Interior's orders, acted as sole authority.[95] In some cases, instead of following the relevant legal regulations, local authorities and citizens applied individually to the Ministry of Interior regarding their problems. This unstable environment and the lack of regulatory enforcement disrupted the restitution process. Additionally, the rise of the Kemalist nationalist movement in the city in 1919–1920 put a halt to this process.

In the final analysis, this restitution process directly affected the national resistance movement in Aintab, so much so that the famous battle of Aintab against the French—which resulted in the gifting of the honorific prefix *Gazi* (veteran), renaming the city as Gaziantep on 8 February 1921—seems to have been as much the organized struggle of a group of genocide profiteers seeking to hold onto their loot as it was a fight against an occupying force. This resistance sought to make it impossible for the returning Armenians to stay in their native towns, terrorizing them in the hope of causing them to flee. In short, not only did the local notables, landowners, industrialists, and civil-military bureaucratic elites lead the resistance movement, but they also financed it in order to cleanse Aintab of Armenians.[96]

The historiography of Aintab written by nationalist local literati purports that after the entrance of the Turkish army into the city, the Armenians—feeling humiliated by the betrayal of their French allies—subsequently sold their goods and properties and migrated to Syria along with the French forces.[97] However, in reality, the Kemalist government declared in November 1922 that the goods and assets of Armenians who did not return to Turkey in three months would be forefitted and seized by the state. The same government also did not recognize the validity of passports issued by the French authorities.[98] During these turbulent years, some Armenians *had* been able to sell their properties – however few these people may have been. Although the sales had been made under compulsion, and for prices considerably lower than their real value, the fact that they had been technically "purchased" gave a color of legality to their new Turkish owners. As for the properties that had been (briefly) restored to Armenians, which they now had to leave behind, these were henceforth listed under the rubric of "abandoned properties" according to Abandoned Properties Laws (*Emval-i Metruke Kanunları*). As such, they were now at the government's and local administrations' disposal.[99]

Moreover, the violation of the Lausanne provisions and reintroduction of CUP liquidation laws at the domestic level, as well as bilateral agreements with France on the international level, ensured that Aintab-Armenians who had been deported in 1915–1916 or fled later with the departing French forces could neither retain title to their lost property nor gain compensation for it. Thus the Republican regime was linked to its CUP predecessor with its persecutory economic policies, personnel, and ideology.

The nouveau richer of Gaziantep not only became influential figures of the national resistance and the Republican period, but some also emerged as the new captains of industry in the city. For their active participation in the war against the French, they were rewarded with abandoned properties, which they acquired for a pittance. Following the orders of Mustafa Kemal, Armenian properties were distributed to these people,[100] and they formed the foundation of the city's new bourgeoisie.

This English translation of *The Heroic Struggle of Aintab*[101] presents us with the detailed history of the Armenian struggle for survival in Aintab between 1918-1922. It is a unique and significant work because it is based on detailed eyewitness accounts of *real* people who were in the city at that time.

Ümit Kurt, Aintab [Gaziantep]
24 Nov. 2017

ENDNOTES

1. In its place, *Teceddüt Fırkası* (the Renovation Party) was founded by the Unionists present at the final CUP party congress on 11 November. Although the party officially denied that it was continuation of the CUP, its takeover of CUP assets, such as its organizational networks, real estate (the clubs), and cash undermined the credibility of this claim. Eric Jan Zurcher, *The Young Turk Legacy and Nation Building: From the Ottoman Empire to Atatürk's Turkey* (London, New York: I.B.Tauris, 2010), p. 198; Zurcher, *The Unionist Factor: The Role of the Committee of Union and Progress in the Turkish National Movement 1905-1926* (Leiden, E.J. Brill, 1984), pp. 72-73. The party was closed and its members were banned from politics.

2. On the periods in office of these governments, established by seven different grand viziers, see Tarık Zafer Tunaya, *Türkiye'de Siyasi Partiler, Cilt II, Mütareke Dönemi* (Istanbul: Hürriyet Vakfı Yayınları, 1986), p. 37.

3. In the 1919–22 periods, the court-martial active in Istanbul in all tried sixty-three cases, and prosecuted approximately two hundred defendants. For more detailed information on this topic, see Vahakn Dadrian and Taner Akçam, *Judgment at Istanbul: The Armenian Genocide Trials* (New York: Berghahn Books, 2011).

4. *Osmanlı Belgelerinde Ermenilerin Sevk ve İskanı (1878-1920)* (Ankara: Devlet Arşivleri Genel Müdürlüğü, 2007), p. 396.

5. BOA.DH.ŞFR 92/205, 21 October 1918, cited in İbrahim Ethem Atnur, *Türkiye'de Ermeni Kadınları ve Çocukları Meselesi 1915-1923* (Ankara: Babil Yayıncılık, 2005), p. 173. This order was repeated on 5 November 1918. BOA.HR.SYS 2569/1 in *Osmanlı Belgelerinde Ermenilerin Sevk ve İskanı*, p. 400.

6. BOA.DH.ŞFR 92/207, Cipher telegram to Edirne, Erzurum, Adana, Ankara, Aydın, Bitlis, Aleppo, Hüdâvendigâr, Diyarbakır, Sivas, Trebizond, Kastamonu, Konya, Mamuretülaziz, Mosul, and Van provinces; and Urfa, İzmit, Bolu, Canik, Çatalca, Karesi, Kale-i Sultaniye, Menteşe, Teke, Kayseri, Kütahya, Karahisar-ı Sahib, İçel, Batum, Kars, Erzincan, Eskişehir, and Niğde provincial district governments, 22 October 1334 [1918].

7. *Osmanlı Belgelerinde Ermenilerin Sevk ve İskânı*, pp. 397–98.

8. BOA.DH.ŞFR 92/235, a coded telegram sent by the IAMM to the Provinces of Edirne, Aleppo, Sivas and the Provincial Districts of Urfa, İzmid, Bolu and etc. dated 23 October 1918.

9. BOA.DH.ŞFR 608/20, 28 December 1918.

10.Ibid.

11. Ibid.

12. "Antep Savunması", *Gaziantep Kültür Dergisi*, 10 (109): 1967, p. 4; Kevork A. Sarafian, Պատմութիւն Անթէպի Հայոց [Badmoutiun Ayntebi Hayots -

History of Aintab Armenians] Vol. II (LA: Union of Aintab Armenians, 1953), p. 45; M. Abadie, *Türk Verdün'ü Gaziantep: Antep'in Dört Muhasarası* (Gaziantep: Osman Nuri Tuzcu Eğitim ve Kültür Vakfı, 1999), p. 26; Ali Nadir Ünler, "Antep Savunması", *Gaziantep Kültür Dergisi*, 1 (1): 1957, p. 10. According to some sources, Aintab was occupied by British forces on 17 December 1918; see Ahmet Hulki Saral, *Türk İstiklal Harbi, Vol. 4, Güney Cephesi* (Ankara: Genelkurmay Harp Tarihi Başkanlığı, 1966), p. 50; Eyüp Sabri (Akgöl), *Esaret Hatıraları (Bir Esirin Hatıraları, Gaziantep'te İngiliz Tecavüzünün Başlangıcı ve Türk Üserasına Zulüm ve İşkenceler)*, Nejat Sefercioğlu (ed.) (Istanbul: Tercüman, 1978), p. 13; Ramazan E. Güllü, *Antep Ermenileri: Sosyal-Siyasi ve Kültürel Hayatı* (Ankara: IQ Yayınları, 2010), p. 296; Stanley E. Kerr, *The Lions of Marash: Personal Experience with American Near East Relief, 1919-1922* (Albany: State University of Albany of New York Press, 1973), p. 35; Ali Fuat Türkgeldi, *Mondros ve Mudanya Mütarekelerinin Tarihi* (Ankara: Güney Matbaacılık ve Gazetecilik, 1948), p. 67; Zeki Sarıhan, *Kurtuluş Savaşı Günlüğü,* Vol. 1 (Ankara: Öğretmen Dünyası, 1982), p. 79.

13. Sarafian, Պատմութիւն Անթէպի Հայոց, Vol. I (LA: Union of Aintab Armenians, 1953), p. 1071.

14. Lutfi Levonian used to be a member of the faculty in Central Turkey College. He and his family members were exempted from deportation. He served as the head of the government Commercial High School in Aintab. His brother Adour Levonian served in the Ottoman army during the war and his two sisters Mari and Nuritsa were teachers in the Turkish schools; see *ABCFM* 16.9.6.1, 1817-1919, Harvard University, Unit 5, Reel 674, Vol. 2, Part 1, No 369; Harutyun Nazarian, Եղեռնէն վերապրողի յուշեր [Yeghernen Verbroghi Housher or Memories of a Survivor the Genocide] (Aleppo: 2009), p. 15.

15. Պատմութիւն Անթէպի Հայոց, Vol. I, p. 1071.

16. CAB 24/145, *Eastern Report*, 26 December 1918, p. 170.

17. Պատմութիւն Անթէպի Հայոց, Vol. I, p. 1072. Indian Cavalry Corps served under General Allenby in his successful advance from Egypt to Aleppo. There were three squadrons of Indian Cavalry lodged in Central Turkey College in December 1918. *The Missionary Herald*, 116 (1): 1919, p. 159.

18. Stina Katchadourian, *Efronia: An Armenian Love Story* (Princeton: Gomidas Institute Books), p. 159.

19. Sarkis Laleian (ed.), Յուշամատեան նուիրուած Ատուր Յ. Լեւոնեանի - Ինքնակենսագրութիւն եւ դրուագներ իր կեանքէն ու գործէն [Houshamadyan nvirvadz Asdour H. Levoniani - Inknagensakroutiun yev trvakner ir gyanken ou kordzen or Memoir Dedicated to Adur Levonian: Autobiography and Episodes from his Life and Work] (Beirut: Shirag, 1967), p. 37.

20. Eyüp Sabri (Akgöl), *Bir Esirin Hatıraları*, p. 30.

21. FO 371/4174, no. 102551 and FO 10991/M.1159 from the high commissioner in Istanbul, Arthur Calthorpe, to Lord Curzon, Istanbul, 27 June 1919, concerning official documents in the possession of the district governor of Aintab seized by the British military authorities on 4 February, 1919.

22. ATASE, Arş 1/105, Dosya No: (6)-2, K1 255, Fihrist: 5/1 cited in Ayhan Öztürk, *Milli Mücadele'de Gaziantep* (Kayseri: Geçit Yayınları, 1994), p. 31; Mustafa Nurettin Lohanizade, *Gazi Antep Savunması* (Istanbul: Kastaş Yayınları, 1989), p. 18.

23. Ibid.

24. Պատմութիւն Անթէպի Հայոց, Vol. I, p. 1075.

25. FO 608/95, *General Headquarter Intelligence Summary*, 4 March 1919, p. 15.

26. Ibid., p. 15.

27. Ibid., p. 15; *Supplement to General Headquarter Intelligence Summary*, 1 April 1919; Պատմութիւն Անթէպի Հայոց, Vol. I, p. 1075; Sarkis Balabanian, Կեանքիս տաք ու պաղ օրերը : (Այնթապ-Քեսապ-Հալէպ) [Gyankis Dak ou Bagh Oreru - Ayntab-Kesab-Haleb or The Hot and Cold Days of My Life: Aintab, Kesap, Aleppo] (Aleppo: Shirag, 1983), p. 149; Յուշամատեան նուիրուած Ատուր Յ. Լեւոնեանի, p. 41.

28. BOA.DH.ŞFR 609/14, 1 January 1919.

29. Ibid.

30. Daizâde Ahmed Hurşid Effendi was involved in the *Kuva-yi milliye* (National Forces) and provided financial support for the forces of national struggle. He was also one of the prominent local notables who seized a number of Armenians properties during the deportation; see Bibliothèque arménienne Nubar, Paris (hereafter BNu)/Fonds A. Andonian, P.J. 1/3, file 4, Aintab, "The Deportation of Armenians in Aintab," pp. 11-17.

31. Eyüp Sabri (Akgöl), *Bir Esirin Hatıraları*, p. 15.

32. Hüseyin Cemil Bey, son of Kethüdazâde İbrahim Effendi of the *ayan* (notable) and graduate of the American College, published this newspaper with his friends in protest of the British arrival to Aintab, the predicament of the country, and the excesses of Armenians. Eyüp Sabri (Akgöl), *Bir Esirin Hatıraları*, p. 24. This newspaper was raided and shut down again by the French during their occupation in November 1919. Even though the newspaper continued to be published intermittently after April 1920, it was dismantled following the surrender of Aintab to the French due to starvation. The mottos of the newspapers were "Aintab is Turkish and will remain Turkish" and "Aintab is the fortress of Turkishness." Uğurol Barlas, *Gaziantep Basın Tarihi, 100. Yıl* (Karabük: Özer Matbaası, 1972), p. 25; Barlas,

"Gaziantep'te Gazetecilik," *Gaziantep Kültür-Aylık Fikir ve Bilgi Dergisi*, 1 (8): 1958, p. 8.

33. Պատմութիւն Անթէպի Հայոց, Vol. II, p. 52; Celal Pekdoğan, "Acı Zerdali Çekirdeği Ekmeğinden Uvralı Buğday Ekmeğine," in Refik Duru (eds.), *Gaziantep 'Dört Yanı Dağlar Bağlar'* (Istanbul: Yapı Kredi Yayınları, 2007), p. 126.

34. Պատմութիւն Անթէպի Հայոց, Vol. I, p. 1074; Katchadourian, *Efronia*, p. 159; Յուշամատեան նուիրուած Ատուր Յ. Լեւոնեանի, p. 45; Balabanian, Կեանքիս տաք ու պաղ օրերը, p. 149.

35. Ibid., p. 1074; Eyüp Sabri (Akgöl), *Bir Esirin Hatıraları*, pp. 24-25. Eyüp Sabri asserted that the hopes and ambitions of the British forces for Aintab increased due to the overall presence of a remarkable tranquility upon their arrival, at which point they were met with no resistance whatsoever from any side. On the contrary, every single British need was provided for, along with constant propaganda on their behalf. This was done partly through the intermediary of some of the municipality functionaries but mainly by the permission and directives of the district governor Celal Bey, whom Sabri labeled "a collaborationist." Ibid., p. 14. Eyüp Sabri stated that the support given by the local government to the British occupation forces under the supervision of Celal Bey caused the increase of British military forces in Aintab (Ibid., p. 14) and also see Hüseyin Beyaz, *Antep Savunması Günlüğü* (Istanbul: Engin Matbaası, 1994), p. 124. It is interesting to note that both Eyüp Sabri and Celal Bey, whom the former openly accused the latter of collaborating with the occupying forces, were members of the CUP. Celal Bey was notably a founding member of the Aintab Branch of CUP; see "Celal Kadri Barlas'ın Dilinden, İttihat ve Terakki Cemiyeti Nasıl Kuruldu?", *Gaziantep'i Tanıtıyoruz* 2 (2): 1963, pp. 16-17 and Yener, "Celal Kadri Barlas'ı Kaybettik," *Gaziantep Kültür Dergisi*, 6 (68): 1963, p. 177.

36. Eyüp Sabri (Akgöl), *Bir Esirin Hatıraları*, p. 27.

37. Ibid., pp. 28-29.

38. BOA.HR.HU 43/61, 15 C 1337 (18 March 1919), *Osmanlı Belgelerinde Ermeniler (1915-1920)* (Ankara: Başbakanlık Devlet Arşivleri Genel Müdürlüğü Yayınları, 1995), pp. 222-24; M. Oğuz Göğüş, "General Faik Taşçıoğlu'nu Kaybettik," *Gaziantep'i Tanıtıyoruz*, 1 (2): 1952, p. 17. At that time, *Teminat* was one of the local newspapers that was printed in Aintab. In *Teminat*'s 22 and 25 January 1919 issues, it was stated that the accountant of Aintab, officers of the Land Registry and Pious Foundations offices, as well as two leading figures from local notables were surrendered to the commander of British occupation forces by the district governor Celal Kadri Bey. These people were sent to Aleppo for investigations regarding their roles in the deportation of Armenians from Aintab; see BOA.DH.ŞFR 613/100, 5 February 1919.

39. Sedat Bey was a teacher at a CUP *idadi* (high school) in Aintab.

40. Hüseyin Bey was a retired major.

41. Eyüp Sabri (Akgöl), *Bir Esirin Hatıraları*, pp. 19, 41; BEO 4595/344573, 14 and 24 Teşrinievvel 1335 (14 and 24 October 1919); DH.İ.UM 19-9/1-35, 1338 M 27 (22 October 1919).

42. Ibid., p. 45.

43. Enver Behnan Şapolyo, *Kemal Atatürk ve Milli Mücadele Tarihi* (Ankara: Berkalp Kitapevi, 1944), p. 224.

44. BOA.HR.SYS 2704/11, 31 December 1918 and BOA.DH.EUM.AYŞ 32/16, 11 February 1920; Edouard Brémond, "La Cilicie en 1919-1920," *Revue des Etudes Arméniennes*, 1 (3): 1921, pp. 309, 311; Du Véou, *La Passion de la Cilicie*, pp. 66, 90-91 cited in Vahram L. Shemmassian, "Repatriation of Armenian Refugees from the Arab Middle East, 1918-1920" in Richard G. Hovannissian and Simon Payaslian (ed.), *Armenian Cilicia* (Costa Mesa, CA: Mazda Publishers, 2008), p. 432; Zaven Der Yeghiayan, *My Patriarchal Memoirs* (Barrington, R.I.: Mayreni Publications, 2002), p. 191; Doğan Avcıoğlu, *Milli Kurtuluş Tarihi*, Vol. I (Istanbul: Tekin Yayınevi, 1977), p. 115.

45. Brémond, "La Cilicie en 1919-1920," pp. 309, 311; Du Véou, *La Passion de la Cilicie*, pp. 66, 90-91 cited in Shemmassian, "Repatriation of Armenian Refugees from the Arab Middle East, 1918-1920," p. 432.

46. *Times* (London), 16 January 1919.

47. FO 371/3405, 199352/55708/44, Sykes to FO for Boghos Nubar's information, 2 December 1918 cited in Shemmassian, "Repatriation of Armenian Refugees from the Arab Middle East, 1918-1920," p. 425.

48. Ibid.

49. *Darakir* (Deportees), Aleppo, 25 December 1918. Detailed lists of potential repatriates originating from various localities are found in France, *Archives du Ministére des Affaires Etrangéres*, Nantes, Beyrouth: Cilicie 1919-1921, Cilicie-Alep, cartons 319-331; APA, Files 42. Kilis was a district of Aintab in 1918.

50. Founded in early 1917, the Armenian National Union (ANU) brought together various Armenian organizations and political parties in Egypt. After the Mudros Armistice, the Allies promoted the creation of other ANU chapters—the French in Cilicia and the British in Syria—because of the need of interlocutors who could fairly claim to represent the diverse components of Armenian society. As soon as the armistice was signed, both General Allenby and Georges-Picot, the French commissioner, encouraged the formation of the branches of the ANU in all of the Allied-occupied areas in which there was an Armenian population. In Cilicia, the ANU and the representative of the Paris-based Armenian National Delegation, Mihran Damadian, were—in the view of

the French administration—quasi-official spokesmen for Armenian interests. Vahé Tachjian, "The Cilician Armenians and French Policy, 1919-1921" in *Armenian Cilicia*, p. 542, footnote number 4.

51. BCA/TİGMA 272.00.00.74.68.37.5, 9 January 1919.

52. *Archives of the Armenian National Delegation* (cited hereafter as AND), in the BNu/Fonds, Microfilm/1, "Statistiques des Arméniens d'Alep."

53. Nazarian, Եղեռնէն վերապրողի յուշեր, p. 17.

54. APC/APJ, PCI Bureau, 367, list of the regions where the Armenians and the Greeks were repatriated, cited in Raymond Kévorkian, *The Armenian Genocide: A Complete History* (London: I.B.Tauris, 2011), p. 748.

55. Barsamian and Gedzvanian on behalf of Ehnesh refugees to Aleppo ANU chairman and members, 16 January 1919; Barsamian on behalf of twenty-five Ehnesh refugees to Aleppo ANU chairman and members, 13 February 1919 in Shemmassian, "Repatriation of Armenian Refugees from the Arab Middle East, 1918-1920," p. 424. Clouscard's announcement in Armenian regarding repatriation of Armenians to Aintab and Marash, 12 May 1919. See also Clouscard to President of Inter-Provincial Committee of Aleppo, 8 June 1919 cited in Ibid., p. 424.

56. NARA/RG 84, Vol. 83, *Correspondence, American Consulate, Aleppo, 1919*, Jackson, Political and Economic Conditions, 31 May 1919; NARA/RG59/867.00/897.

57. NARA/RG59/867.48/1316, Jackson to Secretary of State, 23 August 1919; Harutyun Simonian (ed.), Հաւելուած Այնթապի Հայոց Պատմութիւն [Havelouadz Ayntabi Hayots Badmoutiun or Collected: History of Aintab Armenians] (Waltham: Mayreni, 1997), p. 105.

58. These figures reflect Armenian, British, and French sources. Turkish sources reduce these numbers to 20,000 - 30,000. Population figures for the Ottoman Empire have always been controversial, and the rich literature for these estimates is too extensive to list here. See some sources: Yervant Babaian (ed.), Պատմութիւն Անթէպի Հայոց, [History of Aintab Armenians] Vol. III (LA, Union of the Armenians of Aintab: April Publishers, 1994), pp. 11-12; Sarafian, *A Briefer History of Aintab: A concise history of the cultural, religious, educational, political, industrial and commercial life of the Armenians of Aintab* (CA, Los Angeles: Union of the Armenians of Aintab, 1957), p. 11; Kemal Karpat, *Ottoman Population (1830-1914): Demographic and Social Character* (Madison Wisconsin: University of Madison Press, 1985), p. 176; *Arşiv Belgeleriyle Ermeni Faaliyetleri 1914-1918*, Vol. 1 (Ankara: Genelkurmay Basımevi, 2005), p. 655.

59. This number includes 4,000 Aintab Armenians who were already exempted from depotation and had never left the city. Kevork Barsoumian, Պատմութիւն Այնդապի Հ. Յ. Դաշնակցութեան 1898-1922 [Badmoutiun

Ayntabi H. H. Yashnagtsoutiun, 1898-1922 or History of Ayntab A. R. F., 1898-1922] (Aleppo: Tigris, 1957), p. 331. Archpriest Nerses Babaian who reached Aintab on 21 November 1919 from his exile estimated the Armenian population in Aintab at 17,000–18,000; see Nerses Babaian (ed.), *Pages from my Diary*, Yervant Babaian (ed.) and Aris G. Sevag (transl.) (Los Angeles: Abril Printing, 2000), p. 31.

60. Ibid., p. 51.

61. Karaian, "On the Number of Armenians in Aintab in 1914" in Պատմութիւն Անթէպի Հայոց Union Committee of Aintab was formed in early 1919. It was composed of seven elected members: Dr. Hovsep Bezdjian, chairman (Armenian Protestant); Yeghiazan Benlian, secretary (Armenian Orthodox); Dr. Kevork Arslanian, treasurer (Armenian Catholic); Mushegh Hadidian, consultant (Armenian Protestant); Nerses Ishkhanian, consultant (Armenian Protestant); Kevork Leyleguian, consultant (Armenian Orthodox); Bedros Merdjenian, consultant (Armenian Orthodox). The Armenian National Union was founded for the purpose of managing community and religious affairs in Aintab; see Պատմութիւն Անթէպի Հայոց, Vol. I, p. 1080.

62. CAB 24/96/4, 15 November 1919, Dispatch from Civil Commissioner, Mesopotamia, to Secretary of State for India, p. 21.

63. "Թուրքերուն զէնք կը բաժնուի - Քիլիսէն կը գրեն" [Tourkeroun Zenk gu Pazhnoui: Kilisen gu kren or Arms are Being Distributed to the Turks: They are Writing from Kilis], Ճակատամարտ [Jagadamard (Struggle)], Constantinople (Istanbul), 16 July 1919.

64. Ibid.

65. Ünler, *Türk'ün Kurtuluş Savaşı'nda Gaziantep Savunması* (Istanbul: Kardeşler Matbaası, 1969), p. 15; Ömer Asım Aksoy, *Türkçe Bir Hayat* (Istanbul: Yapı Kredi Yayınları, 1999), p. 36.

66. Պատմութիւն Անթէպի Հայոց, Vol. II, p. 51.

67. Yaşar Akbıyık, *Milli Mücadele'de Güney Cephesi (Maraş)* (Ankara: Kültür Bakanlığı, 1990), pp. 48-52; Gotthard Jaeschke, *Kurtuluş Savaşı ile İlgili İngiliz Belgeleri* (Ankara: TTK, 1991), p. 46.

68. Պատմութիւն Անթէպի Հայոց, Vol. I, p. 1080; Mustafa Budak, *İdealden Gerçeğe, Misak-ı Milli'den Lozan'a Dış Politika* (Istanbul: ATAM Yayınları, 2003), pp. 116-21.

69. BOA.DH.ŞFR 648/44, 11 October 1919; Պատմութիւն Անթէպի Հայոց Vol. I, p. 553; Nerses Tavoukjian, Տառապանքի Օրագրութիւն [Darabanki Orakroutiun or Diary of Torment], ed., Toros Toramanian (Beirut: High Type Compugraph – Technopresse, 1991), p. 195; M. Abadie, (Lieutt-Colonel Br.), *Les Quatre Sièges d'Aintab (1920-1921)*, (Paris: Charles Lavauzelle, 1922), p. 30; Zekai Güner, "Antep Savunması ve Ali Şefik Özdemir Bey'in

Faaliyetleri," *Zonguldak Karaelmas Üniversitesi Sosyal Bilimler Dergisi*, 3 (6): 2007, p. 51.

70. Պատմութիւն Անթէպի Հայոց, Vol. I, p. 1080; Balabanian, Կեանքիս տար ու պաղ օրերը, p. 150; Nazarian, Եղեռնէն վերապրողի յուշեր, p. 21; National Archives of Armenia, Catalogue No: 430/1/824, 28 April 1920.

71. Պատմութիւն Անթէպի Հայոց, Vol. II, pp. 52-53; Abadi, *Türk Verdün'ü Gaziantep*, p. 30; Sarafian, *A Briefer History of Aintab*, p. 152. The Legion had been formed in Egypt as the *Légion d'Orient* (The Eastern Legion) on 15 November 1916, under the command of Allied officers to assist in the war efforts against the Ottoman armies. It was the Armenian Legion that first entered in Cilicia in late 1918. For detailed history of Armenian Legion; see *Tenth Anniversary Booklet of the Armenian Legionnaires* (Cairo, 1928); Dickran H. Boyajian, *Armenian Legion: Historical Memoirs* (Watertown, MA: Baikar Press, 1965); Krikor Ajemian, *Pages from the Battles of Marash* (Cairo, 1928); Aram Karamanoukian, *Les Etrangers et le Service Militaire* (Paris: Padena, 1978); Manoug Baghdasarian, *Memoirs from the Days of the Cilician Legionnaire Movement* (Boston, 1943); Kerr, *The Lions of Marash*.

72. BOA.DH.ŞFR 649/89, 1 November 1919; Պատմութիւն Անթէպի Հայոց, Vol. II, p. 54.

73. ATASE, İSHK, Box: 48, File: 151, No. 3562. Indignation of the Local Populace to the French Occupation of Marash, 25 November 1919, cited in Yücel Güçlü, *Armenians and the Allies in Cilicia 1914-1923* (Salt Lake City: The University of Utah Press, 2010), p. 116.

74. Nazarian, Եղեռնէն վերապրողի յուշեր, p. 21.

75. John E. Merrill, "Pen Pictures of the Siege of Aintab," *Envelope Series*, 23 (3): 1920, p. 3; Պատմութիւն Անթէպի Հայոց, Vol. III, p. 52; "Gaziantep Savunması," *Gaziantep Kültür Dergisi*, 10 (109): 1967, p. 22; Fatma Ülgen, "Reading Mustafa Kemal Atatürk on the Armenian genocide of 1915," *Patterns of Prejudice*, 44 (4): 2010, p. 377.

76. Sabahattin Selek, *Anadolu İhtilali*, Vol. II (Istanbul: Kastaş, 2000), p. 702. See also Avcıoğlu, *Milli Kurtuluş Tarihi*, Vol. 4 (Istanbul: Tekin Yayınları, 1997), pp. 1382-83; İlhan Tekeli, "Osmanlı İmparatorluğu'ndan Günümüze Nüfusun Zorunlu Yer Değiştirmesi ve İskân Sorunu," *Toplum ve Bilim*, 50 (1990), p. 62; Çağlar Keyder, "İmparatorluk'tan Cumhuriyet'e Geçişte Kayıp Burjuvazi Aranıyor," *Toplumsal Tarih*, 12 (68): 1999, pp. 4-11.

77. In fact, from April to June 1919, Colonel Brémond, chief military governor in Cilicia, promulgated three decrees that formed the legal base of the restitution to the Cilician Armenians of all confiscated movable and immovable properties; see Tachjian, "Cilician Armenians and French Policy 1919-1921," p. 545.

78. Ünler, *Gaziantep Savunması*, p. 18.

79. Ibid., pp. 17-21; Ünler, "Gaziantep Müdafaası," *Gaziantep Halkevi Broşürü* (Gaziantep: Halk Fırkası Matbaası, 1935), p. 94; "Ahmet Muhtar Göğüş," *Gaziantep'i Tanıtıyoruz*, 3 (4): 1968, p. 20; Bilgehan Pamuk, *Bir Şehrin Direnişi: Antep Savunması* (Istanbul: IQ Yayıncılık, 2009), p. 136; Պատմութիւն Անթէպի Հայոց, Vol. II, p. 52. Other members were Dr. Hamid, Dr. Mecid, Bülbülzâde Hacı Abdullah, Kepkepzâde Şakir, Hasan Sadık, Müftü Bulaşıkzâde Müftü Hacı Arif, Fahreddin Hoca, Mısrizâde Nuri, Hoca Abdullah Edib, Fazlı Ağazâde Nuri, Izrapzâde Şefik, Zaafizâde Mazlum, Şeyh Ubeydullah, Müftüzâde Hayri, Mevlevi Şeyhi Mustafa, Dai Ahmed Ağa, Hacı Hanefizâde Abdullah, Ahmed Muhtar and Celal Kadri Hacı Ömer Zade, Mehmet Ali, Mahmud Budeyri, Dai Ahmed Ağa, Pazarbaşı Nuri, Sadık Effendi, Kahramanzâde Hacı Mehmed, İncozâde Hüseyin, Timurzâde Rıfat, Kepkepzâde Abdürrezzak, Hacı Hilmi, Hacı Hüseyin Ağazâde, Körükçüzâde Mustafa, Mehmet Hayri, Mutafzâde Abdülkadir, Attarzâde Abdullah, Sait Ağazâde Mustafa, Musa Kazım, and Vice Mayor of Aintab Refik Bey.

80. "Gaziantep'i Tanıtıyoruz," *Gaziantep Kültür Dergisi*, 3 (2): 1968, p. 3.

81. Պատմութիւն Անթէպի Հայոց, Vol. II, p. 85.

82. There is an enormous amount of Turkish and Armenian literature on the Turkish-French war in Aintab. For instance, see Ali Sancar, *Gaziantep Muharebeleri* (Istanbul: Harp Akademileri Basımevi, 1962); Sahir Üzer, *Gaziantep Savaşının İç Yüzü 1 (Kılıç Ali Devri)* (Kayseri: Sümer Matbaası, 1949); Üzer, *Gaziantep Savaşının İç Yüzü 2 (Özdemir Devri)* (Ankara: Doğuş Matbaası, 1952); Hulusi Yetkin, *Gaziantep Savaşı Hatıralarından Derlemeler* (Gaziantep: Işık Matbaası, 1962); Yetkin, *Kurtuluş Destanı* (Gaziantep: Mürüvvet Matbaası, 1959); Yetkin and Mehmet Solmaz, *Şehit Şahin* (Gaziantep: Güneş Matbaası, 1965); Burhan Bozgeyik, *İstiklal Harbinde Gaziantep* (Gaziantep: Şehitkamil Belediyesi, 1998); Adil Dai, *Harbin Kahraman Çocukları* (Gaziantep: Gaziantep Üniversitesi Vakfı Yayını, 2000); Dai, *Olaylarla Gaziantep Savaşı* (Gaziantep: Gaziyurt Matbaası, 1992); Göğüş, *Gaziantep Savaşı* (Gaziantep: Gaziyurt Matbaası, 1971); Lohanizade Nurettin Mustafa, *Gazi Antep Savunması*; Öztürk, *Milli Mücadele'de Gaziantep*; Barsoumian, Պատմութիւն Այնդապի Հ. Յ. Դաշնակցութեան 1898-1922 [Badmoutiun Ayntabi H. H. Yashnagtsoutiun, 1898-1922]; ՊՊատմութիւն Անթէպի Հայոց, Vol. I, II, and III; A. Gesar, Այնթապի Քոյամարտը, [Ayntabi Koyamardu or The Self-Defense of Aintab] (Boston: Hairenik, 1945); *Pages from My Diary*.

83. National Archive of Armenia, *A Letter from Catholicate Deputy Der Nerses Tavoukjian to Arshak Chobanian*, 14 November 1921, Catalogue No: 430/1/842; *A Letter from Catholicate Deputy Der Nerses Tavoukjian to Monsieur Briand, President of the French Republic Council in Paris*, 16 November 1921, Catalogue No: 430/1/844; FO 608/278, British Armenian Committee, Cilicia,

8 June 1921, pp. 181-82; Balabanian, Կեանքիս տաք ու պաղ օրերը, p. 151; Պատմութիւն Անթէպի Հայոց, Vol. II, p. 308.

84. Cited in Güçlü, *Armenians and the Allies in Cilicia 1914-1923*, p. 144.

85. BNu/Fonds, *Notes Sur La Cilicie*, p. 1; National Archive of Armenia, *A Letter from Catholicate Deputy Der Nerses Tavoukjian to Arshak Chobanian*, 14 November 1921, Catalogue No: 430/1/842, p. 6. In his significant letter to Chobanian, who was in Paris at the time, Tavoukjian underlined how they had been abandoned by the French and how the French did not fulfill their promises to protect the security of life and property of the Armenians. He also directed criticism toward himself for how naïve they were to believe the promises of the French civil and military authorities to not leave them to the hands of nationalists in Aintab. He also stated in his letter, "The French sacrificed Armenians to the enemy [The Kemalists]." Tavoukjian asked the French authorities to provide protection for their exodus from Aintab and places for Armenians to settle, as well as to assess the values of their houses and give this money to their owners (Ibid., pp. 7-9). For a similar letter written by Nerses Tavoukjian and sent to the President of the French Republic Council on 16 November 1921, see National Archive of Armenia, *A Letter from the Catholicate Deputy Nerses Tavoukjian to the President of French Republic Council*, Catalogue No: 430/1/844, 16 November 1921.

86. Ibid., p. 3; National Archive of Armenia, Catalogue No: 340/1/716, 19 April 1921; Tavoukjian, Տառապանքի Օրագրութիւն, pp. 352-53; Nazarian, Եղեռնէն վերապրողի յուշեր, p. 67.

87. Պատմութիւն Անթէպի Հայոց, Vol. II, p. 306.

88. BNu/Fonds, *Notes Sur La Cilicie*, p. 1. As of 14 November 1921, according to the number given by Der Nerses Tavoukjian, there were 8,500 Armenians in Aintab; see National Archive of Armenia, *A Letter from Catholicate Deputy Der Nerses Tavoukjian to Arshak Chobanian*, 14 November 1921, Catalogue No: 430/1/842, p. 9.

89. Պատմութիւն Անթէպի Հայոց, Vol. III, p. 307; Tachjian, "The Expulsion of Non-Turkish Ethnic and Religious Groups from Turkey to Syria during the 1920s and early 1930s," in Jacques Semelin (ed.), *Online Encyclopedia of Mass Violence*, http://www.massviolence.org/IMG/article_PDF/The-expulsion-of-non-Turkish-ethnic-and-religious-groups.pdf, p. 6. According to the report of the British Consulate in Aleppo, as of November 1922, there were still 3,000 Armenians living in Aintab; see FO 371, "Diplomatic Records: Report on the forced exile of the remaining Armenians from Aintab and Marash," 15 November 1922; National Archive of Armenia, Catalogue No: 430/1/838, 1922; ATASE, İSHK, Box: 1706, File: 72, No. 1440. French Plans for Evacuation, 29 November 1921, cited in Güçlü, *Armenians and the Allies in Cilicia 1914-1923*, p. 145.

90. ATASE, İSHK, Box: 1758, File: 154, No. 1602. Entry of Turkish Troops into Adana, 5 January 1922, cited in Güçlü, *Armenians and the Allies in Cilicia 1914-1923*, p. 152.

91. Tachjian, "The Expulsion of Non-Turkish Ethnic and Religious Groups from Turkey to Syria during the 1920s and early 1930s," p. 6. The last Armenian, Sarkis Tutundjian left Aintab for Aleppo in 1936. Պատմութիւն Անթէպի Հայոց, Vol. III, p. 307.

92. FO 608/95, *General Headquarter Intelligence Summary*, 4 March 1919, p. 17; Donald Bloxham, *The Great Game of Genocide: Imperialism, Nationalism, and the Destruction of the Ottoman Armenians* (Oxford: Oxford University Press, 2005), p. 152.

93. *Zhamanag*, 11 December 1918, No: 3381.

94. BOA.DH.ŞFR 96/195, 15 February 1919.

95. Eyüp Sabri (Akgöl), *Bir Esirin Hatıraları*; Göğüş, *İlk İnsanlardan Bugüne Çeşitli Yönleriyle Gaziantep* (Ankara: Cihan Ofset, 1997); Yener, *Gaziantep Yakın Tarihinden Notlar.*

96. For realization of the same process in Adana; see Damar Arıkoğlu, *Hatıralarım* (Istanbul: Tan Matbaası, 1961), p. 100.

97. Yetkin, *Gaziantep için Söylenenler*, (Gaziantep: Yeni Matbaa, 1969), p. 46; Mitat Enç, *Selamlık Sohbetleri* (Istanbul: Ötüken, 2007), p. 70; *Gaziantep Kültür Dergisi*, "Gaziantep Savunması," 10 (118): 1967, p. 234. In the 1927 population census, there were fifty-five Christians living in Gaziantep. The number of Armenians was forty to forty-five. *1927 Yılı Umumi Nüfus Tahriri*, Türkiye Cumhuriyeti Başvekalet İstatistik Umum Müdürlüğü, 28 October 1927, Fascicule 1-2, Ankara 1929.

98. BNu/Fonds, *Notes Sur La Cilicie*, a report from the president of the Commission of Immigrant dated on 12 February 1922, Larnaka.

99. For detailed analysis of abandoned properties laws and regulations, see Akçam and Ümit Kurt, *The Spirit of the Laws: The Plunder of Wealth in the Armenian Genocide* (New York and Oxford: Berghahn Books, 2015) and Kurt, "The Plunder of Wealth through Abandoned Properties Laws in the Armenian Genocide," *Genocide Studies International* 10, 1 (2016), pp. 37-51. Indeed, the homes "abandoned" by Armenians in Cilicia were put into the hands of a Turkish committee appointed by Hamit Bey, undersecretary of the Ministry of Interior and a former governor of Trabzon and Diyarbekir, to be kept for them. This arrangement was to continue for a year, in the event any Armenians returned. By the time these homes were confiscated by the Kemalist government in 1922, Armenians of Aintab had already crowded into the three enormous camps at İskenderun, Aleppo, and Beirut; see Service Historique de l'Armee de Terre (hereafter SHAT), Armée du Levant, 4H 175, Dossier I, *Rapports et correspondance relatifs a l'évacuation de Cilicie* (March 1921-April

1922); Clair Price, *The Rebirth of Turkey* (New York: Thomas Seltzer, 1923), p. 192.

100. These include Hüseyin Cemil Göğüş, Hakkı Kozanlı, Taşçızâde Abdullah, Nuri Patpat Besim Bey, İnco oğlu Hasan Agha, Özdemir Mehmet Emin Ağa, Çulhalar Şıhıoğlu Mehmet Emin Agha, Mennanzâde Mustafa, Molla Mustafa, Kürt Hacı Ali, Müftü zade Arif Effendi, Daizâde Ahmed Agha, Nuri Pazarbaşı, Piafzâde Abdülkadir, Mehmet Hayri, Hacı Ömerzâde, Mehmet Ali, Mahmud Budeyri, Dai Ahmed Ağa, Pazarbaşı Nuri, Sadık Effendi, Kahramanzâde Hacı Mehmed, İncozade Hüseyin, Timurzâde Rıfat, Kepkepzade Abdürrezzak, Hacı Hilmi, Hacı Hüseyin Ağazade, Körükçüzâde Mustafa, Mehmet Hayri, Mutafzâde Abdülkadir, Attarzade Abdullah, Sait Ağazâde Mustafa, Musa Kazım, and Vice Mayor of Aintab Refik Bey. Interview conducted with Aykut Tuzcu on 19 November 2014 in Gaziantep.

101. Այնթապի Հերոսամարտը [Ayntabi Herosamardu] appears in Kevork A. Sarafian (comp. and ed.), Պատմութիւն Անթէպի Հայոց, Vol. II (LA: Union of Aintab Armenians, 1953).

The Heroic Battle of Aintab

Kevork Baboian

originally edited and prepared for publication by
Kevork. A. Sarafian

translated with a new introduction by
Ümit Kurt

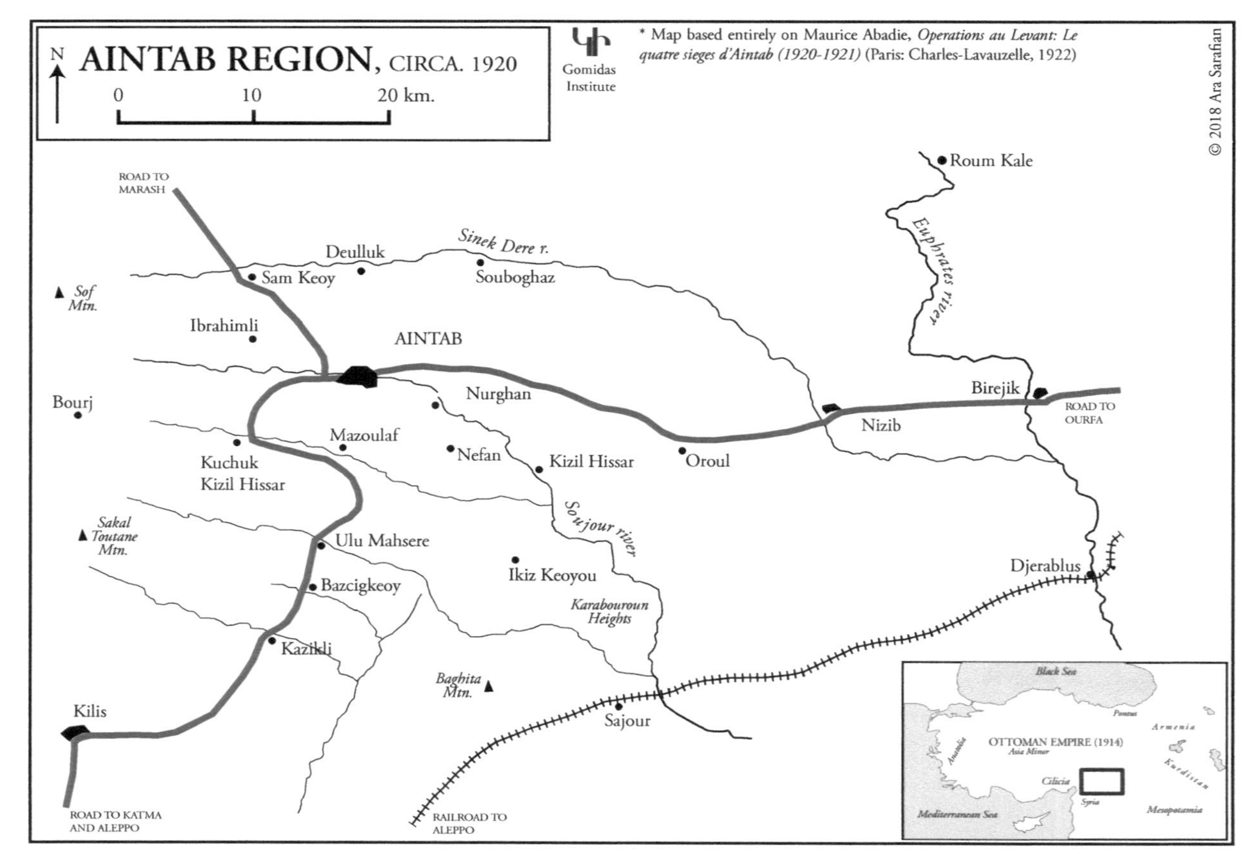
N
AINTAB REGION, CIRCA. 1920
0
10
20 km.
Gomidas Institute
* Map based entirely on Maurice Abadie, Operations au Levant: Le quatre sieges d'Aintab (1920-1921) (Paris: Charles-Lavauzelle, 1922)
© 2018 Ara Sarafian
ROAD TO MARASH
Sinek Dere r.
Deulluk
Sam Keoy
Souboghaz
Sof Mtn.
Ibrahimli
AINTAB
Bourj
Nurghan
Mazoulaf
Nefan
Kuchuk Kizil Hissar
Kizil Hissar
Oroul
Soujour river
Sakal Toutane Mtn.
Ulu Mahsere
Bazcigkeoy
Ikiz Keoyou
Karabouroun Heights
Kazikli
Baghita Mtn.
Kilis
Sajour
ROAD TO KATMA AND ALEPPO
RAILROAD TO ALEPPO
Roum Kale
Euphrates river
Birejik
ROAD TO OURFA
Nizib
Djerablus
Black Sea
Pontus
Armenia
OTTOMAN EMPIRE (1914)
Asia Minor
Anatolia
Kurdistan
Cilicia
Syria
Mediterranean Sea
Mesopotamia

Introduction by Kevork A. Sarafian

The Defense of Aintab: The Verdun of Anatolia

"Le Verdun de l'Anatolie" is the title of a chapter from an important French book which recites the story of the battle of an outnumbered French force against the Kemalist troops in the city of Aintab.* This battle takes place between two unequal forces.

The book describes how, on April 1st, 1920, a newly arrived French battalion in Aintab goes to Kilis, taking with it the heavy artillery and part of the detachment a French soldiers at Aintab. The Turks, seizing the opportunity to attack the Armenian quarter of the city, first destroy the French troops and then annihilate the Armenians.

The Armenians of Aintab, who were prepared wholeheartedly to resist the Turkish forces, courageously defend their positions for 15 days, despite the scarcity of fighters and ammunition. During the early days of the battle, the French simply observe the situation and remain at their posts at the American College [Central Turkey College] in Aintab. The Armenians not only defend the Armenian quarter, but occupy the American institutions, as well as the Latin Franciscan monastery where 150 Armenians had found refuge.

The Ghevont Yerets † of the heroic battle of Aintab, the priest Rev. Nerses Tavoukjian, the father of the prelate of the American-Armenians, Archbishop Diran, informed the Catholicos of Cilicia, Sahag Khabaian, about the situation in Aintab with a letter sent on April 25/27, 1920, beseeching him to make representations to the French central authorities. It is worth quoting an excerpt from that letter here:

> When the French Colonel was convinced that his troops could safely cross the Armenian street and reach the Latin monastery, he dispatched 25 soldiers to defend it. Likewise, he provided 15 soldiers for the American institutions. Armenians also defended those institutions courageously. This battle continued for 15 days

---

* [Paul Du Véou, *La Passion de la Cilicie*, 1919-1922, Éditeur: Paul Geuthner, Paris, 1938], (pp. 229-248).

† [St. Ghevont Yerets of the 5th century preacher and warrior who stood against the Persians who wanted Armenians to renounce Christianity.]

> and nights as the Turks attacked relentlessly from all sides. According to the testimonies of participants, by the night of Maundy Thursday, the three hour battle had turned into a complete war. Thank God we were always successful and the Turks did not break through our lines. On the other hand, our boys captured many of their positions, always repelling their attacks. On April 16 and 17, French troops arrived from the East and West. The fight somewhat stopped for two or three days, but no significant changes occurred. Since yesterday, the French have not helped us either by providing soldiers or sending ammunition.
>
> We helped the French by protecting them from the Turkish attacks, yet they didn't do the same for us.

The war continued, and the French were compelled to fight the Kemalist *chetes* [irregular soldiers or bandits] who wanted to annihilate them. The details of this war were written down by one of our co-workers, the late Kevork Baboian. What we wish to say here is no more than stating the unforgettable truth, that had the Aintab Armenians not taken up arms in the first days of the war, had they not roared "Death or Freedom" against the Kemalist forces, had they not relied solely on their courage and God's help, the Armenians of Aintab – approximately 17,000 souls – would have certainly been ruthlessly massacred.

After some time, the Turks signed a peace treaty with the representatives of the Armenians of Aintab. The French remained helpless and alone, and during the days of this short cease-fire, the Armenians prepared their positions and amassed supplies without wasting any time. During this volatile period of neutrality, the strategic policies adopted by the Armenian National Committee of Aintab are worthy of praise as much as the heroic soldiers who fought bravely on the battlefield.

However, when the Armenians saw that the French were in a tense situation and the Turks were not abiding by the terms of the ceasefire agreement, they wholeheartedly went back to the battlefield and stood by the French army which was desperate for their help.

This is the reason why the French author calls the battle of Aintab, the "Verdun of Anatolia," because the Armenians and French stood firm alongside each other against the bullets of the fanatical Kemalist forces. The Turks also called the battle of Aintab the "War of Verdun."

Another book, *La Passion de la Cilicie* (The Passion of Cilicia), describes the courage and loyalty of the Armenians.

> When the Turkish commander saw what was happening, he threatened to destroy the Armenian positions. Gunfire was exchanged along the length of the street, and the Armenians joined us, because this courageous people, roused by protecting their homes, did not want to hear and speak about neutrality any more and vowed to win or die by our side. The leader of their committee came to our command post to place his soldiers under Andrea's command. Andrea accepted their loyalty and testified that until the end of the siege, this detachment fought marvelously and attested to courage and complete loyalty rarely seen.

As a historical note, we should mention that we have in our possession the official document sent to one of the two the commanders of the Armenian heroes of Aintab, Mr. Adour Levonian.

> Lieutenant-Colonel Andrea, the commander of the French troops, sends his compliments to Mr. Adour Levonian and his soldiers for their magnificent display of courage and perseverance throughout their fight alongside the French. Through their relentless labor, they were able to transform the city into a stronghold, holding back the enemy despite their constant attacks.
>
> Lieutenant-Colonel Andrea thanks the Armenians for the precious aid they provided to the French soldiers during the long months of the siege.

Thanks to the research of Reverend Joseph Barsoumian, this valuable book [The Passion of Cilicia], whose acquisition demanded arduous efforts, was finally found in the library of one of the dentists living in Lyon, Mr. Kevork Nigoghosian. This voluminous book not only gave descriptions of Cilicia's evacuation and the massacres at Marash, Hajin and Adana, but also numerous documents which shed light on the strategic and political intrigues orchestrated by the French high authorities.

This book shows every aspect of the crime Franklin Bouillon committed when he evacuated French soldiers and gallant Armenians from Cilicia. One reads with anguish, the grand statesman and patriot Aristid Briand's poignant declaration in the French parliament on June 25th, 1920:

> Alexandretta and Cilicia: a magnificent position, a formidable point on the Mediterranean, the control of which is vital for France's future... To depart (interrupts Briand in the French parliament), to depart from that region, after bringing the Armenian survivors of the massacres there, to depart after what happened to the Syrians,

> do you know what this means? This means that thousands of people, women and children, will be massacred, because the French flag will be absent. I say that France has no right to behave in such a way (Applause from the "Rightists" in the hall).

However, despite Briand's humanism and far-sightedness, people like Franklin Bouillon led a chivalrous France in wrong directions, and France left Cilicia after witnessing the massacres of Armenians in Marash, Hajin, and Adana. The heroic Armenians of Aintab, after fighting against the Kemalist forces for many months, were obliged to evacuate the newly liberated city, hand in hand with the French, and found refuge in neighboring Syrian cities.

The slogan, which used to echo through the mountains and valleys of Cilicia, was heard no more, "The mother of Armenians, France our hope."

There are two more books which shed light on the heroic battle of Aintab and the events of Cilicia: Robert Norman's *Colonnes dans le Levant* [Columns in the Levant], published by Charles-La Vauzelle and Cie, Paris, and Lieutenant-Colonel M. Abady's *Les Quatre Siege d'Aintab, 1920-1921* [The Four Sieges of Aintab, 1920-1921], published by Charles-La Vauzelle and Cie.

These two books describe the French military operations and both are important for those interested in military studies. We believe that our assistant, the deceased Kevork Baboian, when working on his project, "The Heroic Battle of Aintab," had *Les Quatre Siege d'Aintab, 1920-1921* and Robert Norman's *Colonnes dans le Levant* in mind.

During the early months of the battle, the French commander Flye Sainte Marie sent the following motivating announcement dated 26 April 1920:

> To the Armenians of Aintab,
>
> I am happy and congratulate the Armenian people of Aintab for the courage they displayed and will continue to exhibit in the future. I also congratulate them for their organizational spirit and valorous strength.
>
> It is now imperative to demonstrate two grand military qualities, which are composure and coolness.
>
> God will secure success. I will continue my efforts to find a way to get out of the chaotic situation which has lasted for over a month.
>
> Flye Sainte Marie
>
> 26 April, 1920

Chapter 2

The Occupation of Aintab by the Entente Powers.

The Armistice of Mudros, signed on October 31st, 1918, secured the sanjak of Aintab for the Turkish authorities. However, according to the 7th article of the agreement, the Entente Powers reserved the right to reoccupy those lands if the security of their armies was threatened. For that specific reason, the British had occupied Kilis and Aintab in January 1919, as well as Marash and Ourfa in February of the same year.

The aforementioned occupation fanned Turkish impertinence with claims that the occupation was illegal and assertions that not a single event jeopardizing the peace had occurred there. However, the well-organized British troops silenced them and peace was restored. It was during these times that deported Armenians started to return to their native towns and rebuilding their devastated homes. The British, after restoring peace in the town, started taking steps to improve the economy of the city and promote self-sufficiency among its inhabitants. By order of the British commander, the immovable and movable properties of Armenians confiscated by the Turks during the deportation were returned to their rightful owners. People who attempted to disturb the peace were sent to Egypt and weapons in the possession of Turks were confiscated. Various road construction projects began in order to provide jobs for the people. Frankly, throughout that short period of British occupation, the prosperous financial situation of the people of Aintab, and particularly that of Armenians, was restored. Devastated houses were rebuilt and Armenian craftsmen started to work immediately. Armenians, having barely survived the horrors of the Syrian deserts, hoped to finally live in a period of peace and prosperity.

In October 1919, the Entente powers, for their own reasons, decided to concede the territories under British control to the French. The British were unhappy with this arrangement, since they did not wish to lose areas replete with natural resources. Thus, the British encouraged the Turkish and Armenian elements of these territories to start protests and refuse the French mandate. Such a proposal perplexed the Armenian community, since they had looked upon the Entente powers with gratitude. Consequently, the Armenians adopted a position of neutrality. Neither a British or French occupied of Aintab made a difference to them. The

Armenians were only looking for physical security and peace. However, the British were annoyed by the position adopted by Armenians.

On the suggestion of the former captain of the Intelligence Bureau, Hassan Rifki, the Turks sent a letter to the Sultan and General Allenby on October 12th, 1919, expressing their wish to see British armies hold Cilicia.

In reality, the Turks wished neither the British nor the French to maintain control. However, given the Turkish government's secret treaty with Britain, they preferred the latter over the French. The terms of this agreement were the following, as they became clear when they were published in the French newspaper, *Efler*, through M. Briand's efforts.

The Treaty was signed in September 1919, when the British were still on Cilician territories, but it was only declared on February 11th, 1920.

> Article 1. The British government will safeguard Turkey's complete independence under its patronage.
>
> Article 2. Constantinople will remain the seat of the Caliphate and Britain will control the Dardanelles.
>
> Article 3. Turkey will not oppose the formation of an independent Kurdistan.
>
> Article 4. Turkey will assist in Britain's control over Syria and Iraq by providing the necessary force and promising to offer the Caliph's and Sultan's moral support to the Muslim peoples of the British Empire.
>
> Article 5. The British Government promises to provide the semi-constitutional Turkish government with the necessary police force in order to protect it against nationalist movements.
>
> Article 6. Turkey renounces its demands for Egypt and Cyprus.
>
> Article 7. This treaty will have a personal and covert character and the British government will support the proposals of the Turkish delegates at the peace conference.
>
> Article 8. As soon as the terms of this treaty are agreed upon, His Majesty the Sultan will sign a treaty with the British government based on this agreement.

The Turks saw that the British desire to remain on Cilician lands meant little, and that faced with French persistence, the British were forced to withdraw and concede their positions to the latter. The Turks also realized that with the withdrawal of the British forces, they would have more favourable circumstances for action. They never wished for a French mandate.

The aforementioned Turkish mentality can be understood from the expression that circulated among them: "Cholera has gone, the plague will come." On October 27th, 1919, the Turks voted in favor of the following draft agreement:

The Grand Convention of Aintab

> During the armistice, not one of the Entente powers occupied Aintab. Yet, two months later, the British sent a battalion as protection for their army stationed in Aleppo.
>
> The British saw with their own eyes that we, the people of Aintab, respect law and order and love peace, and that we protect the property and honor of our fellow Christians, as we do our own.
>
> We have heard that the British will be withdrawing from Aleppo as well as from Aintab.
>
> We are very pleased with the British, since their withdrawal from Aintab demonstrates that they respect our independence and rights.
>
> The British assert that 90% of the population of Aintab is Muslim, more than a thousand villages are Turkish and Muslim and that all immovable property belongs to them.
>
> Therefore, based on Wilson's principle, they should consider that our country is not part of Syria and that they should let us decide our fate.
>
> We will not permit any other occupation after the British withdrawal.
>
> For sake of humanity and civilization, we request that you present our justifiable rights and wishes to the conference.
>
> On behalf of the Convention,
>
> Mayor of Aintab,
>
> M. Loutfi

During this same period, another telegram was sent to the high command of the occupying French army on behalf of the commander of Diyarbekir's 10th Battalion commander Jevdet Bey with the following message:

> Diyarbekir, October 29th, 1919.

We are pleased to hear that the British troops have withdrawn from Aintab, whose occupation was already a violation of the terms agreed upon in the Armistice treaty and was unjustly implemented.

In the meantime, we hear that the French have already come to occupy Aintab in their place.

Considering the friendly relationships developed between France and Turkey for centuries, the fact that all the Turkish intellectuals and statesmen have received a French education, that our country has benefited from France many times, and that we owe our economic progress to it, we feel compelled to express nothing but our deepest gratitude towards France.

As to what pertains to our mutual interests, we are sure of the sympathy that the French feel towards Turks and we are proud to see our French friends besides us.

However, in this hour, when the peace conference strives to reach a conclusion by signing a peace treaty with Turkey, the French occupation of the hitherto British held lands and the publication of such news in some Egyptian and Syrian newspapers has brought forth great agitation and stimulated suspicions among the public.

This agitation has resounded substantially in my region and protests are taking place everywhere against the Entente powers.

This new occupation is illegal, no matter from what aspect it is viewed, whether for the implementation of the Armistice terms or the adoption of a precautionary stance, and it will not grant rights to the majority in this region, in other words, to the Turkish or Muslim elements.

On behalf of the people of my region, I voice my protest against this injustice.

In order to remedy this injustice, by respecting the principle of national self-determination and appealing to the principles of liberty and the fraternity of the civilized human race attributed to France, I am certain that my commander will uphold justice by evacuating the territories in question.

In the meantime, please allow me to draw your attention to another point.

Unfortunately, these foreign occupations "corrupt" the non-Muslim peoples, who have been well treated by us for centuries.

The enthusiasm and joy of the Armenian prefecture established in Adana are sufficient for me to assert my opinion.

The conscription of non-Muslim elements into your armies will give rise to misunderstandings and injustices to the Muslim population of these areas.

Even from the first day, I have been aware of such conduct by the Armenian population of Aintab.

We trust French justice. Nevertheless, such reports and provocations will multiply and, as a result, will stir up hostilities amongst the various elements.

These events will hurt the feelings of the majority of the Muslim population and your occupation will have no other benefit than to cause us agony, something that is certainly against your interests.

Commander of 10th Battalion, Commander Jevdet

Despite the efforts of the Turks, the French entered Aintab on October 20th, 1919, and the last British troops withdrew at the end of the same month. In order to avoid any interruption during the transfer process, which would have been disastrous for the Christian community, the French rushed to put the city under their protection with a small force commanded by Lieutenant-Colonel Flye Sainte Marie, comprising the 412th Artillery Brigade, an African "Hunters" squad and the 3rd Battalion of the Armenian Legion.

(A division of the 412th Artillery brigade and the "Hunters" squad, as well as the first battalion of the Armenian Legion also occupied Marash).

Let us mention here that the Kemalist movements had already begun during the British occupation. Citing Wilson's famous principle of people's right to self-determination, Turkish statesmen and military personnel first conferred in Erzurum on August 7th, 1919 and then in Sivas on September 11th, 1919 in order to discuss the question of the complete independence of Turkey.

After the Sivas conference, the Committee for the Protection of Rights of Rumeli and Anatolia was formed with Mustafa Kemal Pasha at its head. He exploited the dissensions of the Entente powers on economic and political matters in order to strengthen his position and bolster the rise of the *Milli* movement with Enguri [Ankara] at its center. The government at Constantinople, including the Caliph and his supporters, were considered by Kemal and the Milli government as traitors who surrendered the fatherland to the Entente powers. The Milli government was filled with animosity towards the Greeks who landed in Izmir, the Italians who occupied Adalia (Antalya), the British who wanted to create an independent Kurdistan and dismember Syria from Turkey, the Armenians who wanted independence for their fatherland (i.e. the eastern provinces), as well as the French who meddled with administrative affairs in Cilicia. Finally, the new Kemalist government, relying on its newly formed army, wanted to find a propitious solution for the aforementioned problems, either through diplomacy or military force. Do we need to add that diplomatic negotiations made the Kemalists realize their dream and carried them from one success to another, bestowing them the reputation of being national saviors and heroes? The British were already aware of this movement and when the Kemalist organization started to operate in Aintab, the local commander notified his superior, whose answer, according to the testimony of an American missionary was, "Close your eyes and pretend that you have not seen it." After that, during a Turco-British meeting, the British made the following important declaration to Mutasarrif Jelal and his companions:

> The French cannot send more than 30,000 troops to Syria and Cilicia, whereas the soldiers of Kemal Pasha will arrive to Aintab and its vicinity at the beginning of spring.

The organizers of the Milli movement of Aintab were Ragheb Bey, police chief Esad Bey, Dr. Hamid Bey, Avni from Marash, Eshref Effendi, Hoja Hamdi Effendi from Marash, Kebkeb Zadeh Abdurreshad Effendi, Marak Zadeh Sherif (a thief and a criminal from the lower classes), Keorukchu Zadeh Ahmed and Ahmed Moukhtar, whose crimes committed with Hussein Jemil as members of the Ittihad were known to the Armenian community of Aintab.

Among the moral supporters and financial sponsors of the aforementioned people, we can recall, Bazarbashuh Zadeh Nouri, Hoja Zadeh Ferid, Haji Oemer Zadeh Mohammed Ali, Kahraman Zadeh Haji Mohammed, and Komiser Halil Injo Zadeh Hussein from Kilis from the Turkish nobility. These men and others were the ones who poisoned the Muslim population of Aintab with the venom of hatred and stirred them up against the Armenians and French.

Chapter 3

The French Entry into Aintab

(Important events from November 1st 1918 to January 1st, 1919)

On October 29th, 1919, the French commander Flye Sainte Marie entered Aintab and was greeted by joyful crowds and applause. The Armenians, as a grateful people, contributed to the welcome with a cheerful reception. The Turks did not participate and withdrew to their quarters. They were furious at the newly arrived French army, the major part of which consisted of volunteers in the Armenian Legion. The detachment commander greeted the Armenian community with a brief oration from the balcony of the Muslim hospital. His speech was translated by an Armenian volunteer. The commander declared:

> I bring peace to the Armenian and Muslim people who have both suffered. I bring this peace through France and the flag that it symbolizes, which I am holding in my hands. You will be happy and peaceful under our governance.

Not a single Turkish statesman or ordinary person was present at this speech. On the other hand, the attitude of Armenians stirred feelings of resentment among the Turks to such an extent that they still reflected on it several months later.

The following day, on October 30th, the French command-post organized a few consultative meetings.

1. With the British, General Veyd and Flye Sainte Marie drafted a placard according to which the French were replacing the British while maintaining the same responsibilities and jurisdiction.

2. With the Turks, General Veyd introduced Sainte Marie to Turkish notables, Mutasarrif Jelalettin, his lieutenant Sabri Bey and Sheikh Mustafa.

3. With the Armenians, whose representative body was the National Union consisting of A. Babigian, L. A. Levonian, Dr. K. Arslanian, K. Leylegian, K. K. Karamanougian, A. Jebejian, Y. Benlian, Nazaret Fesdekjian and B. Milletbashian.

The day after these meetings, on November 1st, the French received the following complaint:

To the Commander of the newly arrived French army of Aintab:

Two days ago, I was informed of your arrival in Aintab with a few soldiers and officers.

During my daily visit, I understood that you have come to Aintab with the intent of occupying it.

After the fall of Aleppo, and despite the terms of the Armistice, the British commander unjustly came to Aintab in order to maintain the peace in the occupied areas, and to provide his cavalry with safe shelter for the winter. Eventually he went on to occupy Marash and Ourfa.

The British only wished to maintain peace in the land they occupied, without meddling in our internal administrative affairs. They have not interfered in anything and have shown impartial conduct towards the Christian and Muslim communities. Peace prevailed in the country during their tenure of 11 months.

Today, the British, who are forced to withdraw from Aleppo, are also forced to leave this region.

You surely know the agreed terms of the Armistice, according to which the Aintab region remains inside Turkey's borders and the demarcation line passes through Mislimiyeh. Aintab and its outskirts remain under Turkish sovereignty. According to the terms of the Mudros Armistice signed on October 30st, 1918, the Entente powers have the right to occupy regions that are essential for the security of their armies in case of fighting. According to the first article, the Entente powers reserve the right of occupation in case of massacres. The other articles are concerned with other aspects of the Armistice.

The occupation of Aintab, where neither fighting nor massacres have occurred, is unacceptable to us and we request that you leave.

I am sending a copy of this complaint to the Commander of the French occupation Army of Aintab, Colonel Flye Sainte Marie, and another one to the Turkish government of Constantinople.

Please accept etc.

Aintab, November 1st, 1919

Vice Mutasarrif

Sabri

Arrival of French troops in Aintab.

On November 2nd, the command post of the French occupation army of Aintab received the following telegraph from Marash:

> After an eight-month occupation by British troops, the region has been occupied by French troops since October 20th.
>
> During the British occupation not a single event occurred which violated our national and religious rights.
>
> Relying on the well-known civilization and uprightness of the French people, we maintain that the change or transfer of the occupation to the French has not given rise to any change of feelings towards you in our hearts. However, the majority of your army consists of Armenians, who are native to Adana, and who, as soon as they arrived in Marash, displayed considerable enmity towards the Muslims there.
>
> Their rudeness has been confirmed by reports from the police administration and the testimonies of French and British commanders.
>
> Let us list the events in question.
>
> a) While passing through the market and city streets, they have insulted the Muslim religion, and dishonored a Muslim clergyman they encountered, regardless of his status as an

Ulema and his venerable *kisvet* (a garment worn by Muslim hojas).

b) They gathered, armed, in front of the Uzun Oluk bathhouse, and attempted to unveil Muslim women. After the outcries of the latter, three Muslims called Haji Imam, Said Effendi, and Hafar Kabul Oghlu hurried to their aid but were badly injured with bayonets and bullets. They also assaulted T. A. Effendi and beat Zulfi Kiar Oghlu Hussein Chavush.

c) On the way to the garrison, they shouted that they would slaughter the Muslims and enslave their wives.

d) Tragic events have occurred, like the assassination of a Muslim refugee (near the city), immediately after a declaration of protection made on your behalf; and finally, the maltreatment of a large Muslim majority by a small minority, though the latter are aware of the ability of the former to teach them a good lesson when religious and national feelings are dishonored.

To encourage dreadful events (massacres), they have created some agitation, in order to ascribe them to Muslims later on. However, despite all this, the Muslim people knew how to maintain their calmness.

In order to maintain the peace of the region, we have informed the central government and the occupying army of these inflammatory events.

In his reply, the commander expressed his astonishment and assured us that similar events would not be repeated in the future.

Although he has made this promise, there are still Armenians in the occupying army who are known for their crimes, with similar events occurring every day. We have the right to think that the honor of the Muslim people is unsafe. We report this state of affairs to you for your information.

If our sound and legal demands are not taken into account, our firm determination is to make our complaints heard by the Supreme Court.

We await your response.

Marash, 2 November 1919

(Signed by 11 noblemen)

The exchange of French for British troops at Aintab (4 Nov. 1919). The Eighteenth Indian Lancers withdraw as French and Armenian troops stand at the roadside.

The Turks had tortured an Armenian Legionnaire a day before sending this protest.

November 5th. A courier came from Zeitun and informed us of the danger threatening that city, as the Turks were massing forces in Elbistan, preparatory to beginning their attacks.

November 7th. The Ottoman flag over Akyol garrison was brought down by a Turkish policeman at the command of a French lieutenant with the approval of the British. The Islamic Committee complained and forced the policeman to resign. Despite Colonel Flye Sainte Marie's intervention, the policeman was not reinstated. The Turks contended that the policeman was punished for a different reason. After this, the French command wrote to the Turkish government that thereafter no Ottoman flag would be raised.

November 8th. The Armenian Legionnaires were sent away from Aintab on the insistence of the Turks, and Algerian soldiers were brought in to replace them.

November 9th. The following circular issued by Kemal Pasha reached Aintab. It was sent by telegraph to Adana, Sis, Mersin, and Jebeluh Bereket's National Association of the Protectors of Rights:

> Aintab and Marash, which were occupied by the British despite the terms of the Armistice and then evacuated, are now reoccupied by the French. The government is forced to complain to the Entente powers about this occupation which violates the rights of the local population, and which, in turn, has started to organize meetings to show the whole world that even the smallest part of the Ottoman Empire will not be dismembered from it.
>
> Therefore, with this circular we inform the administrations and central bodies of the Committee of the National Association for the Protection of Rights, as well as the leaders of the local councils, that they should protest to the representatives of the Entente Powers and galvanize public opinion in Europe and the United States by stating that the aforementioned places are part of Turkey and are now occupied by the French. Moreover, they should request immediate restoration of peace.
>
> November 9th, 1919
>
> Executive Body of the Committee for Protection of Rights of Anatolia and Rumelia.
>
> Mustafa Kemal.

November 13th. The commander of the French army in Cilicia, Colonel Piépape and Colonel Norman, passed through Aintab and visited the governorship where they were received coldly. The Turks served neither coffee nor cigarettes. On the same day, the French command received the following telegraph from Severeg.

> November 13th, 1919.
>
> We were pained to receive news of the occupation of Marash, Aintab and Ourfa. This is a violation of the terms of the Armistice and International Law.
>
> Events following the occupation, such as killings, attacks and the punishment of those who complained, terrified the Muslims.
>
> We warn you that if you don't put an end to such incidents, we are ready to fight until the last man.

On behalf of the Central Committee for the Protection of National Rights,

Jevad

November 20th. Three Armenian orphans escaped from Mr. Travis's orphanage and started wandering the streets. Turkish policemen arrested and imprisoned them as incendiaries. The release of these innocent boys only became possible after ceaseless appeals by the French high command.

November 27th. The Mutasarrif complained about the French flag raised over the occupied buildings, claiming it to be a violation of Ottoman sovereign rights.

November 28th. A protest note was sent to the French by the Islamic Committee, stating that sheltering too many Armenian refugees filled with a spirit of revenge in Aintab was dangerous for the maintenance of peace.

November 29th. A small French cavalry unit, while patrolling along the Marash-Islahiyeh road, was attacked 15 kilometers south of El-Oghlu, leaving behind one dead and two wounded. The assailants were never found.

November 30th. The French took the police staff under their control, which infuriated the Turks.

December 5th. The French received the following letter on the occasion of the aforementioned event.

Diyarbekir, December 5th, 1919.

To the Command of the French Occupying Army,

I was informed that, citing an extended section of the 4th article of the Armistice, you have suggested taking the police administration and gendarmerie of Aintab under your control.

Only one armistice was signed in Mudros. There are no extra articles and I do not recognize any extension to the Armistice terms. Had there been such a thing, my government would have notified me about it. Therefore, I protest at your violation of the Armistice terms signed with the participation of the British on October 31st, 1918. The terms of this Armistice have also been published in Aintab.

Similarly, I have heard about a person called Captain Andre, who was sent from Osmaniyeh to Marash, where he has suggested to the Mutassarif that he should participate in the administrative affairs of the city.

The British, during their occupation, did not meddle in the internal affairs of the government.

You announced, in your declaration published in Aintab, that the French occupation would be exactly like the British one. Therefore, you must not ignore your declaration.

Your High Commissariat in Constantinople has announced to the Turkish government that this change in occupation is not the result of an official decision, but rather an exchange between French and British soldiers.

Our government at Constantinople considered this declaration as a guarantee, whereas your commanding officers at Marash, Aintab, Ourfa and Berejik are operating against its terms.

No peace has been signed with Turkey yet. We have nothing in our hands, except the Armistice terms agreed upon at Mudros. Any violation or extension to the terms of this armistice is unjust and unacceptable to us.

Therefore, we complain to the whole of civilized mankind about your military operations. Turkey is a country in the east, where French literature and science were the most widespread for many centuries. Our country has benefited from the French economy. In the financial sector, Turkey is France's oldest friend.

I want to make you comprehend that for the sake of your country's interests, beware of doing things which will break the Turkish nation's heart.

Kindly accept this letter and order the cessation of meddling in our internal affairs.

Commander of the 13th Battalion of the Turkish Army, Jevdet

December 9th. General Keret arrived in Aintab.

December 10th. There was trouble in Marash. Suleiman Pasha prepared to hold the road between Aintab and Islahiyeh with 800 men.

December 14th. A military parade took place at the crossroads between Marash and Kilis in honor of General Keret to which Turkish noblemen, the Armenian National Union and American missionaries were invited. The Turks completely refrained from attending, and only Mutasarrif Jelalettin was present with his few companions. There were 70 participants at the parade on behalf of the Turkish gendarmerie, but they disappeared even before the parade started. This was ignored by the French command, and when the French commander nervously asked the Mutasarrif where had they gone, the latter replied, "They returned to the city." However, upon the commander's question, "Who gave them permission?", no answer was given, because it was a volatile situation and turmoil was imminent. The parade ended hastily. The Islamic Committee sent the following emphatic complaint, "The French occupation is a blow to our independence and against our national wishes."

December 15th. Posters were stuck to walls along the streets of Marash, begging the people for war against the French. There was agitation everywhere. While Muslims started to arm themselves, the placid French behavior was seen as a sign of weakness.

December 22nd. Tensions escalated in Marash, as trade and all work stopped. Some orders arriving from Constantinople claimed that the French, similar to the British, would be staying where they were, otherwise there would be bloodshed.

December 23rd. A brigade heading to Marash was involved in a fight at Bazarjek. Threatening Francophile Turks, the nationalists became very active in distributing and transporting arms and munitions, highlighting key positions and killing Armenian travelers leaving the town.

December 25th. Rumors started to circulate that Ghelej Ali Bey was ready to march on Marash with his 12,000 regular troops. This served as propaganda to draw the Kurds into the war.

December 29th. Armenians were threatened with slaughter. The government blamed the Christians.

December 30th was the Grand National holiday. We could consider this date as the official Turkish declaration of enmity, which supposedly coincided with the 600th anniversary of rise of the Ottoman Empire. The town markets were decorated with flags. The French allowed the demonstration to take place on the condition that demonstrators didn't cross to the western side of Transversal Street. Despite this warning, thousands gathered outside the College gates and infiltrated positions Demonstrators with flags, sanjaks [religious banners], drums, silly musical instruments and barbarous chants wandered around the French and Armenian quarters until nightfall. The French watched the

Babylonic chaos with interest, where the expression of barbaric instincts resembled the cavities of the sewers. Endless insults were uttered. No popular gathering had been as horrific and ugly as this furious Muslim crowd. It was a mixture of barbarity, fanaticism, brigandage, insolence, virulence and ignorance.

The Turks thought they had won, whereas the French and Armenians simply observed the drama.

Starting with the French arrival in Aintab, this was the atmosphere of the town for two months, an unstable situation with signs of an imminent uprising. The fever and terror of war were everywhere. The Turks divided the town into areas called *Semt*s, with each appointed chief holding the title of "Semt Reisi." After the deportations, the unfortunate Armenian people, having barely witnessed a year of rest, were getting ready to be thrown anew into the flames of battle. It was winter, the weather was cold and snow had fallen. The Armenians resorted to self-containment: Armenian families were moved from Turkish streets to Armenian ones, while Armenian merchants and tradesmen started to transport their merchandise to their houses. These precautions contributed greatly to the later success of the defense of Aintab.

Chapter 4

On the Eve of the Critical Days

(From January 1st to April 1st, 1920)

January1st. The eve of the battle of Marash, the shops were closed and the streets were fortified with barricades.

January3rd. An unprecedented panic began in Aintab fuelled by the events in Marash.

January 5th. There were fervent speeches and demonstration on the occasion of Ahmed Moukhtar's election as deputy.

January 6th. A protest note was sent from Bazarjek to the French, with the following points:

1. The French, with the cooperation of Armenian *chetes* (irregular troops) and their artillery have burned and destroyed the village of Jejel, damaging it greatly.

2. The French cavalry, arriving at Karabeyekluh, wanted to requisition provisions from the villagers without paying their cost, and when the villagers refused, they were beaten and abused.

3. A French cavalryman killed a nobleman called Kara Ali when the latter was returning to his house in Karabeyekluh. They add that two other people had accompanied him, but we do not know whether they are dead or alive.

4. French soldiers located near Akhir Dagh have killed two Muslims on their return from the forest where they had gone to collect wood.

5. The French have been arming the Armenians for two months, ceaselessly providing them with artillery, ammunition and weapons, storing them in Armenian houses and churches, thus turning them into fortified barricades, the sole purpose of which is the massacre the Muslim community.

6. There are no thieves here, only armed men, whose purpose is to operate against the violators of our national rights.

7. We protest against the term "thief" and the aforementioned savage acts.

8. We demand an end to this gruesome situation.

9. We declare for the last time, that we will be forced to resist all the movements that offend our national rights, holding all those who trample upon them to account.

(Signed by the 7 noblemen of Bazarjek).

On January 8th and 9th, the Colonel suggested that the Armenian National Union sends a letter to Marash as an expression of their support for the French soldiers.

The French efforts to restore peace in Aintab and its vicinity between January 9th and 21st had no effect. The Turkish *chete*s blocked the roads and streets, and they cut down the telegraphic wires. No messenger could pass through Marash. The Ak-Su Bridge was destroyed.

A whole French cavalry unit, commanded by Lieutenant Frinzi, disappeared with no trace.

January 21st. During the evening, at 5 o'clock, a French soldier (an Algerian), going to the French bakery, tried to unveil a Muslim woman who was accompanied by her 16 year-old son. Following this sacrilegious act, the boy attacked the French soldier, who killed him with his bayonet.

When there is tension between two nations, an ordinary event, or some casual or careless behavior, can rally forces whose collision can lead to war. A small incident can set such machinery in motion. This incident clearly showed the secret intentions of the Turks. The day following the death of the young boy stirred the fanatical temper of the Muslims and resulted in a massive funeral ceremony. A noisy crowd followed the coffin. Insults were heard, addressed to the French and Armenians. That insignificant boy became the man of the day and was counted amongst Turkish national and religious heroes. After the funeral, a threatening note was sent to the French command, even though it had promised to pay 400 Ottoman gold liras to the parents and relatives of the victim, as well as harsh punishment for the soldier responsible for his disgraceful behavior.

The Turks were not satisfied because they considered the French proposal a sign of weakness and wanted to demand additional compensation.

On the same day, the Mutasarrif suggested to the French command that a mixed Turkish-French force should ensure the security of the city in order to prevent any further friction or incident.

January 29th. During this time, the newly elected Armenian National Union comprised Dr. K. Arslanian, Hagop Mouradian, Nazareth

Fesdekjian, Soghomon Arevian, Khoren Varjabedian, Hagop Melkonian, Krikor Jebejian, Hagop Murekian, Dikran S. Mesrobian and Yervant Aginian (from the refugees). Colonel Flye Sainte Marie suggested that the heads of the three denominations should join them. These were Padre Mariano (Catholic), Rev. D. Nerses Tavoukjian (Armenian Apostolic) and Rev. Yenovk Hadidian (Protestant).

It was during this time that the sorrowful news of the Marash massacre spread through Aintab. Until then, there had been no news about the heart-rending Marash massacre. Even the French did not know anything about it.

Rumors that Marash had been bombarded by Norman's and Keret's forces, that two thirds of the city had been burnt down, that the majority of its population, about 10,000 Armenians and some Turks, had been slaughtered, started circulating in Aintab. Moreover, news arrived that the survivors were in very miserable condition because food and shelter were lacking, as well as the winter conditions. The French had lost around 700 men in the mountains around Marash and retreated because of food shortages. Their retreat was even more tragic than the battle. The Turks had demanded their surrender. However, the French refused and left the city on the following day, taking with them 2-3,000 Armenians, who suffered heavy losses because of the snow.

The events at Marash had two benefits. One, they delayed the battle of Aintab, because the Turks were as bewildered as the Armenians. Second, the Armenians, anticipating the danger awaiting them, began taking some precautions.

Until this date, the Armenians trusted the French troops, with the expectation that during any incident, the latter would distract the Turks with a few bombardments.

January 30th. The National Union decided to send two men, one to Aleppo and the other to Adana, to demand help for Aintab from the other committees. Moreover, it decided to contact Dr. Altounian, Damadian and the National Delegation to find a solution for the deadlock.

January 31st. Two Algerian soldiers went to the grand market to buy some groceries. They had a small argument with a shop-keeper. The result was that all the shop-keepers surrounded them, and the Grand Market (Arasa) soon became impassable. The soldiers, who felt threatened, resorted to their handguns. The crowd pulled back, while the soldiers slowly moved back and found shelter near two policemen, who confiscated their weapons, making them vulnerable to the crowd's fury. The soldiers fell, exhausted, under the rain of blows from sticks and were transported to the governorate in a ghastly state. The crowd, still dissatisfied, attacked the few remaining Armenian craftsmen in the grand market. The uproar got worse by the minute. Some shouted "to arms", and others rushed to their houses and shops to bring out their weapons. In this chaos, the following phrases were heard many times: "Brothers, let us first kill the *giavours* (infidels) among us, and then march against the French." Some of the Armenians craftsmen were injured that day, others were captured, and a few barely escaped, finding shelter in the Armenian streets. However, Turkish Nationalist leaders dispersed the crowd, stating that the hour of the battle had not yet arrived. *

The National Union reported these events to the French command, who wanted to pacify the much agitated people by stating: "These are ordinary events that happen on a daily basis in Paris. The killing of 10 to 15 Armenians cannot be considered the beginning of a war. The Armenians should go back to the market calmly and we should try to win the friendship of the Turks."

The French command knew that these were not ordinary occurrences. However, such noises were of no importance to Flye Sainte Marie, whose ear was more accustomed to the sound of German 42s. He wanted to buy some time and delay the fighting as much as possible, since reinforcements were unlikely to arrive from the outside. The wind was blowing, snow was falling and the roads were impassable.

February 1st to 5th. Four Americans who were traveling from Aleppo to Aintab were slaughtered near Besh-Geoz and buried on the spot. Their bodies were later transported to Aintab and surrendered to the College. A non-military state official demanded that a Turk hand over his weapon. When the latter refused, panic arose once more and led to the injury of two Armenians, A. Poladian, and H. Barbaraian.

February 6th. The following people from Sasoun were killed at the northern and southern water mills of Soret Mezreh, as well as at Bostanjek and Kerel: Hagop, Kevork, Guiro, Khacho, Garo and Arshag.

* During this event, seven Armenians were injured and one disappeared.

February 7th. The National Union met with the General Staff (Etat-Majeur) at the invitation of the French commander. Turks were also invited but did not show up. They sent the colonel a letter complaining about an Armenian who had supposedly attacked a Turkish gendarme in Kozanleh and claiming that, after the Marash events, they were afraid of meeting the general staff, fearing potential arrests.

The National Union was informed by a Turkish source that six guard houses would be established in the Armenian streets.

February 8th. A meeting took place in the governmental building, in the presence of Colonel Flye Sainte Marie, Captain Reno, Mutasarrif Jelalettin, Turkish notables, a few members of the Islamic Committee (Jemiyet-i Islamiyeh), Armenian notables and the National Union.

The French commander expressed his regrets to the Turks who had not replied to his invitation. The Turks mentioned the intemperance of an Armenian named Artin who had insulted a Turkish gendarme as an excuse. The Colonel pointed out that there was no need to establish guard houses in the Armenian quarter, and that he would take the appropriate measures concerning this matter. After the Colonel left, a debate took place between the Turks and Armenians discussing Armenian withdrawal to their streets as well as their reluctance to open their shops etc.... On this matter, Mr. H. Mouradian, in reply, remembered two events, the first being the torture of some Armenians when a few French soldiers were beaten, and, secondly, the injury of two Armenians as a result of a Turkish gendarme demanding the surrender of restricted weapons from a Turkish civilian. These events inspired the Armenians with distrust of the Turks. Similarly, it was pointed out that the Turks had stored forbidden weapons in their shops. In the end, it was agreed that, in order to bring about solidarity between the two elements, a joint committee composed of Turks and Armenians would be formed.

February 11th. Four Turks injured a 61 year old Armenian called Kevork Ashjibedrossian, wounding him in the back, in the street located between the guard houses of Sou Bourjou and Balekluh. At the same time the French command received the following letter from a man called Shahin Bey, a leader of a *chete* group:

> It is obvious that the rebellion at Marash is the result of General Keret spreading hatred between the Turks and the Armenians. Similarly, the failure of the French to maintain peace locally and

> prevent the assassination of four Americans on February 11th has been confirmed. Currently, the traffic between Aintab and Kilis is safe. Besides the French, everyone can pass through the aforementioned towns safely (here we omit the insults addressed to the French)
>
> Commander of the occupying army of Kilis, Shahin

February 13th. A Turk stabbed and injured an Armenian called Haroutioun Bogharian.

February 16th. Following the National Union's insistence, the Mutasarrif promised to investigate the case of the Turks who had wounded two Armenians.

The chancery of the Armenian National Union and a few other notables, as well as Padre Mariano, Rev. Nerses Tavoukjian and Rev. Y. Hadidian appeared before the general staff, taking with them Mr. H. Vosguerichian as translator at the Colonel's invitation. The Colonel expressed his anger, stating that the Armenians were not being obedient and would force him to fight. He claimed that the Armenian reluctance to go to the market was detrimental to the Armenians.

The Rev. Nerses Tavoukjian responded to the Colonel with the following words on behalf of the National Union:

> Commander, we obey you and it is for this reason that we remain silent against all this violence. You tell us to go to the government building and come to an agreement with the Turks. However, we, the Armenians, know that a couple of years ago, many went there and never returned. Hundreds were slaughtered in that building and their children did not even know the secret of their tragic death. Despite knowing all this, it is only to obey you that we go there, endangering our lives. You tell us to go to the market. We have tried too many times and suffered each time. We cannot force the people to be slaughtered day and night. Can you blame a people whose fate, over many centuries, has been death at the hands of Turks?
>
> As for the claim that it is the Armenian people who will be the cause of a Franco-Turkish conflagration, we say, open up the roads and behold, we will take the staff of exile into our hands again, ignoring the snow and storms, and go to a place where the Entente powers have sufficient strength to protect us. Children and adults hand in hand, we will go from one village to another,

> visiting each town until we find a tranquil place. Then, you will be free to deal with the Turks as you see fit.

The Colonel was deeply affected by this response and pointed out that although such a reply was rough, he wished that we waited a little longer and made further sacrifices so that everything could be restored. The National Union debunked the rumors that accused it of becoming Communist. One of the attendees also pointed out that the Turks had suggested forming a coalition to expel the French from Aintab.

The Colonel replied, "One could only laugh at such a suggestion."

February 17th to 28th. During this period, the orphanages of Elbeyli Oghlu, Millet Khan, and Nazar Agha were moved to the Armenian streets in the city and re-established there. Reports were coming from Marash that, after three weeks of fighting, the French had been forced to withdraw to Islahiyeh, taking thousands of Armenians with them. The retreating column had suffered many losses due to the snow and cold. More than 150 French soldiers were captured in Marash by the Turks. This bewildering news led to new measures in Aintab.

Armenian notables met the Turks at the government building at their invitation. The following Armenian delegates were present: Rev. Nerses Tavoukjian, Padre Mariano, Dr. K. Arslanian, N. Fesdekjian, G. D. Melkonian, G. Murekian, Y. Aginian, Dr. H. Bezjian, Bedros Ashjian, Hovhannes Levonian, Hovhannes Jebejian, Hovsep Arakelian, Bedros Milletbashian, Hagop Karamanougian, K. Leylegian, Khoren Bey Nazaretian, Hovsep Kendirjian, Sarkis Karamanougian, Dr. Chamichian and Dr. Kr. Khalfeian. The American delegates were Dr. John Merrill, Dr. Shepard, etc. The mutasarrif provided some information on political matters and then reflected on the Marash events in such an emotional manner that some of the Turks who were present lamented. The mutasarrif concluded that his wish or intention was to prevent the occurrence of similar events in Aintab, and that this was only possible with the mutual accord of the Turkish and Armenian elements of the city. Thus, it was agreed to form a committee [*Imtizaj Komision*], the purpose of which was to settle future disputes between Turks and Armenians peacefully. The second suggestion was to form an aid committee for Marash, amass relief supplies for the needy, and send it off through the American Red Cross.*

The mutasarrif suggested that the Armenians, when any problem arose thereafter, should not contact the French but go directly to the government. He stated that any appeal through French intermediaries would arrive late and the government would be incapable of adopting the appropriate measures in time, be they an investigation or an arrest. Mr. Hovhannes Levonian replied that the Armenians have never had such an intention, i.e. they have never ignored the Turkish government and, as before, would maintain civil conduct with the Turkish authorities.

Ahmed Moukhtar (a known Ittihadist and nationalist leader) said that the Armenians of Aintab had no right to offend them because of the deportation issue. The Turkish people assumed no responsibility for those measures, because the government during that period executed the orders of the Bab-i Ali. They were only a tool.

In response to these comments, Dr. Merrill expressed himself in the following way. "Until the end of 1914, the Turks maintained their national honor inalterably, treating the Armenians as Ottoman subjects. However, as a result of the deportations, they have lost their honor." These audacious words and expressions greatly infuriated the Turkish state officials. In the end, Rev. Nerses Tavoukjian suggested leaving past matters to history and discuss the present situation and the measures to be adopted for a better future.

These mutual accusations continued for a couple of hours. Some of the Turks alluded to the reluctance of some Armenian shopkeepers to go to the market, thus contributing to mutual suspicious between the two communities. The reply was that Turkish shopkeepers should remove all those weapons that the government has banned from their shops and refrain from expressions which would only add anguish to the already affected hearts of the Armenians. After the exchange of opinions, it was decided that the government would adopt every measure to maintain the peace of the city. After the meeting, some men left the government building and went to the grand market to address the Turkish people assembled there. The Mufti stated, loudly:

---

* Later on, the following people were appointed to the Imtizaj Komision on behalf of the Armenian National Union: Dr. Hovsep Bezjian, Hovsep Kendirjian, Hagop Karamanougian, B. Milletbashian, Khoren Bey Nazaretian, Hovhannes Jebejian, Hovhannes Levonian and K. Leylegian.

> Compatriots, we and the Armenian notables have met and decided to prevent the fate of Marash befalling Aintab. The people of Marash, today, are on the verge of death, having no food and shelter. A box of matches costs 20 kurush, and from this we can visualize the misery they are living in. Therefore, I suggest you stay calm and refrain from turning our beautiful city into ruins.

After the mufti's statement the people passed through the market and the Armenian quarter in a procession and later dispersed.

The reader will understand from the above lines as to what had led to the efforts to bring about an agreement. Near the Karatar Bridge, four Armenian travelers were butchered and the criminals were neither pursued nor arrested. The Turks continued to arm themselves. On February 28th, a blacksmith called Yeghia, disappeared. Turkish "terrorists", under the pretext of buying iron, took him to an unknown area of the city and strangled him brutally. The body of the victim was never found. In the end, an ultimatum composed of four articles was sent to the French by four Turkish notables. The Turks promised to maintain peace in the city if the four conditions were met.

1) The Armenian Legionnaires must be removed from Aintab.

2) There should be no interference in Turkish administrative affairs.

3) No reinforcements should be brought into Aintab.

4) There should be no preparations for the movement of any detachment, not even through Aintab. Two Turkish battalions should come to Aintab and help maintain peace and ensure safe passage for traffic.

The French, noticing that the situation was getting serious, accelerated their fortification efforts. The American College, Muslim hospital, and Beyaz Ahmed's Hotel were transformed into fortresses; barricades and tunnels were built, and trenches dug.

It had now been a few months since the Armenians began taking precautionary measures in order to best defend themselves against potential attacks and massacres. A body was formed to attend to this situation. Its first task was to divide the Armenian quarters of the town into sections where it appointed commanders and fighters. It established secret guardhouses in domestic buildings to watch the movements in the streets, especially that of Turkish guards and gendarmes who were supposedly maintaining peace in the city. People were appointed who would immediately erect barricades if an incident occurred and, for that reason, the necessary stones and wood were stored in nearby houses. Adour Levonian and Avedis Kalemkerian supervised the job zealously. They also tried their best to register the stock of ammunition and weapons the people possessed.

In the history of the heroic battle of Aintab, what brought honor to the Armenian craftsmen was the manufacture of bombs, which contributed greatly to Armenian successes. The Armenian National Union, whose previously mentioned members were two or three representatives from each of the three political parties, ordered the production of 100 bombs. Thanks to the National Union's diligent actions, the people of Aintab enjoyed good government and many Armenian lives were saved in many critical moments when they were on the edge of the abyss. It was through the actions and efforts of this body that the troops received direction and were inspired by a national spirit.

March 2nd. A Turk named Ali was killed in front of Painter Sarkis's house. The heads of the three Christian sects visited the mutasarrif and promised to support any investigation so that such a minor event would not give rise to inter-communal tensions.

On the same night, Turkish night-guards forcibly abducted the night-guard of the Armenian street called Kastel Bashuh. The Armenian guard barely managed to escape.

March 3rd. After the placement of a placard announcing that Constantinople was in Turkish hands and that the Muslim population should stay calm – otherwise it would be deprived of its political rights, great chaos ensued. A large crowd gathered at the grand market. They tried to force the government to signal the beginning of a war in Aintab. However, the time had not come yet, and the people had to wait a little longer. In the end, Turkish notables and nationalist leaders succeeded in dispersing the crowd with great difficulty because there were other matters still to be arranged. There was ammunition to be transported; some organizational matters were still incomplete; officers and captains were providing the civilians with military training in various buildings; and Turkish *mullahs* were still exciting the nationalist sentiments of the

Kendirli Latin church.

people through their sermons in the mosques. They stated that "The Armenians of Aintab should die like the Armenians of Yetesia [Ourfa]."

Here we should add that the Turks made a strategic error by exciting the civilian people against the Armenians because the latter, relying on the French, used them as a shield against the Turks, and the Turks were not able to use their swords successfully against the French later on.

This error was realized by a Turkish military expert called Kelej Ali who, despite his ceaseless attempts to stop the Turkish-Armenian war that had already erupted, could not stop the fighting because it was already too late. According to Kelej Ali, the Turks should have attacked the French in the first instance and then turn against the Armenians afterwards.

March 5th. A group of men grazing some French mules were attacked by Turkish chetes four kilometers to the West of the city. One of them was killed, and the other two wounded. The Turks refused categorically to sell provisions to the Armenians. The boycott worsened.

March 6th. Under the pretext of searching for a body in a water pit, the Turks entered an Armenian house on Sahra-Arduh street and, after confiscating a hand-gun and a rifle, took the owner to the government building. Panic broke out among the Armenians. Had the Turkish gendarmes not chosen a shortcut, they would have been in a dangerous situation. The owner of the weapons was released that night in order to put an end to the people's rage.

March 7th. A few French soldiers had gone hunting and Turkish chetes opened fire on them and killed two. The incident was barely a few kilometers away from the city. The remaining soldiers barely escaped and returned to the city to report the event to the French command. A French brigade rushed to the scene, but it was of no use. The following day, the funeral of the fallen men took place in the Latin Church [Kendirli] with great mourning.

March 10th. An American Red Cross team was transporting provisions to Marash under the supervision of Turkish gendarmes. However, those same gendarmes ended up confiscating the provisions and sharing them with other Turkish chetes in Besh-Geoz.

March 20th. A large number of armed villagers attacked the city from every direction. The killings continued outside the city. The chief of the Badavi ashiret [tribe], being friendly to the Armenians and the French, fought against the Turkish chetes and died during the fight.

March 19th. The Colonel was invited to the telegraph-office to contact the leader of the nationalist movement in Marash, who demanded the immediate withdrawal of the French from Aintab. The Colonel replied that he had come to Aintab according to the will of the Entente powers and promised to let the powers know about the nationalist leader's request. The chete leader insulted the Colonel in his telegraph. The Colonel informed the Armenian population of Aintab about this exchange through Mr. Mouradian and exhorted them to remain calm.

March 22nd. This day was a watershed for the Armenian people who had tolerated every aggressive act of the Turkish people. The Armenians also started to show enmity towards the Turks and made them understand that this time they would extract a high price for their lives. After the terror of the deportations, the slaughter houses of Deir-ez Zor, and every misery that the Armenian people suffered, the last remaining fragments of the Armenians wanted to show the threatening Turkish nationalists that this time their actions wouldn't remain unpunished. The Turks were not yet satisfied drinking Armenian blood. This time they would drink poison from the hands of their victims.

During this same time, an Armenian from Sepasdia named Karekin was arrested because of a cartridge issue. When Karekin, under the supervision of Turkish gendarmes, was passing the Akyol guard house, his older brother and some relatives begged the police chief for his release and promised to pay the requested monetary fine. The police chief abruptly refused and asserted that they would take him to prison. At that time the prisons were full of Turkish criminals. The Armenian prisoners, who were a minority and sentenced for minor offences, were thrown amongst these criminal gangs who would satisfy their beastly instincts with them. Knowing that this was the case, the arrested man's brother and relatives were upset and reluctant to allow their 16 year old brother to be confined in such a prison. Given the police chief's refusal, the relatives went to a place called Kiulhan Damuh and hid behind the cupola, watching the street where the policemen and their prisoner would pass.

When they were passing through that point, the Armenians attacked it. The assailants immediately assaulted the gendarmes, confiscated their weapons, and freed the boy. The gendarmes escaped and compelled the chetes and Turkish soldiers located a hundred meters away to flee Aintab. The Turks were greatly affected. This time the Armenians were displaying a different quality. The following day, 20-30 gendarmes sent by the government besieged the Kiulhan Damuh area and, after arresting all the Armenian shop-keepers located there, took them to the government building.

The Armenians of Aintab went to the church in large numbers and demanded that the freedom of all the prisoners be obtained by the National Union, otherwise they would arrest 14 Turks, instead of four, and would attack the Kozanluh guard house at night, capturing all the gendarmes and soldiers in it.

That same night, the Turkish government surrendered the arrested individuals to their relatives, receiving a note signed by the latter, attesting to their safe release.

On the following day, the devious Turks sent the following protest note to the French, stating that:

> All responsibility for these events rests solely with the Armenians. We have behaved calmly, not giving rise to any perilous events. The disobedient and rebellious Armenians render disciplinary actions by the government impossible. We are unable to restrain any disobedience and punish them.

Khoren Bey mediated the return of weapons confiscated by the Armenians and the case was closed.

March 26th–28th. Colonel Andre arrived in Aintab, clearing the Kilis road from chetes. Their leader was Shahin Bey of Aintab and his body was handed over. Colonel Andrea entered Aintab around nightfall on March 28th.

March 29th. The commander of the second French battalion ordered the mutasarrif to post some placards on walls in the streets. The Turkish crowd immediately removed them and painted them with blood.

March 30th. Colonel Andrea and the mutasarrif had a meeting.

This was the situation in Aintab and its vicinity until April 1st. The situation was so volatile that even a small spark would have ignited a war.

Chapter 5

The Three Pillars of the Heroic Battle of Aintab

(April 1st to 30th, 1920)

Before delving in the details of the battle of Aintab, it is necessary to acquaint our readers with the three individuals who made such a great contribution to the self-defense of the city.

It would be wrong for the reader to think that we want to ascribe the success of Aintab's self-defense to just a few people. This would be a great injustice to those living and martyred individuals who performed heroic deeds.

Therefore, the glory of the victory in Aintab belongs to no one, but to all. The child, the orphan, the widow, the old, the young, the craftsman, the teacher and the intellectual all had their roles to play. All played their part in the heroic defense against the Turkish chetes. Despite this, we should still not forget to praise the contribution made by the three leaders who displayed unique qualities of deliberation, organization and planning.

Whose is the victory? The colossal ship struggling against the ocean waves or its captain? They are both mutually related and important. Therefore, by recognizing the leaders' as well as the Armenian community's honor, we can remember the role played by the people and the aforementioned three people.

The first, Rev. Nerses Tavoukjian. He was a short, dark clergyman, with a round head and piercing eyes, behind which his wisdom was conspicuous. He was an assertive and experienced person, born and raised in a poor family, who had climbed the social ladder, recognizing the advantages and imperfections of all. He received his primary education at the Franciscan School in Aintab, and that prepared him for the Catholic priesthood. However, he became a clergyman in the Armenian Apostolic Church, pursuing his education at Central Turkey College. He later became a graduate of Armash monastery. He was a fervent Armenian who hated the Turks because of the genocide. He was the preacher of love and forgiveness, yet he never forgave to the atrocities committed by the Turks.

During his youth, he became famous for his courage and had a tumultuous life. For that reason, he had come to know every kind of human vicissitude and understood the psychology of every type of person as well as how to find ways to get along with them. The drug addicts of his time respected him too. He used to laugh at threats addressed to him and would stand imperturbably against any attack. He was audacious in publishing the principles that he believed in. His decisions were the result of long deliberations. He always based his decisions on evidence.

During the war, when there was a matter of life and death, he would never lose his cool, even when the most thoughtful people had lost their reason and were rushing to find a solution.

He was a politician without being a strategist. When the community had put its hopes on the French, he believed in his people. Knowing Turkish psychology, he recommended the stick, harsh force, and the doctrine of "an eye for an eye." He had lost his faith in French willingness to protect the Armenians of Aintab, especially after the events that took place in Marash. I remember the priest's ghastly pallor during the most critical days of the war. Immersed in deep thoughts, he spent sleepless nights trying to make decisions. To do this or that? To say yes or no? Accept or refuse?

He was the epicenter of political, economic, religious, and administrative issues, as well as an adviser to the Military Body. The Provisions Committee looked to him at critical moments. Before any negotiations were conducted, the people appealed to him. Being the center of all this, he had the unique ability to explain matters clearly. He was the means of communicating with the French. This priest knew how to talk to the Colonel, was the bridge of reconciliation between Turks and Armenians, and the one person who had the audacity to talk to them confidently.

Many, during the most critical moments of the Armistice, refused to accept the invitation of the Turks. He alone went and gave them explanations. He had a bizarre method of working with the Military Body and exonerating them at his meetings with the Turks. He rendered these services wholeheartedly, although he knew that he might never return from Turkish offices.

The second, Mr. Adour Levonian, was a tall, magnanimous, affable and honest young man. He was clever and quick. He was also audacious and industrious with a military bearing. He was everywhere. His soldiers loved him.

He inspired trust and moral vigor everywhere. He always stood on the front line and led his soldiers during an attack. He had an aptitude for

Armenian community leaders. Father Nerses Tavukjian *(left)* and Adour Levonian *(right).*

strategy, without having political aspirations. He therefore succeeded in the former and failed in the latter.

Let us move to the third person, Mr. Kalemkerian. He complemented Mr. Levonian. He was of average height, robust and vigorous, around 30-35 years old. His qualities included assertiveness reaching a level of stubbornness, sagacity, and extreme audacity during battle. During the critical moments in the fighting, when anger often led to miscalculations, he remained calm.

He was the son of an artisan, whose hand-made objects were famous for their good quality. His family had been famous in Aintab for many generations. Kalemkerian's work was regarded with admiration as masterpieces of bronze and silver.

Although he had never been a soldier, he displayed military qualities. He investigated the weak points of the enemy during the Armenian self-defense, personally led attacks he knew would be successful, and tossed grenades at his opponents. He displayed his audacity, coolness and

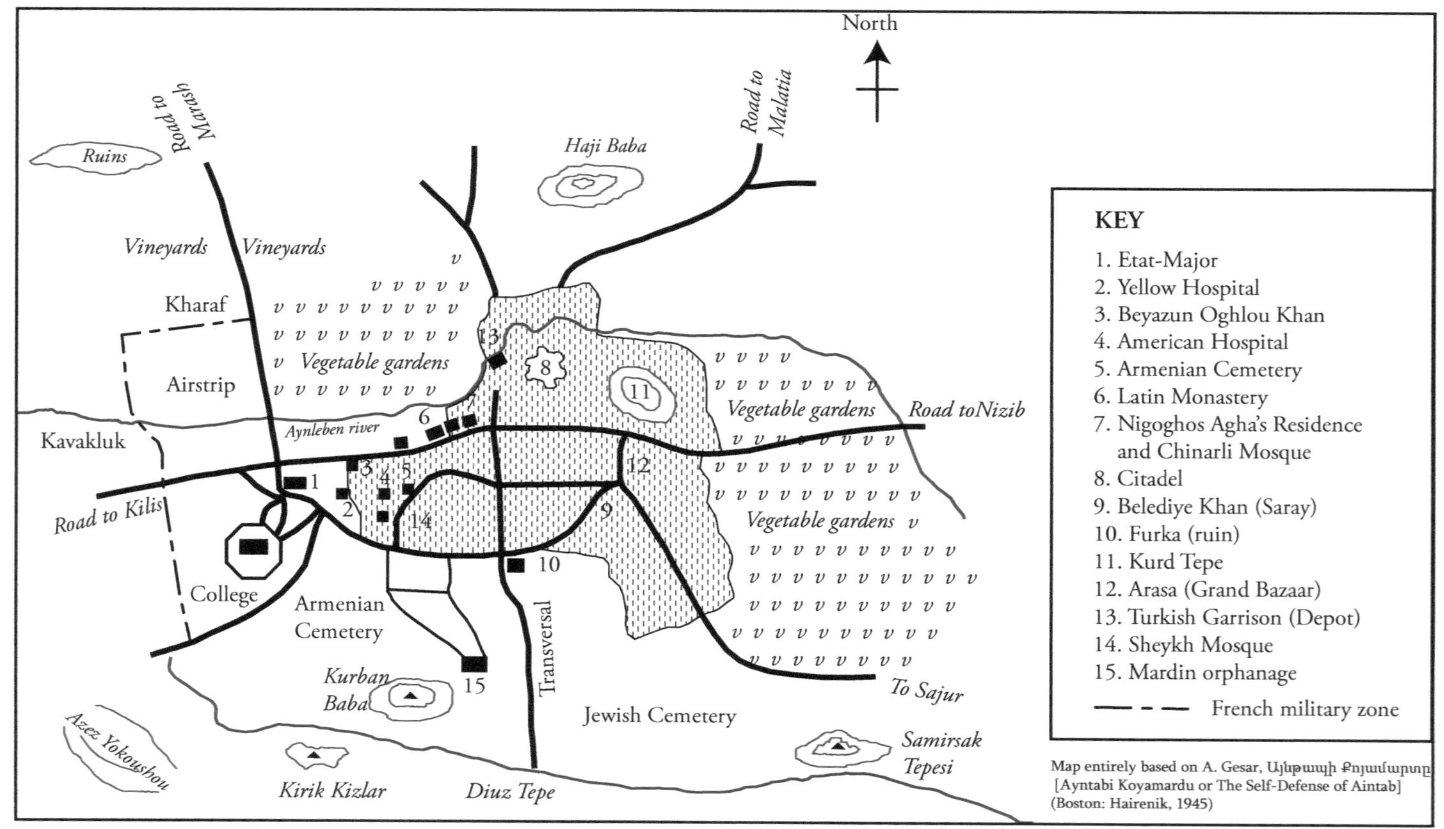
KEY
1. Etat-Major
2. Yellow Hospital
3. Beyazun Oghlou Khan
4. American Hospital
5. Armenian Cemetery
6. Latin Monastery
7. Nigoghos Agha's Residence and Chinarli Mosque
8. Citadel
9. Belediye Khan (Saray)
10. Furka (ruin)
11. Kurd Tepe
12. Arasa (Grand Bazaar)
13. Turkish Garrison (Depot)
14. Sheykh Mosque
15. Mardin orphanage
French military zone
Map entirely based on A. Gesar, Այնթապի Քոյամարդը
[Ayntabi Koyamardu or The Self-Defense of Aintab]
(Boston: Hairenik, 1945)
North
Road to Malatia
Haji Baba
Road to Marash
Ruins
Vineyards
Vineyards
Kharaf
Airstrip
Kavakluk
Road to Kilis
Aynleben river
Vegetable gardens
Vegetable gardens
Vegetable gardens
Road to Nizib
To Sajur
Samirsak Tepesi
Jewish Cemetery
Transversal
Diuz Tepe
Armenian Cemetery
Kurban Baba
Kirik Kizlar
College
Azez Yokoushou

sagacity when he threw enemy grenades back to them. He saved many people from death by such feats. He did not participate in attacks he did not agree with.

These were the three men who played a large part in the heroic battle of Aintab. There were also others, who also served well, and we will refer to them in the coming pages.

The Map of Aintab

A map of Aintab's location gives an idea of the beauty of the city. No other neighboring town presented the spectacle that this city enjoyed. Aintab was completely made of stone, thanks to nearby quarries. Almost every kind of stone was to be found there for very low prices.

If one looked at Aintab from above, one could see that the city was established alongside three hills. The hills ran from west to east. The middle hill, which was smaller than the other two, sloped towards the north and was near the hill forming the western end of the city. These two hills to the west comprised the Armenian quarters, while the third, which was the biggest one, was located to the east and comprised the labyrinth making up the Turkish quarter which extended north and south.

The first two hills were separated from the third one by a wide avenue created by the Turks who, as we have previously recalled, destroyed the beautiful Armenian houses there during the deportations. The Turkish government loved to always make such improvements at the expense of the Armenians. However, the existence of this avenue rendered great service to the Armenian fighters. This was the best position for Armenians to (partly) dominate over Turkish positions. This avenue, which we will name "Transversal", extended from north to south and crossed the three streets which divided the city into three sections from west to east. The first one of these streets was called Pasha, which extended as far as the Kozanluh guard house. From there, it entered the grand market, passing in front of the Ferkah buildings and the government building called Belediyeh Khanuh.

The second one began from a glade called Eshek Kasteli, passed through Akyol, then Eblahan and Ibn Eyyoub market, where the Ibn Eyyoub mosque with its famous minaret were located. Then, it entered the Balekluh market, passing in front of the Y.M.C.A. building, from where it proceeded to the Alay Bey market, Kharadnuh Bazaruh and the grand markets, taking a straight route. The minaret of the Eyyoub Oghlu

Sourp Asdvadzadzin Armenian Apostolic church.

mosque overlooked this last section of the street. This road was 300 meters long, stretching from the mosque's entrance as far as the grand market.

The third avenue began at the start of the road to Kilis, which entered the city through a passage across the Akyol guard house and the mosque. It continued as far as a place called Kiulhan Damuh, from where it headed towards Nigoghos Agha's house and Chinarli Mosque by bending towards the Latin Church, finally reaching the Sou Bourjou guard house. From there it stretched to the Kara Geoz market and the Kondurajuh and entered the grand market through the bazaar.

As we have shown, these three avenues converged at the grand market (Arasa), where, dividing into two lines, the first went out of Sharakusdi Street to the south-east, with the second, diverting north, passed through Millet Khanuh, Kalealti, and Dabbagh Khaneh.

There was a great web of sewers and water canals under these avenues and their branches spread under all the street and continued all the way to city's exit.

The French were mostly located in the College and the Chitji Kharaf during the war. The College, established on a small hill, was located on the western side of the Armenian hills, whereas the Chiftji Kharaf, which was on the western side of the road to Marash, was to the north of the College.

The following places were located on the road to Kilis, where the Armenians had overall control as far as the corner of Transversal Street: the Beyaz Ahmed Hotel (where the French were stationed), Shaban, Balian's house and the Akyol Mosque facing the houses belonging to the Manushagians and Babigians that overlooked the Ayn Leben glade, the house with the balcony on Ferajeh Street, the Latin Church on the other side of the road (the French were located there too), the row of houses belonging to Kaleaghasi, and the Leylegians' house. Facing them were the Chinarli Mosque and Nigoghos Agha's house where the Turks were located. The houses belonging to the Karamanougians, Pilibos Effendi Sarkissian, Hovsep Effendi Kendirjian's buildings, Habib Effendi Kurkjian's houses and those owned by Patanian were located on the corner of Transversal Street. The buildings from Kaleaghasi to the Patanians were occupied by the Turks. Thus, one side of the street belonged to the Armenians, the other to the Turks. Kayajik Street overlooked this avenue and ended abruptly at the glade called Choukour Bostan. Any attack at this point was impossible, whereas the Turks and Armenians faced each other around Balekluh. Half of the market belonged to the Armenians, the other half to the Turks. The Y.M.C.A. building and Yaghoubians house overlooked these streets. The Y.M.C.A was on a promontory and ended at Balekluh market. The Turkish positions were lower up to this point, whereas those of the Armenians were higher. The long southern line was very precarious for the Armenians. Their positions at Kozanluh Teyirbe were less insecure because of the dispersed position of the taverns, behind which was a wood, so the Turks' line of retreat was within our firing range. Here, facing us, was the Ilian Tavern. Our important positions were Topbashian's steam mill and the Barsoumian College building.

It was extremely dangerous for the Armenians to go between Kozanluh Teyirbe and the Sheikh Mosque and its vicinity. In fact, the Turkish and Armenian positions were mixed to such an extent that drawing a map of it was impossible. One part of a building could belong to the Armenians, the other to the Turks. The upper floor of a house could be occupied by Turks, the lower one by Armenians, and vice versa. There were dozens of houses in a similar situation. On this longest and most dangerous front, the most important Armenian positions were the Kozanluh Mosque, occupied a few days before the fighting started, the Bilemjians' and Simon Agha's houses, the buildings and houses located in the vicinity of the Arslanian' house and, on the other (west) side, all the houses that were located at the end of Soghanluh Boujaghi Street. On one side of Sheikh Mosque were some Kurdish houses in which the Turks had taken up positions. The Armenians were protected by the American orphanage and the tall buildings surrounding it. This was the most worrisome front for the Armenians. This concern was borne out on the 17th day of fighting, with Norman's entrance to Aintab. We will discuss this later.

The Armenian front-line positions to the west were protected by the French and were secure. The Armenians were surrounded to the north, south and east and it was only the western side that was safe.

Chapter 6

April 1st

Colonel Andrea's battalion entered Aintab on March 28th after skirmishes against Turkish regular and irregular forces for four days on the road to Kilis, around Ajar, Munedir, Sineb Sou, Kazukluh, Cheorten, Baluk Sou, Misirjik, Besh-Geoz, Bostanjek, and Elmaluh. The Turks suffered over 100 dead and 300 wounded. Infuriated by this unsuccessful battle, the Turks packed the Turkish streets of Aintab after Andrea's arrival in the city. Colonel Andrea's battalion, after delivering the necessary provisions to the Aintab battalion, headed for Kilis at 6 o'clock on April 1st. Flye Sainte Marie remained in Aintab with a small force. The Turks had already finished their preparations weeks before, though the Armenians were not yet aware of an imminent attack. Thus, a group of women and craftsmen had gone to the market in order to buy provisions. There was no commotion at all. At 7.30, the Turks began a surprise attack and assaulted the Armenians in the market like wild tigers. A gun had gone off near the government building and many gunshots followed it. The terror had begun.

A woman from Sivas and her daughter were attacked while shopping. The daughter received a bullet in the head while the mother was assaulted with a knife. The poor woman barely made her escape to the Armenian streets and informed people of the incident.

Many wounded Armenians arrived one after the other. The trouble had started and the signal for war had been given. The Turks, within two nights, had already withdrawn from the Armenian neighborhoods. Some Turkish families were captured in order to exchange them later for Armenian prisoners. However, some Turkish families did not want to leave the Armenians and remained voluntarily in their homes.

Various heartbreaking reports came in, spreading terror and rage amongst the population. A volunteer named Haigazoun and his French friends were brutally murdered at the Sou Bourjou Street. Their bodies were mutilated. A woman was injured by a bullet near Kezek Teyirbey and was transported to hospital. The Turkish chetes, positioned on the nearby hills, were firing on the Armenian quarter. The son of the Birejiklians was martyred. The poor boy was killed as he passed by a window. This first period of terror ended after a short time and the Armenians immediately set to work. It was here that the miraculous qualities of the Armenians became apparent. The enraged people finished the building work in a few hours, something thousands of laborers could not do in days.

The entrances to the Armenian streets were blocked by high barricades, as well as secondary and other positions. There were also firing loopholes opened. All this was done very quickly. Whatever materials the people found, they piled on the barricades. In some places the old houses were torn down in order to use the stones and tiles for such purposes. The inhabitants of each street worked under the supervision of a mason and thus, after one hour, the Armenian streets were turned into fortresses, ready to confront the enemy. All the houses were connected together through narrow alleys. All the inhabitants of the Armenian quarter had united into a single body. One could wander the Armenian streets like a mole. One could get lost wandering in this labyrinth. For this reason, signs had to be displayed for some positions. The orphans found shelter at a hospital, whereas the widows and the orphan girls were placed inside the most secure buildings.

The men were armed and positioned behind the barricades as the fighting started. The number of Armenians captured in the market was around 45. One part of the Turkish forces attacked the Armenians, while the other marched against Colonel Andrea. The latter had been in great anxiety during the previous few days. He had even prepared his soldiers to retreat. Colonel Andrea confronted some Turkish chetes in Kucuk Kizil Hisar and they were dispersed and returned to Aintab after heavy artillery fire by the French. The French commander started to fortify the hill at Mardin, and an area called Ghourban Baba. The Americans raised their flags on American establishments.

Turkish chetes captured French bakery soldiers at Konak. The Turks did not stop firing throughout the day, particularly from the direction of Sheikh Mosque and its minaret, targeting the American hospital and orphanage. Four Armenians were hit by their bullets. During the silence of the night, the soldiers and guards were placed at various positions. This was how the first day of April ended.

The munitions held by Armenians in Aintab on the first day comprised 140 bombs, 45 Mauser and hunting rifles, around 2–300 Kermaluhs, and 30,000 cartridges. Here are some of the testimonies and eye witness accounts written by survivors of that day.

Testimonies by Witness.

Number 1

The testimony of Nazar Aroian from Ibn Eyyoub Street, living in Kolanjuh Abraham's house, age 45.

On Wednesday, March 31st, I went to the market. Simitji Apo invited me to his shop saying, "Take whatever you need today or tomorrow. On Friday, Saturday, Sunday or Monday attacks will begin in every part of the city when a gunshot is fired as a signal from Sachakluh (a hill in the southern part of the city). Go to your home and don't come out, and don't betray me." After secretly telling me this, he gave me 10 kg of flour and sent me home.

On the following day, on April 1st, I went to the market again. I started to be suspicious, seeing the people all prepared and organized. When I was going to the Boughda Bazar, I heard a gunshot from the government building and people started to run. Christians towards the west, and Muslims to the east. During this exact moment, when cannon fire could be heard from around Kizil Hisar, a *munedig* [a public crier] started to shout: "Those who love Islam and Mohammed, and carry weapons in their hands, should go to Kizil Hisar." The people started to rush there. I hid in a bakery near Boughda Bazar that belonged to the wheat merchant Khourshid Agha. When he was about to close his shop, without seeing me, I begged him to hide me, which he did. At the same time, a horseman came and stated: "Ali Kelej Bey had captured 15 French soldiers, despite the latter's heavy shelling of the Turks. Order the women to prepare soup and 15 meals." Some time later I saw, with my own eyes, the transportation of these provisions to Samsak Tepeh on mules. On this same day, at about noon, Sheikh Mustafa arrived with 60 armed men and took me to the government building. On our way he ordered the Turkish guards to immediately kill anyone who was caught robbing Armenian and Turkish shops. When we arrived at Bazar Yeri, we saw Zenjirli Mustafa and his gunmen standing there. "Why didn't you go?" asked Sheikh Mustafa, "We have sent our soldiers. We will go now" was the answer. One of the men then said, "Their eyes are 'big.' They promise something, yet they don't go. They are scared." They handed me over to the prison governor (Essad Bey), asking him, "Did you find the Armenian prisoners? If they are attacked, who will be responsible?" They then isolated the Armenian prisoners, putting them in a separate room. They took me to the Hakki Effendi police station and ordered the guards to keep me there. I stayed there for a day and night. That day, they brought Avedis Yessaian, Hovhannes Karzaian, Nazar Varoian, Yacoub the son of baker Soghomon, Mrs. Osannah and two other women. They gave us food and we slept comfortably at night. On the following day, they gave us food again, and handed us over to the Armenian streets.

This is my "ifadeh". I confirm it.

Nazar Aroian

Number 2

Avedis Nazarian's "ifadeh." He is one of the inhabitants of Choukour Street, currently living in Levon Hovhannesian's house on Hayg Street.

On Tuesday, April 1st, I went to the market in the morning. The Turks refused to sell me anything I asked for. I came to Kurkji Khan. I was about to buy soap from a Jewish merchant when I heard a few gunshots and saw people running and shouting, "Ortalik Karishduh" (trouble has broken out). The Odabashuh immediately ordered the closing of the khan's doors. After staying there for 15 minutes, the Odabashuh made me leave. I finally arrived at Karageoz, after passing numerous armed men and seeing the bodies of two French soldiers lying on the ground. There was an armed man standing next to the bodies who shouted "Isn't there a Muslim who'll remove the bodies of these dogs? Pour some sand on the blood stains on the road. The guards will be here shortly." Then they pulled the bodies into the khan. I encountered a lot of other Armenians and armed men from that point as far as the Soubourjuh guard house who said nothing. I finally arrived at the Armenian streets.

This is my "ifadeh". I confirm it.

Avedis Nazarian

Number 3

The "ifadeh" of Krikor, aged 15, the son of Hovsep Tejirian, living on Church Street.

I went to Arasa (the grand market) on the morning of the incident to buy wheat. A lot of Armenian men were waiting to buy provisions. Suddenly, a gunshot was heard. Then a lot of Muslims armed with shovels, sticks, and cudgels surrounded us. "You cannot escape this time," they said and began attacking us. When they were beating people, I escaped. I can recognize the assailants if I saw them now. I witnessed the killing of a woman near Ghaduh Kasteli. The Jews were running away barefoot. One of the gendarmes slapped a Jew in front of the old castle, saying, "What are you running from?" A Turk fired six shots at me near the Nazar Agha Khan but he missed and I escaped. I heard, "The French have attacked the city, kill the infidels."

My "ifadeh" is correct. I confirm it.

Krikor Tejirian

Number 4

The "ifadeh" of Yeghsa Haroutioun Aghegian, age 38, one of the former inhabitants of Rahan Street, currently living in Tepeh Bashuh.

On Tuesday morning, April 1st, I went to the market with my neighbor, a refugee woman called Hnazant, to buy wheat. I wanted to buy a veil from a Muslim woman in the bazaar. "It's 30 kurush to you, because you look like an infidel (giavour)" the woman said. I gave up and we went to Boughda Bazar. Around 30 women were waiting in line. I went and stood next to the person who was giving out the provisions. "Wait a little while" he said and sent me back. Just then I heard them talking about a young Armenian, saying, "He has good money. He is good prey." I started to be suspicious and wanted to return home, but my friend convinced me to stay a little longer. Shortly afterwards, 20-25 Turks, all armed, came and searched all of us. We suddenly heard a gunshot, which brought a violent crowd armed with axes and sticks, out of Keomur Bazar. A bullet wounded the Armenian whom I mentioned earlier. Then they surrounded us, saying, "Look at these whores." One of them pulled my veil off, the other stole the money I had in my hand, and the third hit me with a stick as I started to run. They were throwing stones at me from behind, shouting, "Go and call the French. Let them come and save you." On the road, I saw another Armenian killed. I accidentally entered a mosque near Hannajah and a Muslim man threw a big stone at me saying, "Are you the kind of person to enter here?" I left and started to run again. At the Kondurajuh Bazar, I saw a girl fall down with blood on her hair. The Muslims who shot her said, "Look, two more have fallen down" and turned towards us. They let me go seeing that I was wounded. I then arrived at Balekluh by crawling there. A Turkish soldier asked, "How did you get here?" and hit me on the back with his rifle. I finally managed, with great difficulty, to get to the Armenian streets where they took me home.

My "ifadeh" is correct. I confirm it.

Yeghsa Aghegian

Number 5

The "Ifadeh" of Yughaper Aynoghlouian, aged 30, from Giurin, living on Church Street.

On April 1st, I went to the market to get some flour. The shopkeepers purposefully did not sell me any. I then went to Boughda Bazar. Men and women were waiting in line there too. Suddenly, I heard a man (they referred to him as Sheikh's son) shout, "Let those who love Islam and Mohammed resort to weapons. The Armenians are always ours, we can kill them with sticks." After this, I saw that the crowd was armed. Then a policeman killed Hayganush Mergerian from Giurin with his pistol and another wounded my cousin Yeghisapet Aynoghlouian with his bayonet, cursing our religion and the French, saying, "Let them come and save you now." I escaped, disguising myself as a Muslim woman. I encountered numerous chetes on my way and one asked, "Where are you going?" "I have a house down on the street," I replied. "No, don't go there, they have slaughtered all the infidels there," he replied. I did not listen to them, however and ran and came here.

This is my "ifadeh". I confirm it.

Yughaper Aynoghlouian

Number 6

Nvart Najarian from Dikranagerd, aged 25, who lives at Tepeh Bashuh.

On April 1st I went to the market, where I heard a gunshot. One of the Turks there, Ali Effendi, asked, "What is that?" and the other replied, "Don't you know? This time, there's no mercy for women and girls, even babies sleeping in their cradles will be slaughtered. The French are their protectors…" He left after cursing their (French) religion. Just then, Mustafa Agha said, "The government allowed the killing." After hearing this, I escaped. I saw two women lying on the ground, all bloody.

This is my "ifadeh", I confirm it.

Nvart Najarian

Number 7

Noyemzar Senekerim Gemjian, aged 30, from Sivas, living on Hayg Street.

On April 1st, I went to buy wheat. Shortly afterwards, the person serving came and said, "There is no wheat, only corn." I did not buy corn. On my way back, I heard a gunshot. Some people were shouting, "Kill them!" and others, "Run!" Just then I saw a crowd armed with guns and bayonets. The Turks, taking their weapons out of their shops, were going onto the streets. I escaped. I then saw Soubourjou guard house's chauffeur (Haigazoun), his friend and two Senegalian soldiers going to the grand market and asked them, "Where are you going? Come back." "Nothing will happen to us, go home!" they replied. Later on, I heard that they had been killed.

This is my "ifadeh", I confirm it.

Noyemzar S. Gemjian

Number 8

This is the "ifadeh" of Mariam Zadig, aged 35, the wife of one of the inhabitants of Yalenez Khaneh Street.

When I was buying wheat on the day of the incident, I heard, "Mohammed, close the shop!" Then I heard a gunshot and saw a large crowd. I ran and witnessed the killing of gardener Aboujian's sister Yacout at Kharar Bazar. A little further on I saw a woman covered in blood. They started beating me and brought me to the

Rushdiyeh College. There, someone stabbed me in the shoulder and I fell down.

My "ifadeh" is correct. I confirm it.

Mariam

Number 9

The "ifadeh" of Haji Krikor Bogharian, aged 56, from Choukour Oba.

I was at home on April 1st, then went to my neighbor's, Mrs. Ziforah's house. I was talking to her father, Haroutioun Agha, when I heard a gunshot. Deyirmenji Abouj Agha also arrived. Abouj Agha told us about my mother and sister's return home from the market. We went outside to welcome them and they told us, "We hardly got flour." At that moment, we heard another gunshot. I rushed home just when my daughter-in-law was locking the doors of the upper floor. It was then that I heard the third gunshot. She shouted, "Father, I am hit!" The bullet had penetrated her left side. She died two and a half hours later. We hid in the lower floors and heard the Turkish chetes entering the house. We heard gunshots and knew from the sounds that Haroutioun Agha made that they had killed him too. After staying hidden for a day and night, kel (bold) Tavit's son came and took us to the Armenian streets. A few days after our arrival, Mrs. Zifora went back to their house where she saw the bodies of my daughter-in-law and her father.

I testify that my "ifadeh" is true.

Krikor Bogharian

Number 10

The "ifadehs" of Hayganush Khelokian, aged 35 from Kastel Bashuh Street, Santoukhd Demirjian, aged 40, from Giurin, living on the same street, and Haiganush Shehirian, aged 25, from Giurin, also living on the same street.

We went to Boughda Bazar to buy some food on April 1st, a Thursday morning. A Turkish woman said, "These poor women will fall into the trap." Shortly afterwards, when we were buying oil, we heard a gunshot. After that, a policeman, who had a red ribbon tied to his hands, pointed at us, saying, "What are you bastards still waiting for? Kill them! They rely on the French, they

> want independence. This is what it looks like!" Just at that moment a crowd armed with revolvers, knives and bayonets surrounded us. They started beating us. They hit Hayganush on her head and blood started to spill out. We then started to run. Near Kharar Bazar, we saw one of our relatives, Hayganush Terjanian (aged 25), shot in the head and lying on the ground. When we arrived there, Alay Bey, one of the gendarmes, asked the other, "Why aren't you killing them?" "I know which ones to kill," replied the other. Running away, we arrived at Balekluh. There we saw a policeman shooting an old woman with his revolver.
>
> We testify the truth of our "ifadeh."
>
> Haiganush Shehirian, Hayganush Khelokian, Santoukhd Demirjian

These are a few examples of the recorded testimonies showing the barbarity of the Turks. As we have previously said, we have the copies of these tragic testimonies as proof. These show that the responsibility for the fighting fell solely on the Turks.

April 2nd

The night passed silently. The fighting started in the morning. The Armenians shot two Turks at Ayn-Leben wood. The operation to occupy Kozanluh Mosque was initiated before noon. This mosque was a real threat to the Armenians, with its minaret overlooking the Armenian houses nearby. Its firing pits were used to kill an Armenian called Yacoub Allekian. The mosque was located on the most dangerous part of the eastern side of the Armenian positions as we previously described. Sheikh Mosque was on the western side and put the Armenians in a very precarious situation.

The first attack against Kozanluh Mosque started from three sides. The building was impregnable and the Turks could defend themselves. However, an aggressive assault undermined their morale and they started to withdraw. They were about to move all their property out of the mosque when two Armenian fighters, Hovsep Tashjian and Khoren Khayajanian, climbed over its eastern wall and entered it. One had a pistol and the other a two-barreled gun. The Turks seeing this courageous act started to flee, leaving the mosque to the Armenian fighters. After the latter occupied the mosque, barricades were erected at strategic points, with the minaret, previously used by the Turks to snipe at Armenian fighters now under the command of Armenians and threatening the Turks.

Around noon, a prisoner exchange took place on the Y.M.C.A. road. During this whole time, this street became the scene of fierce fighting, though maintaining communication points with the Turks to exchange written messages. During these hours, one side would shout, "Stop firing, there is news," and a representative of the other, holding a white flag, would give or receive a message.

The Turks chose another position to attack in the afternoon: the Latin Church. The Turkish chetes entered Nigoghos Agha's house and also occupied the Chinarli Mosque, Kezek Teyirbesi, the surrounding houses and the ancient mills belonging to the Kurkjians and Sahagians. There were thousands of Turkish regular and irregular soldiers positioned there, waiting for the signal to attack. At about 7:30, the Turks started firing and began a general attack, the target being the Latin Church. The horrific noise of exploding bullets hurt our ears. During those critical moments, the Armenians of Aintab witnessed a heroic deed that had never been seen before. As we previously said, the Latin Church was located opposite the Feraye house that had a balcony and a wide street separated them.

On the first day of the fighting, the Catholic community – 400 people – had assembled there, including those escaping from the market. Among them was a French soldier with his rifle and cartridges.

The Armenians had still no means of communication with the monastery, so the protection of all those people – men, women, and the elderly – depended on the courage of that one soldier. By occupying the monastery, the Turks were going to slaughter all the families, and hence threaten our positions.

The French soldier, who was called Cavalier Solz and was later awarded with the "Militia Medal" for his valor, resisted the attack of numerous chetes, all by himself. He fired ceaselessly from various firing positions, pretending that there was a vast fighting force positioned inside the monastery. The Turks really did believe it. This went on for a couple of hours, as the soldier ran relentlessly from one position to the other, firing ruthlessly at the enemy. He was a brave soldier. When a Turk fell, he would clap his hands, but if he missed, he would tap his head for the loss

Armenians pulling a house apart to use materials to construct fortifications elsewhere.

Women and children help construction of defensive lines.

Armenian defenses during the fighting.

of a wasted cartridge. He got bored with fighting in the yard, so he went up the bell tower, where he fortified his position using the roof tiles and started firing at the enemy from that elevation. He killed dozens of Turks. The people sheltering there admired his bravery. He was a hero protecting the women and children against the Turks. At 9:30, Solz started firing fewer shots, because he was almost out of ammunition. The Armenians across the street saw this and decided to help the hero. After a few minutes of deliberation, they decided that there was no other choice than to "connect" monastery to the Feraye house by erecting a safe passage with two walls on either sides. The work began immediately. This was a very audacious and dangerous plan, because the Turks had the street in their sights. The soldier was tired and all the people there were panicking and very hungry. Despite thousands of flying bullets and the efforts of their enemy to obstruct this initiative, the Armenians began building the walls.

They built a wall greater than the height of an average man in one hour and were thus able to cross the street and arrive at the southern walls of the Latin Church. It only remained for the church wall to be breached. After some effort from both outside and inside, a wide hole was opened and the necessary provisions were given to the needy. Some Armenian fighters also entered the church to rescue the French soldier. So the attack of the Turks on the Latin Church failed completely. We, the Armenians, had suffered one loss: a man who wanted to watch the movements of the chetes and had raised his head above the wall.

After the fiasco at the Latin Church, the Turks concentrated their offensive against the Armenians at Chinarli Mosque. Some Turks had remained in Kaleaghasi and some of the surrounding houses. For the Armenian fighters, the occupation of these few houses and pushing the Turks back to the other side of the street was imperative for their protection. Thus, they started breaching the walls of these houses and occupying them one by one, eventually capturing all the houses in that row. The Turks finally found shelter in the Leylegians' house located at the crossroads. The Turks there had to either die fighting or withdraw to Chinarli Mosque. Seeing the latter choice as the more favorable, they escaped and entered the mosque. The Armenians, by occupying the Leylegians' house, had altered that front in their favor by pushing the Turks back to the other side of the street.

The Turks, enraged by this retreat, undertook a last attack around 11:30 and entered the shops located on the lower floor of the Leylegians' house from where, they thought, they could enter the Armenian streets by destroying some walls. The crowd invaded the stores, shouting, "Allah, Allah!" The Turks looked like furious tigers. For the Armenians, these were very critical moments, because they still had not prepared their firing positions at the walls to prevent the Turks' advance. This time the Armenians were desperate. They were crying for weapons and help, but there were no weapons. Even the coolest fighters were desperate. All visualized the slaughter they would face if the Turks penetrated their positions. At that exact moment, the Armenians resorted to the hitherto untried bombs they had made. A. Levonian, S. Chakmajian and a few others were at the most critical points of the front. The sound of the axes and chisels coming from the other side of the wall could be heard, as S. Chakmajian lit the fuse and threw the bomb in front of the Leylegians' shop. The Turks were busy and didn't notice the bomb, which shook the nearby buildings and houses when it exploded. A. Levonian threw the second bomb, shouting, "It is not the French fighting against you, it is us, the Armenians." The Turks, suffering a few losses and many wounded, retreated once more to Chinarli Mosque. For the Turks, the Armenian bombs were a surprise and after that experience they started to behave more carefully. The Turks had failed and the Armenians were victorious.

Central Supplies Committee, Aintab, 1920. (*left to right standing*) Garabed Karzaian, Haroutiun Panjarian, Hovhannes Araradian, Naoum Dasho, (*left to right seated*) Asdvadzadour Giuleserian, Yeghia Demirjian, Der Nerses Kahana Babaian, Haroutiun Kharajian, Krior Demirjian.

The Turks suffered many casualties during this battle, whereas the moral vigor of the Armenians was at its peak. The French colonel congratulated the Armenians on this victory by sending them a few thousand cartridges. Moreover, he requested that the French soldier who was defending the Latin Church should withdraw from there. However, he sent 30 soldiers to the Latin Church in accordance with the demands of Father Mariano for its protection. Likewise, 12 soldiers were sent to defend the American institutions as demanded by Dr. Shepard. It must be acknowledged that during the 70 days of Turco-Armenian fighting, these institutions were defended solely by the French.

We were aware, through Kelej Ali Bey's placard (posted on the same morning), that the Armenian notables had been invited to Bazar Bashuh Nouri Effendi's house, where it was asserted that the Turks had no hostile feelings towards the Armenians, and that they only wanted to expel the French from their country. The Armenians replied by stating, "Our fight is nothing other than self-defense. Had the Turks only fought against the French, the Armenians would not have intervened". Despite this, the Turks continued the attacks against us until nightfall.

Organizational matters were settled by the National Union. An administration was formed to look after provisions and was made up of Karekin Bogharian, Nerses Babaian, H. Araradian, Haji Hr. Basmajian, Asdvadzadour Guleserian, Krikor Demirjian and Hagop Gemjian. Their role was to provide provisions and supply and distribute relief to the poor and needy. As we will see later, their work was to have as much importance as that of the Military Body.

Second, in order to prevent pillage and plunder, a committee was formed with the following members: D. T. Jebejian, R. Topjian, and Y. Yessaian.

April 3rd

One of the important Turkish positions was Akyol Mosque that the Turks had evacuated because it was situated on our firing line and they couldn't defend themselves there. The Armenians immediately seized it in the morning and placed a few soldiers there.

Monsieur Silve, the commander of the French troops at the monastery visited the Armenian positions with the representatives of the Military Body and gave his evaluation. The French offered 25 Mauser rifles and thousands of cartridges to the Armenians. The colonel saw himself in a real war situation and promised to help the Armenians in every way.

The day ended with a few shots being fired. We had three fighters wounded by bullets from the Sheikh Mosque minaret and other areas.

The Turks resorted to deceit in order to guarantee their success in the future. They started to obstruct the work being carried out on fortifications by Armenian fighters, as well as other diplomatic ploys. For this reason, the Turks invited the members of the "Imtizaj Commission" and Dr. Shepard to Bazar Bashuh Nouri Effendi's house in the afternoon.

Sheikh Mustafa stated on behalf of the Turks that they had nothing against the Armenians and condemned the fighting. He promised to end the shooting and to work for the reconciliation and re-establishment of fraternal relations between Turks and Armenians. However, the real goal of this meeting was to buy time in order to transport ammunition and place soldiers at key locations. The Armenians speculated about the real intention behind such a gathering. They disparaged it and continued their efforts to build fortifications. The Armenians, who knew Turkish psychology very well, could see the Turks' real designs based on their smallest acts. They were more skilful in defensive undertakings than the Turks were.

It was really heartbreaking to see four to five year old children carrying stones with their little hands. Poor childhood…! It was as if they too were feeling the inexorable bitterness of the destiny of their people and the tempestuous demands of life. Married women and widows carried stones, dug trenches and attempted to compensate for the lack of ammunition by building the best barricades. The French really admired our positions. The minarets of the occupied mosques were fortified like real fortresses and served as observation points to spy on every movement that the Turks made.

On this day (April 3rd), a French airplane flew overhead for the first time. The Turks fired a thousand shots at it. The airplane was forbidden to land because the landing zone was dangerous. It returned to its base.

On this same day, the orphans of Mardin orphanage were moved to the American hospital. This orphanage was located on the western side of the hills south of the city at a height of 1,500 meters. The Turks had occupied Samsak Tepeh and Sachakluh and were near Mardin. These southern hills that were covered with Muslim cemeteries facilitated the advance of the Turkish chetes. Mardin had been isolated and had lost all connection with the city and the Armenian positions. The Turks finally invaded the orphanage, where they found no one except some orphans and their American teacher. They requested the doorman's surrender, looked around the whole building, but did not find him. In the end, a Turkish commander allowed them to go to the city. Miss Frearson loaded provisions and furniture on the orphans' backs, as much as they could carry, and brought them to the city. After the departure of the orphans, the chetes ransacked the building and raised their flag as a token of victory.

April 4th

The Turks sent the following letter, the Armenian translation of which we present below:

> To Dr. Shepard, Dr. Hovsep Bezjian, Dr. Haroutioun Kalfaian, Dr. Louder Chamichian, Dr. Kevork Shameyan (Arslanian), Hovhannes Levonian, Hagop Karamanougian, Bedros Milletbashian, Bedros Ashjian, Krikor Sarkissian (dentist), Hovhannes Jebejian and Hanneh Kurkjian
>
> If there are any others, apart from those mentioned above, who would like to honor us with their presence, they are free to attend.

> Honorable Sirs,
>
> I have just received a letter from Sheikh Mustafa of Mevlevi [lodge] informing me of the arrival of Kelej Ali Bey in Aintab.
>
> Kelej Ali Bey wishes to meet the aforementioned men, as well as the Muslim community and official delegates at my house for consultations. In accordance with the decision of yesterday's meeting, we would like you to be here at 3 o'clock.
>
> 4/4/1336
>
> Bazar Bashuh Mohammed Nouri

The Armenians accepted this invitation by sending Dr. Shepard. Ali Kelej prepared a very noble reception and made the following statement:

> We do not have any antagonism towards the Armenians. Our enemy is the French. It is always best for you not to cooperate with the French. We are suspicious of you because many of the wounded were hit by French bullets. You should stay calm. We are sure that this city will remain ours. We will restore peace and establish security. The mutual relationship of Turks and Armenians in this town is known to me. I do not wish the destruction of the city. Do not fire from your positions. I will take my soldiers and leave.

From a strategic point of view, Kelej Ali Bey never really wanted a fight against the Armenians because he believed that after the French defeat, killing the Armenians would be easy. However, what he saw was pointless. The feelings of enmity between the Turks and Armenians had already begun. He had warned his officers about this matter. Thus, the peace efforts undertaken by Kelej Ali, came to nothing because the Turkish military could only be controlled with *oghi* (alcohol) and other transgressions. Dr. Shepard believed in the promises made by Kelej Ali Bey. The Turks, seizing the opportunity provided by this meeting, dug trenches, formed barricades and, specifically, connected the street called Kurd Mahallesi to the Ferkah buildings. Dr. Shepard, however, visited the Armenian positions, exhorting the fighters to cease fire until 12 o'clock. The Armenians obeyed him. Nevertheless, they observed, angrily, the Turkish efforts to dig trenches and move ammunition to the most threatening positions. The Armenians well knew that the Turks considered Dr. Shepard to be a simple-minded American and wanted to use him against Armenian interests. Events were not delayed. The Turks started firing before the ceasefire was over.

The doctor's fury reached its zenith. They had lied to him and to the Armenians as well. Thus, visiting the positions again, he exhorted the Armenian fighters to fire ruthlessly. "Smash their heads in!" he said, and the Armenians started shooting.

Let us mention the doctor's letter to the Turks, sent after the latter's deceitful tactics and lies. It stated:

> I am an Armenian, and hereafter treat me in the way you treat the Armenians. All the Americans here will support the Armenians morally and materially. We will help them in every way and will fight against you by forming a united front with them. Do not think this conduct of yours will be ignored by the American Government.

This letter was sent to the Turks through the Y.M.C.A.

As we previously recalled, the ceasefire was exploited by the Turks to occupy some houses around our most shaky positions at Soghanluh Boujaghi. They even attacked before 12 o'clock, mounting nine or 10 general assaults, with 4,500–5,000 chetes. The battle lasted for almost three hours and is known as the battle of Soghanluh Boujaghi. The Turks attempted to advance by firing ceaselessly. The bullets were flying like hail. When Haroutiun Naneian, holding a bomb in his hand, wanted to cross the Pisherjians' kitchen from the most advanced section of the Armenians' positions, he was killed by the bullets of Turkish chetes who were positioned behind the southern wall of the kitchen. Another Armenian fighter, Soghomon, died at the same spot. The mere bodies of these fighters terrorized the Turks, who rushed to cover them up. The Turks did not succeed penetrating further at this point. The bodies were later recovered by Hovsep Tashjian.

Chapter 7

The Armenian "Revenge" Cannon

This front was more than 150 meters long and defended by only 80-90 fighters with seven to nine regular rifles. The rest were common hunting guns and revolvers. The fighting continued with the same intensity until nightfall. The Turks were unsuccessful. After an hour's silence, they began attacking more intensely but were repelled by the Armenian cannon shells. What was this famous Armenian cannon? Let me explain to our readers. From the first days of the fighting, the Tutunjians' house was used as a repair center for weapons and ammunition. This served as the core of a future arms factory and armory. During this fight, the Armenians had the idea of a making a cannon, a project which was entrusted to an Armenian blacksmith called Geoyian. During these critical hours, its planning and construction was an urgent matter for a community fighting for its survival. It was known that a widow from Aleppo had a sewing machine on which there were tubes having a diameter of eight centimeters. These cylindrical tubes, one meter in length, were brought to the Armenian craftsmen. They sealed one end of each cylinder and bored a hole for the spark. Being very heavy, the cylindrical roll was transported using a two wheeled carriage. It looked exactly like a cannon. That is why it was the called the "Revenge" cannon. And our "Revenge" had nothing more attractive than its frightening sound.

The roar of this cannon repelled many attacks. This cannon was first used on the night of April 4th, during the Battle of Soghanluh Boujaghi against the barbaric attacks of the Turkish mob. The fighting started with an awful, deafening noise, so loud that nothing else could be heard. Some fighters carried the cannon to a hall near the Apkarians' house. This was the best place that could be found to serve as a firing position since it simultaneously covered Soghanluh Boujaghi and Kurd Mahallesi streets. The cannon was set up and fixed with ropes and stones. The cannoneers aimed at Kelesh Khoja's house, filled the cannon's barrel with 50 dirhems of gunpowder, wadding and some pieces of iron. At the commander's signal, all the fighters left the hall and went outside, positioned themselves against the wall, and waited for the explosion. The commander ignited the spark. A few seconds later an awful explosion was heard and the cannon fired the projectiles onto the Turkish and Armenian streets. The Turks took it to be a real cannon, and a few shots were sufficient to silence them. The humorous part of this was that after we went back inside after each shot, we would find the barrel of the cannon skewed completely to one side and the ropes loosened. The fighters would immediately adjust its position, clean it, and prepare it for the next shot. Our first bombardment caught the attention the French commander, who asked on the telephone whether the Turks were using artillery. After getting the appropriate explanations, he started to laugh and praised the Armenian cannon's achievements. The cylinder that was used to weave wool a month earlier had now become a tool that terrorized the Turks and no one could have imagined that it would make such an awful noise. The French visited the "Revenge" on the following day and photographed it. After the disastrous attack of Soghanluh Boujaghi, the Turks carried out minor attacks on the Latin Church from the northern side of the city but were pushed back by the French soldiers positioned there. The latter threw grenades at the Turkish positions located in Nigoghos Agha's and the Kurkjians' mill, and the Turks fled shouting "Allah, Allah! Help!" During that last attack, the Armenians did not suffer any losses. The enemy was always defeated because of its careless military strategy.

The Armenians built many fortifications inside the hospital and the orphanage. The orphans worked day and night. Some French people even lamented the inexorable destiny of these poor children. Having lost their parents in the deserts of Der-ez Zor, they had come to a place where the same destiny awaited them.

It is worth remembering one of the greatest deeds of the Armenians of Aintab, when they connected most of the city to the general staff building with walls the height of a human being. More than 500 men worked for three days and nights to build this wall, which was considered to be quite a wonder. The Armenian quarters of the city were connected to that building and there was therefore no obstacle in maintaining communications with the French.

Here we should remember the audacity of an old woman called Imanum Mennush who brought honor to the women of Aintab with her heroic deeds.

Vrezh or revenge - the Armenian cannon.

The Armenian quarter was still disconnected from the general staff building and communication was maintained through correspondence. This old woman, a revolver in her hand and a cartridge belt tied to her waist, headed towards the French over a road that was under Turkish fire from the north and east. This meant suicide. The woman, without caring for her life, would go to the French positions, saying, "it takes 40 years to become a brave fellow; who cares about my tatter head?" and brought back a whole bag of cartridges with her, while ignoring the Turkish bullets.

April 5th

Today was silent. Only a few shots were fired. Dr. Shepard went to meet with the Turks at their demands. The Turks resorted to deceit again. Upon his return, the doctor, who was not impressed at all, invited the National Union and the intelligentsia of the city to a meeting and said the following:

> The Turks are nothing to be afraid of and we should not be deceived by their dishonesty. They are a drunken and disgraceful people, and there is utter chaos in the military. That was my overall impression. As to the Armenians (the doctor himself was an "Armenian" too), we should do everything to resist, because when the Americans signed the Declaration of Independence,

Bomb-making.

Repairing arms.

> they did not fall at any obstacle but continued on their victorious path. Therefore we should follow their example. Our will and hard work will triumph against those rascals. It is our duty to do whatever we can.

His words motivated the people there, who decided to distrust the Turks, fortify their positions, continue with self-defense, anticipating any surprises. The following note was also sent to the Turks:

> The restoration of peace in this city is entrusted to the representative of the Entente powers, the French, and the local authorities, i.e. the Turks. Therefore, we request these two bodies to fulfill their responsibilities. In the meantime, we are forced to remain in our positions and continue to defend ourselves until peace is restored.

This historic meeting ended with great enthusiasm.

Here, it is our duty to introduce to our non-Cilician readers the two shepherds who, as human angels, had long served both the Cilician Armenians and the Turks.

Fredrick Douglas Shepard came to Aintab as a medical-missionary in 1888 and worked at the Azaria Smith Hospital as a physician. He had been the mentor to all Armenian doctors. Thousands of wounded and sick people had appealed to him, almost all of whom receiving free medicine and treatment.

The people of Aintab regarded Dr. Shepard as a benevolent person, rather than an exploitative missionary. The poor patients did not even think about paying him.

Dr. Shepard's horse was known to all. All the sick inhabitants of a street would gather round it, to ask the doctor for a consultation and examination when he dismounted from the animal. It often happened that the doctor finished a journey by examining numerous patients. He was a blessing for Aintab and the surrounding area. He was a simple and temperate man, and he used to distribute most of his salary to the poor. I remember that one day he visited one of my poorest classmates. He then recommended the mother to feed the patient with certain required foods and wrote the prescription. Knowing their difficult financial situation, he left the house, having slipped a few coins under the patient's pillow. He did this so that the patient's parents could buy the recommended food.

Aintab American Hospital.

This is an episode from the doctor's life. Similarly, a gang of thieves once approached him and asked him what the time was. The doctor, knowing their intent, pulled out his revolver and replied, "My watch says run!"

The unfortunate doctor, after offering his services, also offered his life to the miserable Armenian people. The death of Dr. Shepard caused great pain among the Armenians of Aintab and the area. During his last journey to Yetesia (Ourfa), he witnessed the massacre of the Armenians and buried his heart in Cilician soil. He had served not only the Armenians, but the Turks as well, who were ungrateful for his sacrifices. They did not honor him and buried him with two Turkish soldiers in 1915.

The son of this generous man, the younger doctor [Jr.], who had come to Aintab, took on the same responsibilities and continued his father's uncompleted work. Father and son were Americans who felt Armenian in their hearts. They always suffered and cooperated with the Armenians. Dr. Shepard's son remained in Aintab until the end of the fighting. Some Americans left, but despite the threats against him, he did not leave. He worked relentlessly to treat the wounded Armenians and French in his clinic. During his free time, he would go to the Armenian positions, motivating the Armenian fighters. He personally participated in some attacks that we will shed light on later.

Let us briefly mention the commanders appointed by the Military Body: A. Levonian, and Avedis Kalemkerian. The other members were M. Mouradian, R. Yaghsezian, S. Jemelian and Hovhannes Merdkhanian.

The Armenian quarter was divided into 11 military regions as follows:

1st region: Y.M.C.A, the area around Bulbul Hoja's house. Captain [*khmpabed*], Toros Anlideligian. Later taken over by H. Semerjian and S. Ekshian.

2nd region. The Red Cross front. First group captain Hovhannes Merjanian, later Hovhannes Merdkhanian, K. Tablaian, and N. Bosnaian. Second group captain, Nazar Demirjian.

3rd region. Kayajik Street. Opposite Turkish positions at Chinarli Mosque and Nigoghos Agha's house, at Leylegians' and Kaleaghasi's houses. The captain was Dr. N. Baghdoian and later K. Maksoudian.

4th region. The Feraye house and its surroundings. Captain Mihran Balian and later, Garabet Parseghian.

5th region. Akyol Mosque and surroundings. Captain Dikran Mesrobian.

6th region. Akyol Street. Captain Haroutioun Panjarjian.

7th region. The American hospital area. Captain Garabet Zadigian, later Sarkis Sheohmelian.

8th region. Soghanluh Boujaghuh. Captain Kevork Svajian, later Adour Chavoush.

9th region. The area around Simon Agha's and Bilemjians' houses. Captain Yacoub Tanielian.

10th region. The area around Ilian's house. Captain Haroutioun Momjian.

11th region. The area around Sheikh Mosque. Captain Avedis Darakjian and Hamalian.

There were 551 soldiers at their disposal, as well as 63 medical orderlies, 81 couriers and 60 corporals.

These arrangements did not remain static throughout this period. The latter regions remained the same, but the others were modified.

Hence the Armenians had a small yet organized military body. Everything was complete. The trenches, roads, tunnels, walls, barricades and crossroads. They all formed a united front against the enemy, who observed the Armenian barricades fearfully from its own trenches.

April 6th

That day and the next few days could be considered to be a time for internal organization. The National Union formed a sanitary committee and appointed Mr. Pierce as its head. Nazar Arslanian and Soghomon Nigoghosian, with Manuel Kendirjian and Movses Kendirjian as assistants, supervised the sanitary arrangements and hygiene of the city.

Second, a workers' unit was formed, under the direction of Roupen Soulahian. He had G. Merjenian, M. Kabakian, A. Seraydarian, and N. Kharadejian as his assistants. Their role was to provide workers to build and maintain fortifications.

Third, a police administration was created comprised of Yeghia Demirjian, Yacoub Kurkjian, B. Kornelios, and Yussif Kadrian. They had 35 gendarmes at their disposal and their role was to keep law and order in the city.

Fourth, in order to complement the fortification works and repair the barricades under fire, a committee was formed of Philip Shishmanian, G. Vahramian, S. Vahramian and H. Poladian.

Fifth, a committee was formed of K. Sarkissian, H. Arakelian, H. Karamanougian, H. Khorabjian, M. Kendirjian, A. Tahtajian, H. Saatjian, H. Yimenjian, G. Kalousdian etc. to record the provisions held by the people.

An important development was the discovery of a secret cellar in the house of a Turk called Shaban. 50 kgs of provisions were transported from that location to the Central Building (Vartanian College at that time) to be distributed to the poor. The confiscated provisions, wheat, lentils, etc. greatly facilitated the job done by the auxiliary committee.

Today the Turks returned the French captives who have already been mentioned. They were at the French bakery during the first day of clashes. There were 25 in total and they were taken to the College.

Captain Reno had a meeting with the National Union today and recommended that the Armenians stop firing because the chetes were to withdraw from their positions. Second, he promised to leave a brigade of soldiers for the protection of the Armenian streets if additional French troops arrived in Aintab. Third, he recommended that great importance be given to the Provisions Committee. He also recommended the use of French cartridges during the fighting and saving the rest (German, Turkish, British, Russian) as reserves. Finally, he promised to offer 7-10,000 bullets to the Armenian fighters.

April 7th

The Turks have been silent for two days. The probability of a sudden attack increased the vigilance of the Armenian fighters. The Turkish mutasarrif sent a letter to the French command around 7 o'clock that night. The letter had only just been given to the Y.M.C.A. courier when a gunshot was heard. Many others followed it and the smell of gunpowder filled the streets. The moon had not yet risen and the darkness of the night was seen as the best moment for the attack, which first began around the Y.M.C.A and then expanded to include the whole Armenian front. The French and the Armenians were both under attack. Thousands of shots were being fired from the mountains and Turks in the city. The attack lasted for an hour and half and was reminiscent of the horrific Chanak Kale nights. Bombs were followed by Armenian cannon shots. Women and children were terrified in the midst of this chaos. Many despaired and were moved to the hospital, while the soldiers prepared to fight with knives and bayonets. The Turks, shouting, "Allah! Allah!" attempted to mount an open attack from many sides. They approached the Y.M.C.A. door with axes. When the door was about to be destroyed, Shahin Chavoush, the heroic Armenian soldier at that position, tossed bombs at the Turks from the Y.M.C.A.'s small courtyard. The Turkish chetes fled, crawling like wounded tigers and found shelter behind the Turkish lines.

We should introduce two of our heroes to our readers now. The first, Shahin Chavoush, and the other, a 14 year old boy from Marash, whose name unfortunately I cannot remember.

Shahin Chavoush, a native of Yetesia, had served in the Ottoman army for 10 years before the 1915 events. During the Ottoman Suez Canal operation in 1914, he was captured by the British and later served as a cavalryman in the British army. He thus had spent most of his life in military service. He was a skilful marksman. He could kill a small sparrow with his revolver from 100 meters. Shahin Chavoush had eyes like a hawk. He was the terror of the Turks and the revenge of the Armenians during the fighting. An important position, like that of the Y.M.C.A., which was under the constant attacks of the Turks, needed a man like Shahin Chavoush. He would walk around the minaret of Ibn Eyyoub Mosque. This minaret is best known to our readers as one of the tallest minarets in Aintab and overlooked the wide grand market avenue. Shahin Chavoush used to climb the minaret day and night and snipe at many chetes. He would be sad when, after climbing the 75 stairs of the minaret, he returned home "empty-handed." The Turks suffered many losses from that minaret. Many followed Shahin's example and that colossal minaret was never left unoccupied. After the armistice, the Turks inquired about the identity of the monster whose bullets never missed their targets. The mullah of Balekluh Mosque, the secretary of the mosque and many others were killed by bullets fired from it. The Turks would approach and look at it in great anger. It oozed the scent of death. Shahin Chavoush was a titan who put himself at the service of a nation yearning for justice.

Many deeds during wars are erased from human memory because they are overshadowed by greater concerns and troubles that follow. Such is the memory of our second hero, a 14 year old boy, who came out of the darkness and disappeared into it. During the horrible night attacks, some telephone wires connecting the church to the French command were severed by bullets. In order to inform the French about our situation, we had no other means than finding a volunteer courier. We were worried and waiting in the telephone bureau when a man introduced a 14 year old boy to Rev. Nerses, stating that the boy would deliver the letter that was lying on the table. The boy was willing to go and he disappeared into the night, taking the letter with him. He returned, panting, 30 minutes later, with a French reply. The priest kissed his forehead and gave him a monetary gift.

The boy told us the following:

> When I left the Armenian positions, thousands of bullets were flying left and right, but I ignored them. However, the French fired at me when I was 10 meters away from the general staff building. They thought I was a Turk. I waived the letter, showing that I was a courier. The French took me to their commander as a captive. I gave him the letter. The commander stroked my face. They wrote down their answer which I brought back with me. He ordered the soldiers not to fire until after I had left. I arrived here safe and sound.

The boy was just telling a simple story. We shook his hand and he disappeared into the darkness of the night, just as he had come from it. The letter from the French commander stated, "Resist. There is nothing to be afraid of. We are under attack, too. Do what you can with your own means."

The Turkish attack on April 7th was a failure. It was a great loss of ammunition for them. They were pushed back everywhere and victory was ours. The Armenian fighters celebrated this victory by singing Armenian songs and hymns from the minarets. After the fighting, when there was a deep silence, these songs created a melancholic atmosphere for the Armenian fighters.

The Turks failed in another attempted attack again at 1:30.

April 8th–9th

There was only sporadic gunfire. However, during such supposedly "peaceful" times, the Turks suffered more losses than they would during tumultuous times. The Armenian fighters eventually understood that their shots were nothing other than a waste of ammunition. It was therefore decided not to fire, unless a Turk could be seen through the loopholes in the barricades. This was a very wise decision in terms of preserving ammunition. After that, many attacks took place without even a shot being fired. The Turks ascribed half of their own gunshots to the Armenian positions. They used to start and end such shooting in vain. The Armenian fighters fired only when they saw a Turk, so claiming the lives of 10-12 Turkish chetes per day. Thus, the Turks lost many men during times we considered to be peaceful. The ranks of the Turkish chetes were full of ignorant villagers and their lack of knowledge of the city also contributed to our success.

The Turks attempted to stir tensions between the French and Armenians through their notes.

Thus, they tried to convince General de La Motte (who was in Kilis) to abandon the Armenians of Aintab because they were Turkish subjects, and if the French refrained from cooperating with the Armenians, they claimed it would be possible to come to a Franco-Turkish agreement.

It is only here that we can understand what Turkish policy meant in the east. The Turks of Turkey had been the experts at such manipulation for centuries. This was how the "Sick Man of Europe" had preserved its moribund existence. For 600 years they had been saying that they were our brothers, that we were the children of the same fatherland, and that it was our duty to unite with them and expel the French. At the same time, they were trying to convince the French to abandon the Armenians. The French, knowing the mentality of the Turks, ignored their appeals.

The National Union placed an official notice on the walls, through which it ordered the official recognition of these organizations.-

1. Committee for Provisions Purchase (Tahriri Erzak ve Mubayaa Komisionu).
2. Provisions Committee (Iase Tevziati Komisionu).
3. Labor Battalion (Amele Taburu).
4. Settlement Committee (Siheyi ve Iskan Komisionu).
5. Abandoned Properties Committee (Emvali Metruke Komisionu).

Likewise, it ordered people not entrusted with any responsibility between the ages of 13 and 70 to serve as workers in the labor battalion wherever necessary. Those who were unable to work would be given 200 grams of wheat and flour daily. Criminals would be punished and made to work forcibly under the supervision of the police.

The National Union established a court to adjudicate on disputes among the people. Its appointed members were Y. Benlian, Bedros Milletbashian, and M. Karamanougian.

April 10th

An Armenian was slightly wounded (I should briefly mention that a list of all the wounded and martyrs is located in an annex at the end of this book. Please excuse me if I do not remember all the names here).

At 10:30, the Turks carried out a major attack on the Y.M.C.A. lasting about 30 minutes. The Turks used their newly constructed bombs for the first time. Two of these fell in the Y.M.C.A courtyard, where an Armenian fighter, without noticing it in the dark, picked it up and began examining the bizarre item. As we gathered around him, we understood that the Turkish bomb was nothing more than paper filled with gunpowder and resembled the fireworks children used during celebrations. These newly-invented Turkish bombs were collected and hung on house walls as ornaments. The Turks started to use tin bombs later on, causing nothing other than loud noises.

Armenian fighters with machine gun.

During that night, violent fighting broke out at Manastir, the Ilian line and Kastel Bashuh positions.

To increase the people's militant spirit, the National Union appointed some propagandists among whom I can recall Prof. Krikor Sarafian, Baligian and Haigazoun Keshishian.

Likewise, Nerses Ishkhanian was appointed as head of the police administration. The Armenian prison was put under the command of this organization.

April 11th

It was Easter, the day of Resurrection, and like other Easters, it became a day of mourning for all. This Easter was the occasion for Armenian mothers to shed tears for their sons, or lament the memory of their fathers, husbands, and grand-fathers slaughtered on the desert sands. It was another day when we tasted tears with our dry bread. We still did not know how many more such Easters were reserved for us.

Rev. Nerses Tavoukjian, H. Mouradian, and Dr. K. Arslanian went to congratulate the commander Flye Sainte Marie on behalf of the National Union for the Easter holiday. He, in turn, congratulated the Armenian people for their calmness and extraordinary organizational skills. He drew the attention of the Armenians to three points:

1. Conservation of ammunition.

2. Perseverance in fortification projects.

3. Food rationing.

At the end, the commander promised to provide the Armenians with a machine-gun as a gift for Easter. This was set up later at the Y.M.C.A position because the Turks were using the same kind of weapon against the Armenians that they had retrieved from the Balekluh guard house.

At this point, we should praise those young Armenians who, during such critical times of siege, succeeded in maintaining communications between Aintab and Kilis and acted as couriers. Many of them were martyred on their way, while others continued their work until the end. On April 11th, one of them, upon his return from Kilis, announced to the Colonel that French reinforcements were on their way to Aintab. However, he also informed the Colonel about the tragic deaths of the French troops in Yetesia (Ourfa). There, the French troops had agreed the following terms with the Turks:

1. The Turks would allow the French to withdraw from that region, without a fight.

2. The Turks would provide the French with the necessary camels and means to transport their heavy loads.

The Turks also promised to provide gendarmes who would lead the French and show them their way out. Despite warnings from the Armenians to distrust the Turks and withdraw the way they thought best, the French accepted the Turkish terms and started to withdraw from Yetesia. The gendarmes assigned to guide them alerted the surrounding chetes who positioned themselves behind big rocks near a valley called "Shebekeh Deresi." When the 500 French soldiers entered the valley, the Turks started firing, and only a few survived. Some Turkish chetes, in order to inform the French at Arab Pounar of the tragic deaths of their friends, tortured and beheaded a few high-ranking French prisoners, and then fixed their heads on long poles and displayed them in the market and streets of Yetesia. These developments created much anger and rage within French circles. The soldiers bound for Aintab were destined to Ourfa, but their orders were cancelled after this tragic news.

Chapter 8

The Occupation of Sheikh Mosque

April 12th

The Turks brought three Muslim clergymen from Marash to consult with the Armenians. Dr. Shepard, Mr. Merrill, and Father Mariano went to meet with them on behalf of the Armenians. The clergymen exhorted the attendees to stop cooperating with the French and unite with the Turks, stating that the former were the reason behind the Marash massacres and, as they had done in the case of Marash, they might abandon Aintab and the Armenians too. This proposal was refused by the Armenians, arguing that the situation in Marash was not the same as in Aintab.

This meeting convened before noon, right after the occupation of Sheikh Mosque. As mentioned earlier, this mosque was located to the western side of the most vulnerable part of the Armenian positions and its minaret had become a great threat to the Armenians from the first days of fighting. Even the orphans and staff in the hospital were targeted by Turkish bullets. Its occupation had therefore become vital for the Armenians for two reasons: first, for the protection of the orphanage and the hospital, and second, for the stabilization of the Armenian front extending to the Kozanluh Mosque. This front was always on the verge of collapse.

The Armenians, armed with bombs, started attacking. After 15 minutes they burnt Hassan's house, which the Turks were using to fire at the Armenian and French positions and threatening the road connecting the city to the general staff building. The Turkish chetes were now fleeing in terror. At 10:30, the Armenians, armed with axes, arrived at the mosque's door from the street on the southern side of the orphanage.

From their starting point to the mosque's door was 100 meters, a distance that the Armenian fighters had to cross under fire. The Armenians, ignoring the danger, went forward and entered the mosque after smashing the door down with their axes. The Turks, suffering many losses, fled and started firing at the position that they had just left. The Armenians immediately started fortifying the mosque. Here, we must remember the names of two Armenians from Aintab who contributed greatly to that operation. The first was a mason called Kahveji (coffee maker) Yussef, and the second, Hovhannes Hamalian. Once the mosque was occupied, they started creating barricades by piling up stones and rocks under enemy fire. In the end, after 8–10 rocks had been smashed by enemy bullets, they succeeded in erecting a barricade and cut the Turkish connection with the mosque.

This victory was greatly celebrated by the Armenians. Everything found in the mosque was confiscated and transferred to the Abandoned Properties Committee.

Dr. Shepard personally participated in this operation and his valorous deeds are worth admiring as much as his benevolence. The eulogies addressed to Admiral Nelson suited him well, "Brave as a lion, gentle as a lamb." We suffered one martyr (an Armenian fighter) and some wounded.

During the night, the Turks mounted a few unsuccessful attacks to recover the mosque, but then stopped.

April 13th–16th

After the Turks pulled back from the vicinity of Sheikh Mosque, the minaret that served as a sniping tower against the orphanage and the hospital was occupied within 30 minutes. The message to the Turks was that their war against international laws could be turned against them. Towards evening, the Turks undertook a one hour and 15 minute attack on the Y.M.C.A. front using old German bombs which did not explode.

People used to a normal life can get accustomed to more abnormal challenges. The peaceful Armenian people were now turning into a warrior nation. However, despite those horrible days, the Armenians still found amusement and joy from daily adventures. For example, a caricature was drawn showing Ali Kelej Bey running towards Marash, with Sheikh Mosque minaret on his back. Such humor served to revitalize the morale of the Armenian fighters.

Newly occupied positions were fortified, the soldiers started to receive their meals from the same kitchen, people entrusted with administrative positions attached insignias to their uniforms, and the Provisions Committee was ordered to buy extra supplies from those who had foodstuffs for more than one month. Opposition to such regulations was to be punished. These decisions were made by the National Union, along with 46 other men, who agreed that those holding provisions for more than a month had to sell them to the nation. They would receive half of the cash value and the remainder in instalments.

April 14th. Dr. Shepard and the National Union held a meeting at the Bezjian's house and decided to send a courier to Kilis and Aleppo, demanding help for Aintab.

The Americans promised to contact the French so that the next column of French reinforcements to Aintab could bring supplies to the Armenian fighters.

April 15th. A woman was wounded in the hospital and a boy was killed by bullets fired from the mountains.

The National Union decided to use the Topbashian mill and adopt a hat design for the fighters and police in order to distinguish them from the Turks.

Third, it decided to form a committee overseeing capital reserves. Its members were Dr. Bezjian, H. Arakelian and S. Jebejian.

Fourth, noticing that some people were unwilling to work, the National Union decided to give a "permit" to each person. People not holding a permit would be tracked down and punished. Unemployed people were obliged to work in the labor battalions, otherwise they would have to pay a fine of two mejidiye [one mejidiye was equal to 20 piaster/kurush] or four okkas of *tsavar* (bulghur) wheat. The responsibility for issuing the permits was entrusted to Khachadour Khachadourian, Kevork Tahtajian, and Khachadour Kavafian.

At about nightfall, the mutasarrif informed the French command through a telegraph message that the chetes had left the city to attack French convoys, and that he had no responsibility for that development.

April 16th

We heard a cannon shot from the eastern side of the city. Bombs were falling on the nearby hills. The Turks, terrorized, started to flee to the north. Then, a machine-gun started firing at the deserters, stopping their escape. The newly arrived French force was Norman's battalion whose entry into Aintab cost the Turks a lot of men. Deserters succeeded, with great difficulty, in finding shelter in Aleppo after wandering from one city to another. The wives and daughters of notable families have been raped by Turkish chetes. These debauched people do not even spare their own kinsmen. This has been the revenge of Armenian on the Turks of Aintab.

The newly arrived French troops besieged the city from the eastern and southern side as far as Mardin, where they united their left flank with the French forces located in the College. For the first time, Flye Sainte Marie used his 6.5cm cannons against the Turkish Kurd Mahallesi positions, forcing them to retreat. After the occupation of Mardin, the Turks, besieged on three sides, had only one way to retreat, which was toward Ferkah to the east. Norman's troops bombarded the vicinity of the government palace, so the French flag was raised over Armenian positions to protect the Armenian quarter.

April 17th. Fresh troops arrived from Kilis. They are Dubiovry's battalion that besieged the city from the northern side and joined Norman's troops.

In the afternoon, the Armenians attacked Bulbul Hoja's house, on the northern side of the Y.M.C.A. This was the only Turkish house among the Armenian positions south of the Transversal. The Turks had opened a trench from Binbashi's house and connected to Bulbul Hoja's house. This attack was led by Avedis Kalemkerian.

The Armenians breached the rear wall of the house. It was easy to make the breach, but entering the premises was difficult, since the Turks were able to outflank us and claim many lives. Fortunately, they left the premises. Mr. Kalemkerian entered and examined the house thoroughly. Finally, he was joined by some other fighters and reached the upper attic, where he found an abandoned barricade. The Turks had opened small air holes on the eastern side of the attic which they had forgotten to block during their retreat. Using these same holes, the Armenian fighters shot dead two chetes who had sheltered at Binbashi's house thinking themselves safe. After the house was occupied, some military measures were arranged. All property there was transferred to the Abandoned Properties Committee and foodstuffs were sent to the Provisions Committee. The Armenians found the Hoja's figs and raisins very tasty, as they were of a really good quality. The Turks had taken a lot of supplies to their soldiers.

April 18th–23rd

There was a house located next to hoja's building that belonged to him. The Armenians attempted to occupy it. The building was first attacked under the leadership of Shahin Chavoush using bombs and then the signal for the assault was given with a blast from a trumpet. After 15 minutes, another blast ordered the ceasefire. A little later, Shahin Chavoush, holding a bomb in his hand, went up to the upper floor of the other building and, after tossing the bomb into the yard, descended down the stairs. There were two or three chetes still remaining on the ground floor. Seeing Shahin Chavoush entering the yard, the chetes fled, shouting, "The infidel has entered!" and disappeared through a firing position in their trenches without even using their weapons. The building was thus secured. The retreating chetes continued firing, but the remaining holes were carefully blocked and our front on the Transversal fully under control.

Through some correspondence with the French convoys, we were informed that the National Union of Aleppo, the A.G.B.U. and Khoren Bey Nazaretian had provided over 1,000 Ottoman gold liras for the purchase of supplies. The flour, rice, salt, and other necessary supplies purchased with this sum had already arrived in Aintab. So, the National Union of Aintab sent a letter of thanks to its benefactors.

The National Union formed a committee of women to explain our situation to the two newly arrived colonels, Norman and Dubiovry. The members of this committee were Mrs. H. Bezjian, Y. Sarkissian, M. Karamanougian, M. Bourounsouzian, M. Mouradian, and Koyoumjian.

April 13th [sic]. General de La Motte arrived in Aintab.

On the 20th, Rev. Nerses Tavoukjian, Dr. K. Arslanian, H. Mouradian, D. Mesrobian, and N. Fesdekjian met the new general who stated the following. First of all, he thanked the Armenians for displaying such bravery and excellent organization throughout the previous 13 days. He announced that the people, who had suffered greatly during the Great War, had already won their fight for justice. Therefore, through their action and efficiency, they were worthy of French protection. He promised to inform General Gouraud in Beirut of this. Moreover, he recommended that the Armenians should be wary of provocations and continue to defend their positions during French operations. He also promised to contribute to supplies for the city by contacting Armenian and foreign benevolent unions so that no efforts would be spared in obtaining wheat for the city. The French would provide facilities for its transportation.

The Armenian delegates also pointed out that the Armenian streets had now turned into theatres of war, and everyone, including all the children, women, and elderly were working to alleviate this problem. However, this situation could not last long, and a lasting solution had to be found.

As for provocations, the Armenians had always taken care to avoid them. On the other hand, one had to remember that the Armenians of Aintab lacked food and weapons. Weapons were often transferred from one position to another, particularly to places where the fighting was intense.

The general, in response, stated that the French did not possess extra weapons, as they did not have an armory, and they therefore could not help the Armenians in this matter. However, he added that the Armenians should not despair, that the day of liberation was near, and that the French would protect their co-religionist nation.

After this meeting, the local French command provided the Armenians with eight to 10 decrepit guns. The Armenians used them after they were refurbished in their arms factory. Until that day, only 80-90 Armenian fighters out of 551 had regular weapons.

At the most desperate moments, the community found ways to strengthen its resolve. Every day, new rumors and lies circulated, as necessitated by circumstances and the needs of the people to believe them. For example, the European powers had decided to occupy Turkey and partition it among themselves; or, a large French force had sailed to Iskenderun and would restore peace after its occupation of these areas. There was always favorable news concerning Armenians, supposedly heard by the woman who did colonel's laundry.

April 21st. The Turks fired at the Y.M.C.A building for 15 minutes without any results.

In order to facilitate the work of the Provisions Committee, the National Union decided to form the following sub-committees:

1. Purchasing sub-committee
2. Selling sub-committee
3. Free Distribution sub-committee
4. Control sub-committee

April 22nd, 10:30 [p.m.]. The Turks opened fired along the line stretching from Ilian Effendi's tavern to the Barsoumian College. This was a bluff to distract Armenian attention because, on that same night, they had started withdrawing from their position called Kurd Mahallesi. They had launched these minor attacks to prevent casualties and made the most of the darkness of the night.

Chapter 9

The Armenian Arms Factory

It is worth providing our readers here with specific details about this "establishment", because the success of the self-defense efforts was largely dependent on it. Under the control of the Military Body, a committee was formed of H. Yaghoubian, A. Mouradian, K. Baghdoian, K. Manoushagian, and H. Panjarjian. This committee worked in the Protestant chapel. This wide building was divided into sections and used by the gunpowder makers.

1. Smelters. They made 25-30 bombs of different sizes every day. They used zinc and copper as their materials. The biggest bombs weighted 360 dirhems, the middle-sized ones 200, and the smallest 100. The latter two were used on the Turkish positions at a distance of 70-80 meters, whereas the big ones were used during attacks in order to bombard the enemy's positions. Their efficiency was tested in caves. They were as effective as the French 7.5cm shells. The Armenians bombs resembled the French ones in having a spring. They caused great terror and claimed many Turkish lives because, in contrast to old French ones that often did not explode, the Armenian bombs exploded immediately. Once ready, the bombs were taken to Garouj Laleian's house. It was his job to fill them with gunpowder. We can say that he was the first to suggest and organize this bomb-making operation. Trained as a gunsmith, he had worked in Ottoman arsenals during the Chanak Kale battle. During the fighting, the Armenians of Aintab benefitted greatly from his talent and expertise. The explosive part of the bomb was composed of potash chloride and "saruh tash." The most dangerous part of the job was the mixing of these two chemicals, because they had to be kept in a humid place, since there was a constant fear of ignition. The aforementioned expert often risked his life making them. 40 dirhems of this mixture was used in each bomb, and the fuse was fixed at one end using a dynamite primer.

2. Primer Makers. The lack of the ammunition compelled us to re-use every cartridge, refilling each one 10-15 times. However, the important element was the primer (located in the base of the cartridge), stocks of which were almost exhausted. Armenian craftsmen made many attempts to create them. However, success was reserved for a jeweler called Kevork Berejiklian. His plan to make them was initially rejected when it was

presented to the French command, since it was deemed too dangerous and possibly fatal. However, the idea had bolstered the confidence of the Armenian craftsmen. In the end, as a first attempt, the aforementioned jeweler made some primers using potassium chloride and mercury and presented it to the head of the armory. The latter tested it by fixing it to a pistol cartridge. However, no sound was heard. Only green smoke came out of the pistol barrel. The success of the experiment was thus in doubt. Nevertheless, a second primer was tested, the cartridge having been filled with gunpowder and a bullet. This time there was a roar as the bullet flew out. It was perfectly successful. The jewelers started working immediately, turning copper into thin metal sheets, from which primer patterns were cut out using dentist tools and then filled with gunpowder. The gunsmiths were thus provided with 1,500 primers a day to use in making cartridges.

3. Gunsmiths. The workers in this section manufactured one gun a week (a Martini). They would restore damaged weapons on a daily basis and return them to the front line positions. Labor was divided: some restored weapons, others made primers and filled cartridges with gunpowder. The gunsmiths used the residue of cannon gunpowder for regular weapons. The Armenian arsenal also worked for the French. Their weapons were also restored there.

4. Blacksmiths. These men built the Armenian cannon, all the necessary tools for incineration, digging, and trench building, as well as the water tanks used by the fire fighters. Another group of blacksmiths worked to melt the copper and zinc retrieved from house balconies.

5. Gunpowder Makers. They worked in a cave. The gunpowder they made was known to us as the type used in hunting guns. Its preparation consisted in mixing 800 dirhems of nitrate with 100 dirhems of sulfur and 100 dirhems of coal. One liter of gunpowder was thus prepared each day and used for revolvers, two-barreled shotguns, and other weapons. Given that this powder was easily damaged by humidity, some people were specifically entrusted with keeping it dry.

6. Other Workers. The remaining men would collect pieces of timber and wood from the different positions in order to prevent any fires that might have broken out as a result of Turkish gunfire. Additionally, they complemented the work of other experts when the need arose. They also made slings for the bomb throwers.

April 23rd

This day became one of the most victorious days for Armenians. A few men entered some Turkish houses intending to plunder them. After entering them, they found themselves inside Turkish lines and, noticing that that part of the city was completely abandoned and no Turkish soldiers could be seen, they informed the Military Body of the situation. The Armenians immediately planned an attack under the leadership of Adour Levonian and Avedis Kalemkerian. The attack started from the direction of Kelesh Hoja's house, where Turkish chetes had been positioned and firing for 22 days. Kelesh Hoja's house was located on the western corner of Pasha Street. The Armenian fighters, after throwing some bombs at the house, entered the premises, but encountered no one. They were puzzled as to where the chetes might have gone. When the house and its surroundings were captured and thoroughly examined, they saw some oil lamps that had just been turned off at the entrance of a cave. At that same moment an Armenian came forward and said that, in his opinion, the Turks might have fled from the Kan Alujdun watercourse. Considering this as plausible, the Armenians immediately ordered the closure of entrances to the water cistern. The primary entrance to the water cistern was located at Ashi Bajeh Mosque, which the Armenians blocked with stones and rocks. This watercourse was a few thousand meters long and extended all the way to Belediyyeh Khan, providing the Turks safe passage. However, the Armenians had erred. The Turks had already abandoned these positions and had only left a few soldiers there, including their commander from Kilis, Arslan Bey. These men were trapped in Kelesh Hoja's house after the Armenians had occupied Pasha, Dashjuh, Barzeh Yanezuh and Kurdish streets. When they heard the explosion of the bombs, they had desperately entered that cave, hid behind a pile of wood and quietly observed the movement of the Armenian fighters and Mr. Kalemkerian. The Armenians, stopping their search on the Water Road, had saved the lives of these Turkish leaders, who were more valuable than common chete fighters. After staying hidden for a while, they moved towards the Turkish positions without being noticed by the Armenian guards. Arslan Bey personally related this story after the armistice.

With the occupation of these streets, the Armenians expanded their territory, and the Transversal became the only avenue separating the Turks and the Armenians. The properties in the occupied streets were transferred to the Abandoned Properties Committee, while foodstuffs went to the Provisions Committee warehouse. Here we must mention the disgraceful event that followed every occupation: the desire to plunder, which was restrained with great difficulty. One faction of the Armenian community thought that plundering the houses of the Turks, who had previously pillaged theirs, was just.

Members of the National Union, Rev. Nerses Tavoukjian, N. Fesdekjian, and Dr. K. Arslanian met Dubiovry and explained the situation. The colonel replied that the Armenians should be careful, especially as the French were not able to help Armenians by providing them weapons and soldiers. However, he added that the French troops in Aintab were sufficient to quell or resist any internal or external attack. The colonel stated that although the French did not resort to direct measures, this situation would not last long. It was their superiors who were in charge and ordered them to behave as they did. After meeting with Colonel Dubiovry, the aforementioned Armenians also met Colonel Flye Sainte Marie, who promised to deliver 500 Egyptian gold liras.

The National Union appointed a Transportation Committee to supervise the movement of provisions from Kilis. Its members were Haroutioun and Hagop Khachadourian and Yessayi Ipekian, with Hagop Murekian and Sarkis B. Nazarian as their supervisors.

April 24th–25th

The departure of the "newly arrived" French troops disappointed the Armenians of Aintab very much. We had expected that the French would occupy the city this time and put an end to our miserable situation. The two enemies that bothered us were hunger and lack of ammunition. French convoys visited the city once every 2-3 weeks, and the supplies they brought were sufficient for only 4-5 days. Everything was almost exhausted: oil, cigarettes, meat, flour. Instead of meat, people started using nuts that the Armenian merchants possessed in great quantities. During the deportation, the Armenians had found the way to eat almost nothing and survive. Meat, oil and wheat were replaced by nuts. Everyone tried to deceive their stomach. With the arrival of the French, the Armenians had greatly benefited from harvesting the crops in Turkish gardens, such as garlic, onions, chickpeas, etc.... With their departure, we were deprived of these foodstuffs. However, all this misfortune did not weaken the moral vigor of the Armenians. They worked for their people, as well as the French. Thousands of workers, widows and orphans, after connecting the college to the city by building a protective wall, were planning to connect the city to the hill of Mardin. Imagine, more than 1,000 workers building a wall stretching from the city as far as the Mardin orphanage. They had to finish it within two nights. Starved and miserable, these people were the embodiment of diligence and productivity. In the morning, the Turks saw a 1,500 meter long wall in front of their positions. This was the first sign of Norman and Dubiovry's departure.

April 26th. Colonel Abady had come to Aintab on the 25th with his staff, replacing Colonel Flye Sainte Marie. On the same day, the Turks sent a letter to Flye Sainte Marie, bearing Ali Kelej's signature. We cannot present the translation of this letter since it is unfit for the eyes of the reader. Those who know Turkish can easily speculate the joyfulness of the foul language and can easily guess what the content of the letter might have been.

After this, on April 26th, the French decided to form a court martial and heavily shell the Turkish quarter. However, a telegraph received on that same morning banned the bombardment. Instead, they decided to attack the Turks with a battalion of Algerian soldiers and two vehicles. The attack was successful. The French soldiers succeeded in even capturing some houses. However, when the Turks encircled them and tried to cut off their escape route, the French pulled back, killing some Turks. This small success was celebrated as a great victory. The use of vehicles in the battle caused confusion and terror among the Turks, who fled without even firing at them. One of the tanks was slightly damaged and was pulled back to the French lines by the other one. During this attack, the French suffered six dead and eight wounded. The Turks suffered much more. The vehicle captain said that he personally killed many Turks with his machine gun.

April 28th

On April 28th, Colonels Norman and Dubiovry's battalions set off to Jarablus. The Turks pursued them until noon and then returned to the city, capturing the positions abandoned by the colonels. The Turks claimed to have pushed back the French by fighting them.

The Turks tried to burn down the Armenian Red Cross positions in the afternoon using poles and sheets dipped in oil or other inflammable liquids. This was the first time they used this tactic. They succeeded burning down a few places at the beginning, but thanks to the vigilance of our fire brigade, the fires were put out. They then tried to burn one or two other places, in order to make the work of the fire fighters difficult. However, they were unsuccessful again. The Armenians adopted a policy of "fight fire with fire" and started burning the Turkish positions at Naum Khayat. That building was easily burnt down as it was completely made of wood. Armenian bombs were thrown at the enemy while this fire burned in order to obstruct the Turkish firefighters and claim as many lives as possible.

Both sides made efforts for weeks to burn down the houses and positions on this front. The Armenians, as well as the Turks, made such attempts using long poles. Sometimes Turkish chetes holding the poles fell behind their barricades, leaving their poles out of reach in the middle of the streets. I witnessed an instance when one Turkish chete was killed by Armenian bullets, leaving three others to complete the attempt, thus leading to the deaths of the other three as well by Armenian bullets. Sometimes, one of the belligerent parties would pull the pole to their side, as their opponents obstructed them with gunfire from the other side, leaving the pole in the street. The street was filled with such poles from Patanians' house as far Chinarli Mosque.

The Armenians burned Mavrit's coffee-house in the evening. This wooden building, which served as an Ittihadist center, burnt down in minutes. Black smoke gathered over the Turkish positions and fell on them like a curse. This was the flame of revenge, the fire in the heart of a suffering people, who now burned the Turkish houses. Terrorized, the Turks withdrew from the Abdo Effendi and Chitji positions in order to save themselves from the burning flames fanned by an eastwards wind, a factor that was well-considered by the Armenians.

The command of the Armenian fire fighters' squad had two water pumps. One had been donated by Dr. Shepard.

The Turks tried, unsuccessfully, to burn some of the positions around the Y.M.C.A building from the direction of the Balekluh market.

April 29th

The Turks sent a letter to the Armenians, French and Americans. The content of the letter to the Armenians was:

> You, as Ottoman citizens, have revolted against your own government. You should know that your acts will not remain unpunished. You are collaborating with an enemy that wants to occupy our fatherland. You therefore have 24 hours to surrender your weapons and accept Ottoman suzerainty, otherwise we will not be responsible for any bloodshed.

The letter sent to the Americans read:

> You have come to our lands for humanitarian purposes. Your position must remain neutral towards this Armeno-Turkish conflict. The French should withdraw from your hospital within 24 hours. You must not treat their wounded. Your neutrality must be displayed by raising American flags over your buildings.

The letter to the French, besides being a collection of insults, contained the following:

> Traitors, thieves, uncivilized, and shameless people! What do you want from our people?

These three ultimatums, giving the recipients a deadline of 24 hours, were signed by Seyfullah as the commander of the Turkish troops.

The Armenian answer was as follows.

The Armenians listed below met at Hayganushian College: four members of the Military Body, H. Arakelian, H. Kendirjian, H. Karamanougian, S. Karamanougian, T. Kupelian, H. Poladian, N. Shirinian, N. Chekjian, Dr. Shepard, H. Bezjian, H. Levonian, N. Ishkhanian, R. Soulahian, B. Milletbashian, Y. Kurkjian and H. Panjarjian, Rev. Karekin Bogharian, Rev. Nerses Babaian, K. Sarkissian, Gh. Ghebligian, M. Hekimian, H. Hamalian, H. Yaghoubian, and H. Araradian refused to surrender any weapons and adopted the note of April 5th, to which the Hatti Humayun of Peyami Sabah was to be attached, condemning the operations carried out by the Turkish chetes as illegal or proscribed by Islam.

The Americans replied in the following way:

> The Armenians are not your enemies. What they are doing is merely defending themselves. As to the French, we cannot expel them because they were sent by the Entente powers.

The French reply was their amusement. They ignored the letter by putting it aside.

The Turkish attitude displayed in these letters was nothing other than an attempt to find a solution to their own desperate situation.

At sunset, bombs started to fall on Mardin Hill and Ghourban Baba. This development was not understood at first, then shortly afterwards bombs started to fall on the Armenian quarter too. The Turks had started, for the first time, to use the mountain artillery they had brought from Rum Kaleh. The 9th Caucasian Army Corps had also arrived. The Turks, relying on this force, had sent the aforementioned letters written with an attitude. The Armenians immediately sheltered in the lower floors of their houses. Some of the shells fell on the Armenian church, the hospital and the surroundings of their positions at Manastir and Akyol. The French retaliated with their 7.5cm cannons and silenced the Turkish artillery by firing 120 shells.

Flye Sainte Marie, taking the rest of Colonel Dubiovry's battalion with him, left Aintab tonight. Most of the Turkish bombs did not explode because they were decrepit and old. They were collected and brought to the armory and the gunpowder in them was used for various purposes. Most of the bombs fired were Russian and the rest were Ottoman.

The Turks started fires again in the evening. This time it was the Leylegians' house that they tried to burn down. The Armenians immediately rushed there with hundreds of buckets and succeed in putting the fire out in 30 minutes. The Turks tried using fire-engines to pump oil on these fires. In the end, however, solidarity and hard-work triumphed over everything.

The Turks attempted to burn down the Yaghoubians' house (on the Transversal) in the morning. The Armenians rushed to put the fire out once more. This is how the night of April 29th ended.

Lieutenant Silva met with the National Union before his departure and told them that he had to comply with his superiors' orders and leave Aintab. He really wanted to stay and fight by the side of the Armenian soldiers. However, military orders had to be obeyed. He told them that he was leaving Aintab with good memories. Father Nerses Tavoukjian thanked the Lieutenant on behalf of the National Union for his support and services to the Armenian fighters and for his bravery.

April 30th

The Turks had occupied all the remaining hills and positions with the exception of Mardin Hill and Ghourban Baba and were getting ready to mount a major attack. The Armenians noticed that the number of Turkish chetes fighting in the streets had decreased. The experienced

Armenian fighters understood this. So, the Armenians attacked Chinarli Mosque from the direction of Kaleaghasi and the Leylegians' house at night.

The reader already knows that the Armenian positions on that side overlooked the Turks. Despite this, the minaret of the mosque caused a lot of headache and damage to the Armenians living in this street. The Armenians fired at the minaret countless times using French bullets. For every three or four shots, a section of the stones would collapse, (the minaret was built of rows of stones), eventually destroying a part of its façade. Exploiting the aperture that was formed as a result, the Armenians tossed bombs into the minaret, weakening its whole structure. The Turks had blocked the windows overlooking the street and were using loopholes to shoot because the mosque was very solid and built of one-meter thick walls. Exploiting the darkness of the night, the Armenians, started using long iron poles to make holes in the dome of the mosque, whose carpet had already been burned. In 15 minutes, the dome was breached, and a bottle of poisonous gas attached to an iron pole was lowered into the mosque through the gap they had made. The Turks fired and the bottle shattered, thus spreading the poisonous gas throughout the neighborhood. The Turks, blinded, started to reach for each other in the mosque. During the chaos that ensued, one of the bravest fighters on that front, A. Chakmajian, tossed three or four bombs into the mosque and they exploded with an awful noise. One then heard the uproar inside the mosque. Based on Turkish testimonies, they lost 70 men after the dome was destroyed. Hiding in the mosque had now become impossible for the chetes, so they thought of surrounding the mosque with high walls and deep trenches, so that the bombs tossed at them would fall into the trenches and not damage anyone inside the mosque. Anticipating their plan, the Armenians stopped throwing bombs from that side. After the ceasefire, when we had the chance to wander about the mosque, we saw thick walls and deep pits that had been built with great difficulty and sacrifice under the constant fire of the Armenian fighters. Chinarli Mosque had become the Chanak Kale of the Turks.

After the Chinarli Mosque attack, the Turks tried to burn the Y.M.C.A and Bulbul Hoja's house, but they failed. During this night attack, when a Turk holding a fire-bomb had come out of his position shouting, "Infidels, I am not afraid of you. Your bullets cannot touch me," an Armenian fighter shot him down. The bullet hit him in the mouth.

The Turks set fire to Yaghoubian's house at midnight, which the Armenians immediately put out. Dr. Shepard personally participated in this effort, working as a laborer and exhorting the other men around him. His presence energized the vigor and motivation of the men. Similarly, our commander A. Levonian was worthy of admiration for his efforts to put out the fires. He also audaciously tossed bombs at enemy positions.

The other important events of April 30th were the following:

The Mutasarrif's representative, Sabri Effendi, demanded the following as a response to our letter:

* The French flags had to be lowered immediately.
* The unconditional surrender of all weapons (this time the deadline was the evening).

Unless these conditions were met, he said he would not be able to guarantee the life and honor of the Armenians.

With this last statement, he meant that the Turks would slaughter the Armenians.

Dr. Shepard presented a letter received from Dr. Lambert to the National Union. According to the letter, Dr. Lambert communicated the decisions of the meeting he had had with General De La Motte, who thought that the fight would last a long time and made the following suggestions:

* The transportation of Miss Frearson's orphans to Aleppo.
* The transportation of all the orphans and widows in the National orphanage and other American institutions to Aleppo.
* The transportation of Armenian refugees to Kilis.
* Permission for those people who wanted to leave for America to do so at their own expense.
* Permission for needy families to leave Aintab in order to facilitate the Provisions Committee's tasks.

As a result of these suggestions, the National Union decided not to organize a general exodus, but permit the departure of those whose absence would not damage the self-defence efforts and facilitate the relief efforts. As to the transportation of the orphans, the National Union suggested to Dr. Lambert that they be sent to Armenian regions.

Colonel Abady let the National Union know that he would be sending an ultimatum to the Turks, according to which, if the latter did not cease their bombardment, the French would destroy the whole Turkish quarter.

May 1st–4th

On May 1st, the Turks took the fight to the Mardin and Ghourban Baba positions. At about 6 p.m., they attempted a minor attack against the French. They also started firing along the whole Armenian defence line, leaving the impression that they were positioned along it with many men. In actual fact, they had concentrated all their force on the surroundings of Sheikh Mosque (a distance of 3,000 meters from Mardin) and the rocky hills of Karatash, 400 meters from the south-east of Ghourban Baba. This time, the Turks had three cannons and many machine guns and intended to put the Armenians as well as the French in a difficult position by occupying the Mardin and Ghourban Baba hills. The shooting continued until nightfall. Nevertheless, the preparations made by the Turks were quite visible. At 5:30, they attacked Mardin from all sides. However, the French soldiers positioned there pushed the enemy back and the Turkish advance was repulsed. The Turks attacked the Armenian positions as well and succeeded in burning down the Patanians' house, located in the north-east of the Armenian positions. The house had a wooden balcony and the fire spread in a few minutes as the Turks continued to pump oil into it from the Andilians' house. The Armenians tried to put out the fire, but in vain. However, they did not despair and tossed bombs onto the Turkish positions in the midst of this chaotic situation.

At midnight, the Turks stopped the pump and a deep silence ensued. Armenian prisoners later told us that one of the bombs tossed at the Turkish position fell among the chetes who were using the pump and caused a fire among them. Rushing to put the fire out, they accidentally used oil instead of water and an explosion destroyed the pump, killing 12 chetes and wounding 15 others. The Armenian prisoner, who related this event, saw the shattered pump on the following day (May 2nd). The fire, after burning down the whole balcony, was put out by the Armenian firefighters and new barricades were built in order to prevent any such fires in the future. During this time, the Armenians noticed a chete who was sitting next to a bucket of oil and waiting. The chete was killed by a shot from the Armenian positions. The Turks did not approach the corpse because of their fears.

On the following day, the Turks punctured the bucket by shooting it and pulled the body inside their lines using a pole with a hook on the end. On the morning of May 2nd, the ongoing battle for Mardin Hill and Ghourban Baba intensified. At about five o'clock, the Turks brought two more cannons to the battlefield, one of which was a 10.5cm gun. They started bombarding the French positions at Chitji Kharaf, the College, the general staff building, the western positions of the Armenian quarter and the houses located on the street called Pert Mahallesi. The aforementioned cannons started shelling the French positions on Mardin Hill and Ghourban Baba from the direction of Sheikh Mosque. The French cannons were inactive because they were stationed on a low hill and could not see the Turkish cannons positioned behind Mardin and Ghourban Baba hills. The bombardment went on for about two hours, after which the Turks concentrated their force facing Ghourban Baba, on the southern side of which Turkish machine guns fired endlessly at the French positions. Just at this time, two brigades of Turkish regular troops attacked from the southern side of Ghourban Baba and made a 100 meters' advance. The French started using bombs, but given the large number of Turkish irregular and regular troops advancing, they could not mount the necessary resistance, especially as the French were deprived of the help of the French troops at the College. At 3:00 pm, the bombardment suddenly stopped and Turkish troops who were shouting "Allah, Allah!" arrived at Ghourban Baba within 15-20 minutes.

Terrorized, some of the Algerian soldiers fled towards the College and Mardin and we, the Armenians, witnessed with much anguish the escaping Algerians and the hellish scene of the Turkish mob firing at them from behind. Lieutenant Bazen lost all hope for the Algerians and desperately tried to muster ethnic-French soldiers in an attempt to protect his position despite having been wounded. However, the advancing Turkish chetes succeed in capturing this position and later executing the French soldiers. The Algerian soldiers were not exempt from this torture. This was despite lieutenant Bazen's pleas, who said to the chete leader, "Do not kill them. They are Muslims like you." "They are worse," replied the Turks. Among the fleeing Algerians, some of whom had fallen in the street, was Sergeant Diash, the only survivor who witnessed his commander and friends' execution, having been forced to leave his position and flee towards Mardin. Using his bayonet, he succeeded in escaping from the chetes who had surrounded him and, despite the thousands of shots fired at him, succeeds in arriving in Mardin. He recounted this tragic event as the lone survivor. The French lost 25 men during this attack, and the bodies of the lieutenant, captains and soldiers were mutilated. The Turks confiscated 300 bombs, 30,000 cartridges, 20-30 rifles and a machine gun.

After the occupation of Ghourban Baba, the Turks attempted to occupy Mardin as well. However, two French machine guns, whose roar still echoes in our ears, obstructed the advance of the Turkish troops. Moreover, the artillery at the College bombarded the occupied positions of Ghourban Baba, ruining the Turkish plan to occupy Mardin.

Around 11:30 at night, the French with 15 volunteers and 12 Algerians who had previously fled, attempted to re-occupy Ghourban Baba and save the mutilated bodies of their friends. However, they were forced to retreat and find shelter in Mardin under heavy Turkish fire. The Turks suffered more losses than the French during this battle because attackers always suffer more casualties than defenders.

The Turks started, after the end of the battle of Mardin and Ghourban Baba, to bombard the Armenian streets once more. The Armenians, sheltering in the lower levels of their houses, avoided the damage caused by the Turkish cannons, especially as the Turkish bombs were old and often did not explode. During the bombardment, the Turks attacked the Y.M.C.A. but withdrew after suffering some losses. The Turkish bombardment wounded three people. Three Turks were killed at Bulbul Hoja's house at this time.

The National Union met with the French general staff to discuss the issue of Turkish bombardment. At the same time, a delegation of women (Y. Sarkissian, M. Sarkissian, V. Antaki, and F. Arakelian) appealed to the colonel to find a solution to the deadlock. The colonel replied that a peace treaty would be signed with the Turks by the end of the month.

At 3:00 a.m., a fire started at jeweler Srabionian's house. It was located on the most prominent point of the Armenian positions and its windows and doors opened towards Choukour Bostan. This house, unfit for self-defense, had been left empty. The Turks had entered it and started the fire. Their entry had not been seen. However, when they left the building, the Armenians punished them by firing a few shots and killing several on the spot. The Armenians did not try to put out the fire, as the house was in an exposed position, and after a few hours, it died out all by itself.

The Turks undertook a few minor attacks on the Red Cross position but they failed. The Armenians fighters were about to go and have a rest in their homes, leaving a few guards at their positions after the torment of the past few days. However, a trumpet peal, full of boding, was heard at midnight. It was the attack alarm. The Turks started attacking again, reminiscent of the general attack of April 1st. The enemy, surrounding the whole Armenian neighborhood, fired ruthlessly. The noise was extremely loud, so that two men standing close to each other and shouting could not hear what the other said. The Armenians did not retaliate and the Turks achieved nothing but a waste of ammunition.

After the attack had continued for a few hours, the colonel informed the Armenians by telephone, that the French would start a bombardment and that the Armenians should be cautious and let the French know if a bomb went off near their positions. The French fired 50-60 rounds from their 7.5 cms artillery towards the Turkish positions on Transversal and silenced them. After the bombardment, letters were sent by the Turks: two letters to the French, one to the Americans, and one to the Armenians.

Chapter 10

The Turkish Ultimatums

These are the translations of the letters addressed to the French:

Aintab May 2nd, 1920

To Lieutenant-Colonel Abady,

I had recommended to your predecessor, Flye Sainte Marie, to leave Aintab and withdraw with all of his troops. I informed him of the detailed demands made by the people.

He acted prudently and left the city with some of his troops. It is very probable that he didn't tell you anything about this. I suggest you leave the city under the following terms:

1) The nation does not wish to see foreign forces on its soil and therefore, if you decide to leave the city by tomorrow (May 3rd, 12 o'clock), I assure you that your troops will not be attacked as far as Kilis.
2) If you choose not to leave, I have to let you know that the place you are staying will be destroyed by our cannons and I doubt that you wish to see blood spilt. You will be responsible for any bloodshed if you don't surrender Aintab and set it free from an unjust occupation.

Please accept my Terms, dear Colonel.

Commander of Armed Forces, Seyfullah

The second letter:

Aintab May 2nd, 1920

To Mr. Lieutenant-Colonel Abady, commander of the region of Aintab,

I have the honor to let you know that I am the leader of a national movement created by the people and I enjoy their trust and blessing.

1) Although the nation is weak and isolated, it won't tolerate and doesn't want the presence of a foreign commander on its soil.
2) The will of the people is firm on this point and its decision is final. If you do not leave the city before 12 on May 3rd, 1920, the Muslims will blockade the city and the roads from all

sides. You will be subject to violent attacks and will be responsible for any bloodshed.

3) I can assure you that if you leave the city, you will not be subject to any attack.

Commander of Nationalist Forces of Aintab and its surrounding

Kelej Ali

The translation of the letter addressed to the Armenians was as follows:

> You should surrender your weapons and raise the Ottoman flag on your roofs as a token of your acceptance of our terms. Also, send a delegation before 12 o'clock to arrange surrender. Otherwise, the Armenian quarter will be bombarded and we will not be responsible for the bloodshed.

This letter was signed by Seyfullah and Kelej Ali

The letter addressed to the Americans was as follows:

1) You should not treat the French wounded.
2) Expel the French soldiers located inside the Hospital (for protection).
3) Take back the Mardin building that belonged to you from the French soldiers.

The French replied to the aforementioned ultimatum with a note to their commanding officers and soldiers:

> The "Commander of Nationalist forces" and "Commander of Mobile Forces" order us to leave Aintab today, before noon.
>
> They threaten us with the most ruthless bombardment and attacks if we do not comply with their demands.
>
> It is beneath us to reply to these threats. We protect the French flag in Aintab and the honor of French soldiers. We will confront them victoriously until the end.
>
> The Turks will not be able to vanquish us. Let each of you stay tranquil and calm in his position and remain firm for any attack.
>
> Long live France.
>
> Commander of Aintab and the region,
>
> Lieutenant-Colonel Abady, Aintab May 3nd, 1920

As for the Armenians, the National Union invited 44 intellectuals to a consultative conference and decided to reply to the Turkish mutasarrif, asking whether, as the representative of the Ottoman government in

Aintab, he acknowledged the status of the aforementioned men (Seyfullah and Kelej Ali) and agreed to their stance. They pleaded with the mutasarrif to put them into direct contact with the Turkish Caliphate in Constantinople. They also stated:

> With this letter, we want the Turks to understand that we are not rebels and that we are the direct subjects of the Caliph. The rebels are the ones who operate against the Caliph's will and orders and fight against us.

The Americans replied in the following way:

> Our hospital is open to patients and wounded of all nationalities. As to the Mardin orphanage, the building has not been at our disposal since April 1st. The French took it from the Turks and not from us.

During this time, the National Union formed a committee to adjudicate on the relationship between the National Union and the Military Body. It was decided that the latter was independent in its actions but had to consult with the National Union prior to any attack.

At 8:15 minor conflicts occurred near the College and around Mardin.

May 4th – 11th

On May 4th, a French plane flew over and opened fire on Turkish positions. However, it became apparent from the gunfire against them that not many Turkish troops were left in the city. Many Turkish soldiers had gone to obstruct the entry of the French convoy on the Kilis-Aintab road, while the Armenians and the French in Aintab were impatiently awaiting the arrival of this force. The French wanted to exchange Turkish prisoners for the mutilated bodies in Ghourban Baba. The Turks refused, saying that their friends were buried according to Turkish rites.

18 kg of explosive materials used for the preparation of bombs exploded by accident today. The building was demolished. This was a heavy loss for us. However, the survival of our two kinsmen at the site was a comfort.

The National Union issued an order according to which the children of poor families were to be vaccinated without charge. It also forbade the destruction of houses. It appointed Mr. H. Poladian as a municipal engineer.

On May 5th, the Turks once more sent letters to the French and Armenians, like the earlier letters, though this time written in a more temperate manner. The French did not reply but the Armenians voted in favor of replying (27 votes in favor, 9 against). The Turkish letter was sent on behalf of the mutasarrif, Seyfullah and Kelej Ali. It repeated the same thing, that the Armenians should surrender. The task of drafting a proper reply was entrusted to Father Nerses Tavoukjian, Levonian, Karamanougian, Milletbashian, Kendirjian, Kupelian, and Fesdekjian.

Two Armenians were slightly wounded in the afternoon in Akyol Street because of the Turkish bombardment. One of the bombs fell on a lavatory and its contents were spread all over the neighboring houses. The Armenians shouted to the Turkish chetes to aim more accurately if that was possible.

The convoy was late, leaving Armenians with provisions for only six or seven days. Future prospects were becoming unclear.

Conversations between Turkish and Armenian fighters.

The readers already know that during these street battles, the Armenians and Turks were separated by distances of only three to eight meters. They were thus able to talk to each other. In order to convey an idea of the popular mindset of the time, some of the conversations that contained insults and often ended with gunshots are recalled here.

> "Citizen, what is your name?"
>
> "Haroutiun. What is yours?"
>
> "Mohammed."
>
> "Mohammed, let me tell you something. You are a stupid nation, and especially the villagers, who are idiots. Your *agha*s eat and drink debauchedly while they send miserable men like you to die like dogs against us."
>
> "You are absolutely right. What do we have against you? We used to live like brothers. Curses be upon those who put us in this situation."

Another Turk shouted from the Chinarli mosque:

> "Citizen, what is your name?"
>
> "Nazar."
>
> "I want to talk to you. But first, promise and make an oath on your honor that we won't shoot each other."
>
> "I promise."

"I am alone in here. My friends went to hold the road to Kilis. If we succeed, may God help you, and if you succeed, may God help us."

A Turk would shout from the Chinarli Mosque:

"Citizen, do you have food? How can you fight with an empty stomach?"

"God knows that we have everything, sardines, sweets, milk. We have plenty of bread and endless raisins and nuts." *

At the same moment, a person bleats like a goat,

"You see, we also have a goat!"

"That is not a goat. It is a donkey with two feet."

Then we heard a gunshot.

"What is that?"

"Let us speak the donkey's language then."

A Turk from the Yaghoubians' house:

"Citizen, I promise not to shoot or throw a rock. I will speak like a man."

"If you don't want to, don't speak. You are free."

"You are Armenians, and us, Turks. We have been living like brothers for 600 years. We do not wish to harm you. Let us not kill each other. Let's be reconciled. If you had united with us, we could have expelled the French in one day."

"We do not need your brotherhood. We trusted you once and you took us to Deir-ez Zor and slaughtered us. What have we done to you for you to slaughter our women and children on April 1st? You have gone beyond any limits. This time we will not spare any of you."

A Turk:

"Citizen, we are bored with this job. When will this war end?"

"When not a single Turk is left alive in the world."

Such conversations ended with shooting.

The local Armenian leaders would become friends with the Turkish captains in many positions and they would promise each other not to shoot and live peacefully. One day one of the Armenian fighters threw a

* The Armenian fighter only received some chickpeas and two pieces of cake-sized black bread as well as a small cup of oil daily. For the sake of national honor, he told the Turk that they lacked nothing.

package of sugar and nuts to the Turkish side. They responded by throwing a package full of plums and other fruits the following day.

The Armenians had been waiting for weeks now. The French convoy was to bring provisions from Kilis but had encountered a large Turkish force at Oulou Mahsereh and had withdrawn, hoping to return to Aintab in greater strength. The Turkish army had many cannons and more than 6,000 regular and irregular soldiers. This retreat was detrimental to the Armenians, because as far as provisions were concerned, almost nothing was left in the city. In order to save us from that dire situation, the French promised to deliver 15 tons of flour to us pending the arrival of the convoy. They were only able to provide three tons, the value of which they demanded later on from the National Union.

May 6th. The National Union formed a committee to deal with the problem of explosives. Its members were H. Berzoudian, H. Ferejian, M. Geoghlanian, and Haserjian.

Upon the suggestion made by Mrs. Foreman (an American missionary), the National Union ratified the members of the Visitors Committee (formed of women), whose task was to supervise the hygiene of the uniforms, beds and houses of the Armenian fighters. The members of this committee were Mrs. Frearson, Marie Bezjian, Hripsimeh Topjian, Z. Baboian, Marie Mouradian, Yester Sarkissian, Behiyeh Shahabian, Yeprouhi Nazarian and Yevkineh Panjarjian.

The National Union appealed again to the following compatriots to increase their donations:

H. Arakelian - a basket of nuts, H. Bezjian - 6 Ottoman gold liras, Simon Agha - 7 Ottoman gold liras, Asdvadzadour Agha - 8 Ottoman gold liras, Nerses Ishkhanian - 3 Egyptian gold liras, K. Sarkissian - 4 Ottoman gold liras, H. Jebejian 30 mejids, M. Karamanougian - 30 Ottoman gold liras, Hanneh Kurkjian - 2000 Kurush. Movses Demirjian refused and B. Ashjian was absent due to illness.

On May 7th, the Turks fired about 30 shells (from 10.5cm cannons) at the Armenian streets and wounded eight people (six minor and two severe injuries). A plane flew over in the afternoon and dropped a package in which the Sultan, the Sheikh-ul-Islam and Farid Pasha condemned the chete acts, urging the Muslim people to act prudently and exhorting the "real faithful" to resist chete actions. Such actions damaged national interests and if the Entente powers killed them, the chetes wouldn't have the right to complain. For a real Muslim, killing a chete was equivalent of doing a good deed. Therefore, chetes killed in the fighting could not be martyrs or *Mujahid* or *Gazi*s.

Such announcements were wrapped around rocks and thrown from the Armenian positions to the Turkish ones. The Turks, however, tore them up and even threw them back wrapped in red sheets, displaying their wish for war.

May 8th and 9th passed with only a few guns being fired. An Armenian woman was killed by her neighbor, an Armenian fighter named Loutfi. That crime infuriated the Armenian community. The National Union decided to punish the criminal.

The National Union continued to receive donations from the following persons: Dr. Chamichian - 4 Ottoman gold liras, S. Baghdasarian - 5 Egyptian gold liras, H. Levonian - 30 litres of nuts, M. Topbashian - 2 Ottoman gold liras, K. Topbashian - 10 Egyptian gold liras, Dr. Hekimian - 1 Ottoman gold lira, Haroutiun Khachadourian - 2 Ottoman gold liras, K. Geoghluyan - 1 Ottoman gold lira, H. Karamanougian - yarn worth 900 kurush, H. Kouzouguian - 5 top tulbend (muslin), Dr. Misirian - 5 Ottoman gold liras, H. Nazarian - 3 Ottoman gold liras, Levon Nazarian - 4 Ottoman gold liras, S. Karamanougian -3 Egyptian gold liras, G. Berzoudian - 44 mejids, N. and M. Manougian - 5 Egyptian gold liras, M. Haserjian - 10 top alaca (?) and H. M. Guleserian - 6 keses of yarn.

May 10th was the end of the first deadline in the Turkish treaty, yet it did not have any influence on the settlement of the Turkish issue. The Armenians eventually started to suffer. The worst enemy was hunger. The director of the American Red Cross, Dr. Lambert, had received an order from the French and Arab governments that the 1,600 orphans located in Aintab were to be transported to Beirut. Thanks to this arrangement, the orphans' share of provisions could be distributed to the people.

The National Union forbade the sale of *oghi* (arak). Wrongdoers would have their *oghi* confiscated by the Armenian authorities.

May 11th–14th

On May 11th, four Armenian prisoners escaped from the Turkish prison and found shelter in the Armenian quarter. The prisoners exploited a hailstorm and the darkness of the night, breached the prison wall and remained hidden in caves the whole night. They found the Armenian positions in the morning and were thus saved.

According to information received from these prisoners, the Turkish *aghas* had left the city and only a handful of state officials remained there. The Turkish people were being forcibly drawn into the war and there was an endless number of refugees. The nationalist troops in the city had gone to block the road to Kilis. The moral vigor of the Turks had dissipated. They feared the Armenians more than they feared the French. The Ibn Eyyoub minaret had become the terror of the Turks. Until then, the number of those who died in that minaret exceeded 12. The Turks claimed that the cause of their failure was the cannon made by the Armenians and showed its wooden frame to their leaders. They had suffered many losses during their attempts to burn down the Red Cross and Patanians' buildings. Those who showed a willingness to surrender to the French were arrested in the city. The Turks had also brought three cannons from Sivas.

Such secret information about the Turks was like opening a curtain. This information bolstered the morale of the Armenians. The news about the weakening of the Turks further stimulated the zeal of the Armenians. More attention was paid to the Ibn Eyyoub minaret and guards were appointed to constantly control the area.

The National Union formed a committee to inspect the monetary accounts of all military and political institutions. Its appointed members were H. D. Melkonian, T. Kupelian, and H. Hamalian.

On May 12th, the Turks opened machine gun fire on the taverns. The Armenians retaliated and destroyed the Turkish barricades.

That night the Turks listened to the speech of a mullah who emphasized the necessity of Armeno-Turkish brotherhood while Armenians replied by referring to the tragic events of the past. They concluded by stating that the basis of Armeno-Turkish brotherhood should have been determined in the past and that it was now very late.

That same night the Turks withdrew from some of their positions by burning down the mills belonging to the Kurkjians and Sahagians on the northern and eastern side of Manastir.

Chapter 11

Miners

Armenian and Turkish miners worked together. As mentioned earlier, the Leylegians' house was across Chinarli Mosque and overlooked it. The house and mosque were separated by a five meter wide avenue. The Turks had been digging a three-meter deep underground tunnel for 25 days, stretching to the aforementioned house. The hammer blows of the Turkish workers could be heard from the Armenian positions, since they were working on rocks. The sound was first heard at "Hamam Pasha", as this position itself was almost subterranean. Such sounds were ignored at first. However, when the miners reached (beneath) the Armenian barricades, Armenians immediately set their own miners to work against them. However, since the Turkish tunnel was too deep, the Armenian miners dug just above the Turks and realized that a second tunnel had been built beneath them. When the Armenian miners finished their work and were heading home, the Turkish sappers started to fill their tunnel with explosive materials and blocked their entrance with rocks and cement.

Early in the morning, when the Armenian miners returned to the tunnel and heard the hammer blows from afar, they immediately understood that the Turkish miners had prepared to blow up the mines. They immediately left the area and informed the Armenian fighters about the situation, who quit their positions and withdrew to secondary positions.

The Armenian fighters had barely quit their positions when an awful explosion was heard, shaking the whole Armenian quarter. The facade of the Leyleguians' house collapsed. The Armenians did not suffer any casualties and the Turks were enraged when they saw another barricade behind the collapsed wall. The Turks had had high hopes on the success of that explosion. They thought they would destroy the whole quarter with that mine, since they had used 60 kg of explosive materials. Their failure was due to the Armenian tunnel that had reduced the effectiveness of the explosion.

The Armenians and Turks started to fight against each other in this manner, i.e. through mines and underground tunnels. Many days of labor and a great quantity of explosives brought almost no results. Once done with the minaret, the Armenians now started to destroy the wall of the mosque. The Turks were shouting, "Do not do it, this is a sacred place", and the Armenians replied that a sacred place cannot be used as a barricade or shelter for criminals. Destroying the thick wall of the mosque was almost impossible, though the windows were completely shattered by bullets. This was still useless, since many walls were built inside the mosque.

The Turks undertook a second mining attempt at the Balekluh market, but failed, since the foundations of the houses were on rocks and the soil was hard. One major concern for the Armenians was the sewer at the Balekluh market. It stretched from the grand market (Arasa) as far as Balekluh, going all the way to the Y.M.C.A, where it deviated to the north in two branches: one to Kayajik Street and the other to Ibn Eyyoub Mosque. However, since these two final parts of the sewage canals were very narrow, no one could enter it, but anyone was able to walk through the other part all the way to the grand market.

To deter such a threat, an underground tunnel was opened from the Y.M.C.A. all the way to the sewage canals and guards were placed at the crossing point. The Turks also removed all the rocks from the canals and placed guards, fearing that the Armenians would use them to attack the Turkish streets at night.

A French Miner

An expert French miner suggested that the Armenians destroy the Chinarli Mosque by blowing it up. Although this plan was deemed to be useless, because of the insistence of a French miner, the Armenians finally agreed to do so under the Frenchman's supervision. The Armenian miners prepared a shaft according to instructions within 24 hours. In order to destroy the building, the French miner placed seven or eight French 7.5 cm artillery shells and some materials prepared by the Armenians that would be fired in the main mine and blow up the building. The Armenians were really skeptical about the success of this operation and the result really proved them right. After the bomb went off, the Turks laughed and mocked our failure. The French miner tried again, placing 14 bombs and other explosive materials inside the tunnel the second time, but he got the same results.

The causes for his failure were the following: first, the Turks had dug many trenches along the wall inside the mosque. Second, the wall of the mosque had a thickness of more than one meter. Third, providing enough explosives to shatter the weight of the wall, which carried the weight of vaulting and the minarets, was impossible.

The Armenians renounced their tunneling plans and opened trenches – a few meters deep – along their positions at Chinarli Mosque, where the Armenian guards could hinder the Turkish miners' plans.

May 13th–14th

The Armenian acts of self-defence inspired hope in the surrounding Armenian towns. The only hope for the Armenians of Kilis was Aintab. Their fate was dependent on the destiny of the Armenians of Aintab, whose nobility and sacrifice could be seen during those critical days. All were obedient, working for the attainment of the same goal. It was a unity of noble spirits, whose work, suffering, and agony may only be understood in the words: "Death for the Sake of Life".

Daily discussions were organized at Ibn Eyyoub Mosque in order to fulfil the intellectual, spiritual and psychological needs of the people.

Armenian craftsmen freely repaired Armenian orphans' shoes. They would also sit down and eat together at the same table, as if the ancient patriarchal system still prevailed. The principle of "all for one, one for all" could not have been applied to a better setting. The common enemy and threat had unified the goals, deeds and concerns of all.

As for the Aintab Armenians' relationship with the French – the Armenians gave up all hope. What they expected from the French did not correspond to reality. The Armenians were working for the French, ignoring the cultural and linguistic differences between them, and the fact that the French lived hundreds of miles away. On the other hand, what did the Armenian signify to the French? They saw the Armenians as Christian Turks who defended their material interests against the plundering Turks and exploited the French, who were fighting for their honor and national interests.

The French were skeptical about the patriotic feelings of the Armenians of Aintab, as if Cilicia was not our fatherland, and the memory of our last dynasty had collapsed under Muslim rule. With this mindset, one of the French captains welcomed me one day, saying, "Two Maltese are equal to one Pole, two Poles are equal to one Jew, and two Jews are barely equal to one Armenian." I do not know how the French had formed this opinion about the Armenians. I only understood that the French thought that they had found an ally they had won through diplomatic negotiations and were using against the Turks. The French told me, "You are stupid. You could more easily agree with the Turks than you could with us. Their culture, language and traditions are much closer to yours than is ours."

The Armenians of Aintab started to understand the French mentality.

I can only say that the benefit of this war was the realization by the Armenians that there was nothing to gain from the French. They were convinced that the Europeans were not concerned about the Armenians and that every nation worked solely in its own interests.

Why was it that the Turks suffered more losses behind their barricades than the Armenians did behind their own? After explaining this, we will proceed with our story.

The Turks used wide and cylindrical firing pits. When a Turkish fighter approached one, he would be spotted by the Armenians and be shot on the spot. The Armenians, however, used funnel shaped firing pits. In other words, those pits were wide on the inside with narrow openings on the outside. This was why it was very rare for an Armenian fighter to be shot behind the barricades.

On May 14th, the death of an armenophile French soldier caused great grief to the Armenian fighters. This soldier had offered Armenians ammunition and had created a close friendship with them. He admired their perseverance and bravery. One day, when the French soldiers, in the presence of French officers, were placing boxes of bombs inside a cave, one of the bombs' safety catches became detached and the bomb fell to the ground. The French soldier, who realized the danger to the lives of the soldiers and officers, immediately picked up the bomb and threw himself out of the cave, but it exploded in his hand. Despite many efforts to keep him alive, he took his last breath at the American hospital. The unfortunate soldier had saved many other lives by sacrificing himself. His bravery and sacrifice was admired by the Armenian fighters.

The Turks attacked the Y.M.C.A. positions by night, using French bombs and rifles, which they had confiscated during the occupation of Ghourban Baba.

The Turks also tried to burn down the houses near Kolaghasuh from the direction of the Chinarli Mosque, but failed.

Chapter 12

More Fires

May 15th–20th

No movement was seen in the Turkish positions during the morning. However, once it was dark, they started a general attack that specifically targeted our eastern and northern positions. The attack from Balekluh to the Y.M.C.A. was repelled with the help of machine guns so that after 15 minutes the fight was taken to the Turkish positions at Chinarli Mosque, where the Turks had stationed the cannon called Ramazan Topu, which caused a lot of noise inside the mosque. In the midst of this tumult, the Turks started burning the Armenian positions that spread as far as the Patanians' house. The fire eventually reached the Leylegians' house that had been partially burned before. The Turks pumped oil onto the fire using a staging they had built and placed next to the minaret. To prevent any further damage, 5-600 people were used to put out the fire. The wooden parts of the neighboring buildings were removed, the secondary barricades fortified and, after the fire was put out, the Armenians demonstrated to the Turks that not even fires, mines or violent attacks could defeat the Armenian positions.

At dawn, we had a martyr who was killed by a treacherous act.

On May 16th, the Turks sent a letter to the Armenians and to the French. They demanded the surrender of the Armenians, whereas the letter addressed to the French contained the following:

> First, your troops have tortured innocent people, something that is against your civilization. Second, we recommend you leave this city, otherwise you will suffer tragic deaths.

The French and Armenians ignored the letters.

A general night attack was mounted again. Machine guns and bombs were used. The Turks had moved the Ramazan cannon to Balekluh, which fired ceaselessly. The fighting stopped after 30 minutes.

Providing the people with foodstuffs was getting harder by the day. There were almost no provisions left and a convoy was only able to bring supplies for a few days. A solution had to be found to ameliorate this situation. The French command therefore decided to send away a convoy of 3,000 people, mainly refugees who did not have a place to stay in the city. This arrangement benefited the people in two ways: first, their rations could be distributed to the remaining people and second, their departure would reduce the burden and responsibilities of the National Union. Natives of the city, whose absence would not hinder the self-defense efforts, would similarly have the right to leave.

It is our duty to recall the institution whose efforts in the relief of the city are worthy of praise and appreciation. That institution was the American Red Cross. The amount of flour and wheat they offered helped the Armenians of Aintab survive for another two weeks.

The Turks fighting against the Armenians and French at Aintab numbered 9–10,000 men. According to a testimony of a Turk, however, 23,000 regular and irregular troops received daily rations. This number was very plausible when the Turks were victorious during battles such as Ghourban Baba. This number was significantly reduced when they were defeated. It follows that determining a specific number for the Turkish fighters remains impossible. It was always changing. Through their dialects, we knew the places they came from. The slaughter of infidels and the plunder of their properties attracted many Turks, Kurds, Cherkez, Arabs and Turkomans from Adiyaman, Malatya, Behesni, Ourfa, Marash, and Kilis. However, such men, after seeing that the infidels confronted them with rifles, left their positions and fled. To prevent any further desertions, the Turks placed special guards at the end of every barricade or trench.

On May 18th, various employees working in the national bodies and committees protested to show the people that there were laws which they had a duty to abide by. Some ignorant people had disgraced a national body, so an executive court (Idareyi Örfi) was formed whose task was to punish all those who failed to fulfil their duties. The National Union placed a notice on the wall concerning this with the following announcement:

> The Armenian National Union, with the approval of the Military Body, has formed an Executive Court.
>
> It is painful to hear about recent disorders in our community and the intemperance of some people towards our national committees.
>
> Such events have the potential to bring about disunity in our nation and agitation in our community. What the Turks failed to

do with their guns and cannons will be realized by our disunity. The Executive court will never stay indifferent to such people and will punish them with its iron fist. Thus, the Executive Court orders the people to remain vigilant about their conduct. You should obey the commands of the police and military bodies, comply with the demands of all national bodies, and facilitate the task of the Provisions Committee.

It is forbidden to destroy houses and protest in the streets. We should not spread false rumors. In other words, we should definitely obey all commands and instructions.

National Executive Court Chairman

A. Kalemkerian A. Levonian

To facilitate the efforts of the Provisions Committee, the National Union started gathering supplies once more. It bought the extra supplies from people who had provisions sufficient for more than a month. It bought one liter of flour for 25 kurush.

Armenian Children during the Fighting

The economic and political misfortunes had led Armenian children to develop resilience to the harshness of their environment. Born and raised during deportations, some had even witnessed the slaughter of their relatives and the red blood spouting from the throats of their mothers and sisters. Thus, fighting and bombardment, and the terror of a prospective massacre no longer affected them. Often, children aged between eight to 12 would organize demonstrations in the empty streets and spread laughter and joy as they passed by.

The children wandering the streets of Aintab were the apprentices of Armenian craftsmen in times of peace and soldiers in times of war.

All these children were conscripted in 1920. They built barricades, carried rocks, exhorted the people, and insulted the Turks.

In May, these children formed a small army, whose spectacle was very amusing, particularly during the dark days of the war. 20 to 30 of them marched in ranks like a squad of soldiers. One lad, who was older than the others, acted as their commander, whose orders they all obeyed with military discipline. As to their appearance, some were barefoot, some wore tattered clothes, but all were armed with wooden rifles and empty cartridge cases in their belts. They also had bombs made of cardboard and airplanes made of tin, as well as wooden horses and machine guns. This was the general picture of this group that marched, almost every day, in the market and streets spreading joy and amusement everywhere.

One of them, a 15-16 year old, who was building a barricade at the most dangerous point of the front line, the Red Cross position, was shot and killed. His death caused great pain and sorrow to his friends who carried his body to the headquarters of the Military Body and gave him a proper funeral with full military honors.

May 20th–25th

Rumors spread on May 20th, that Colonel Dubiovry, had returned to Kilis and was getting ready to return to Aintab with a large force. Such rumors bolstered the morale of the Armenian fighters. Again, the Turks sent a force to hinder the advance of the French reinforcements. This was clear from the few gunshots from the Turkish side. They fired for an hour from the side of Mardin and its surroundings during the night and then stopped.

On May 21st, a French airplane informed us of the imminent arrival of Colonel Dubiovry and a large French force from Kilis, spreading joy within the Armenian community which had been waiting for supplies for so long.

The French bombarded the Turkish convoy that was smuggling ammunition into Aintab. The caravan scattered and the Turks suffered many losses.

On May 22nd, the French troops had already neared the southern side of the city and their cannon could be heard from afar. The Turks controlled Ak-Baba Mountain and the hills of Koerkun, located on the eastern side of the Kilis-Aintab road. Colonel Dubiovry's troops positioned on the Elmaluh and Meshmesh hills were advancing towards the hills of Geneyig. The French occupied Ak-Baba Mountain, dealing the chetes a heavy blow, and making them withdraw to the northern side of Aintab after leaving many dead and wounded on the battlefield. The fighting lasted the whole day.

On the following day, May 23rd, we heard additional cannon fire. In the afternoon, an Armenian courier informed us of the whereabouts of Colonel Dubiovry's troops. During the night, the French bombarded some positions in the vicinity of the city. An organized force from the orphanage in Mardin occupied Ghourban Baba, where it built some fortifications.[*]

Several other positions were also occupied to facilitate Dubiovry's entrance into the city. At night, 30-40 Armenian fighters raided the northern part of the city to capture the Turkish cannon. However, they were barely out of the city when a dreadful trumpet peal was heard. It was about 9 p.m. There was no sign of an attack against Armenian positions, but an awful sound of gunfire from the south-eastern side of the city. Thousands of bullets were flying in the darkness and falling on our roofs. Colonel Dubiovry was entering Aintab from the south-eastern side. The Turks tried to distract the convoy by a surprise attack from Samsak Tepeh. However, despite their attempts, the convoy entered Aintab after fighting for an hour without suffering significant losses. Only a few carts carrying supplies had been left behind, since their loads were heavy and the horses had not been able to pull them up the hill.

These carts were brought to the city on the following day as war booty. The Turkish people, knowing that there were many more carts left behind, rushed to the hills of Samsak Tepeh accompanied by armed chetes. They did not notice the French who had left their barricades the night before and had advanced to the peak of Samsak Tepeh. The Turks, unaware of the presence of the French soldiers, headed towards the peak of the hill fearlessly. Suddenly, the French started firing and the Turks suffered many losses in a very short time. They returned to the city, leaving many dead and wounded behind them. A few carts of provisions cost them dozens of lives.

The convoy reached Aintab in three and a half days. As we have said, the Turkish losses were heavy. A lot of high-ranking Turkish officers were killed too. The fanatical armenophobe called Soylemez Zadeh Mahmoud was killed during this battle. Some translations of Armenian letters were found in his pockets (this man knew Armenian).*

* After the French occupied Ghourban Baba, they retrieved the mutilated bodies of some of their friends slaughtered on May 2nd. The Turks had claimed that they had buried them according to Turkish rites. However, the bodies were just left there and had even served as food for the dogs.

* An Armenian coming from Aleppo, Hovsep Porposian, carried these letters to the National Union, Father Nerses Tavoukjian and a few others. On his way to Aintab, the Red Cross car was captured by the Turks. The latter set the American and an English-speaking Armenians free, but kept Porposian and eventually mutilated him. It is very probable that the letters retrieved from the Turk's pocket were Porposian's letters, given to him for translation.

The convoy had brought a few things for the Armenians. Concerning this issue, Captain Reno met with the National Union on May 24th at 8:30 and stated the following:

> It is extremely difficult to provide the Armenians with supplies in the current situation. Therefore, Colonel Abady orders that 6,000 people leave the city with the convoy. The French authorities will transport them safely to Kilis. After their arrival, General de La Motte will make the necessary arrangements for them. They might then be transported to Adana, Beirut or Iskenderun (Alexandretta). The primary reason of this arrangement is the fact that, under present conditions, it is impossible to provide for all these people with a few supply boxes from Kilis.

To deliberate about this issue, Father Nerses Tavoukjian, Dr. K. Arslanian and H. Mouradian met with Dr. Shepard and Dr. Lambert, who announced the following after they met with Colonel Abady:

> The Issue of the Departure of Some Armenians
>
> Under present conditions, we also find the departure of some people from the city a necessity. The adoption of such measures on the advise of the French arises out of real concerns. Colonel Abady has arranged for the safe conduct of the Armenians as far as Kilis. After that, the necessary arrangements will be made by General de La Motte.

On the same night, a meeting was convened to discuss the departure of 6,000 people. The following statement by Father Nerses Tavoukjian was adopted.

> We will approve the departure of those who wish to leave. However, the men who can contribute to the self-defense of the city will remain here. A special committee composed of three people will control the departure of people. Out of three members, the first will be from the National Union, the second from the Military Body, and the third from the general population. Those who wish to leave must sell their supplies to the Provisions Committee and hand over their weapons to the Military Body.

May 25th–30th

The National Union, complying by the decisions adopted in the aforementioned statement, placed news placards on walls on May 25th.

Such news struck the Armenian community badly. It was the worst thing to hear, after working day and night resisting the enemy for many weeks.

People congregated in front of the general staff building. The cries of women and children and the curses of young men left a horrible impression in the silent, darkness of the night. Then they left. The grieving caravan left and, as if in the midst of the murmur of the trees, we could still see their tears and hear their lamentation as it slowly faded in the night.

The French had decided to move at least half the population of Aintab. Despite the National Union's efforts to receive a written statement from the French to relieve itself from future responsibilities, it failed. The French did not have any official correspondence with the Armenians.

On May 26th, the National Union decided to establish a warehouse to store the furniture of those who had left. It also forbade the free trade of nuts.

On May 27th, General de La Motte arrived in Aintab by air and met with Father Nerses Tavoukjian, Dr. K. Arslanian, and H. Mouradian. The latter explained the city's situation and the state of supplies available to the general. The general made it clear that they did not intend to evacuate the city and, regarding the departure of some people, their only purpose had been to ease the problem of provisioning. It was for this reason that some Armenians left with the convoy. He recommended that those who contributed to the self-defense of the city should remain where they were, while others were allowed to leave. The safe movement of people from Kilis to Adana or Beirut would be guaranteed.

Regarding the general's question as to how long the Armenians could survive with the remaining provisions, the Armenians replied that if an additional 3,000 people left, the remaining 8,000 could survive for 30 more days with the available supplies. The general promised to assist the Armenians in providing them with supplies during the following few days.

Before the departure of the Armenian delegates, the General gave the following information:

1. Izmir and Thrace were under Greek control.
2. Armenia was given to the Armenians, but its borders were not yet clarified. However, he was fairly sure that the vilayets of Bitlis, Van and Erzurum would be included.

3. All the territories located 60 km north of the Baghdad railway from Iskenderun as far as Mardin had been handed over to the French, with Syria becoming a French colony.
4. The status of the vilayet of Adana was still precarious. He believed that it would be handed over to the Turks.

When the meeting was over, the Armenian delegates tasted French sweets and returned to the church.

On May 28th, the National Union met with Colonel Abady, who announced that he was informed through a letter received from General de La Motte, that a 20 day armistice would be signed between Gouraud and M. Kemal's forces on May 31st. The details of the armistice would be negotiated in Kilis between Turkish generals and De La Motte. The Colonel ordered a ceasefire, even if the Turks stupidly started shooting. The Armenians should stay vigilant in their positions and continue their fortification efforts.

Below is a copy of the notice placed on walls by the National Union.

> This morning, an airplane informed us that an armistice has been signed between General Gouraud and M. Kemal's generals from May 31st to June 20th. The negotiations of the terms will be held in Kilis with General De La Motte. Therefore, all firing must cease.
>
> Armenian National Union
>
> Every man must fulfill the duties incumbent on him; otherwise he will be obliged to pay a daily fine of half a mejidiye.
>
> Armenian National Union.

On May 29th, General De La Motte and Colonel Abady announced the following to the Armenian National Union:

> Due to Mustafa Kemal's appeal, General Gouraud has signed a 20-day armistice with the Turks starting from May 31st. Turkish delegates will meet us in order to deliberate on its terms. For us, one of the most important of these terms will be the Turks providing supplies to the Armenians. I strongly believe that the path to peace has begun for this city. If the Turks revoke the terms of the armistice and the war starts again, we will continue to protect the Armenians as before. Although I had suggested to the Armenians the departure of 2,000 to Kilis within three days as a way to ease the problems of rations. However, the situation has

> completely changed and within the next few days the Armistice will be signed. Therefore, I do not see the necessity of their departure.
>
> The Armenians who left with the previous convoy have arrived safely in Kilis and are under the supervision of Captain Virali who is arranging the issue of supplies. I have personally visited them and seen them in a good state. I even recommended that the Americans keep their orphans there. Thus, there are no forces coming from the north to join the Turks.

In the afternoon, the mutasarrif Jelaleddin, Irfan Bey, a policeman, and six gendarmes holding a white flag arrived at the Armenian quarter from their positions at Pasha Street for preliminary negotiations. The Armenian fighters remained at their positions. The Turks did not trust them and demanded the presence of a French officer, and then they all went to the College to meet General De La Motte.

This meeting between the French and Turks lasted between three to four hours. The Turks presented themselves as the victors and made their terms accordingly. They demanded complete authority in the city and the withdrawal of the French from Aintab to a camp far away from the city. They asserted that these terms had been set by Mustafa Kemal.

The Colonel replied angrily that according to the Armistice, the French meant a ceasefire and according to the orders of General Gouraud, the French troops would withdraw to Aintab College, this being what they understood by withdrawal. Similarly, the French would empty Mardin and Ghourban Baba on the condition that the Turks would not occupy it. The Turks, on the other hand, would have the right to occupy positions held by the French in the city like Manastir, Beyaz Ahmed Hotel, and the Yellow Hospital (a Turkish hospital). After long discussions, the Turks left the chamber stating that the French should notify General Gouraud and Mustafa Kemal about these decisions.*

This is the translated version of the armistice terms signed between Mr. De Key and Mustafa Kemal:

---

* When the mutasarrif and Irfan Bey suggested the placement of Turkish gendarmes in Armenian streets, the Colonel replied angrily: "Irfan Bey, do you want an honest agreement? Do you wish for real peace? You should not place gendarmes in Armenian streets so that you do not have problems with the Armenians."

The Terms of the Armistice

According to an agreement signed in Ankara between Mr. De Key and Mustafa Kemal, hostilities will cease for 20 days starting from May 30th, 1920.

The Terms of this Armistice are the following:

1) The French troops in Bozanti and Sis will withdraw as far as the Mersin-Adana road.
2) The French will evacuate Aintab and will withdraw to their camps on the condition that no new attacks will take place against the Armenians.
3) All such evacuations and withdrawals must be completed by the 12th day.
4) The war and political prisoners will be exchanged between French and Turkish authorities who will settle the issue through mutual communications. The exchange should be completed by the 10th day of the Armistice.
5) Free communication should be established between the governor of Adana and the Turkish authorities, and the latter will order its high ranking generals to settle the issue accordingly and establish a link with the commanders of First and Second Army Corps.

As the reader can already see, the terms of this Armistice were very elastic and flexible and for this exact reason it brought about many disputes. In reality, the armistice was nothing other than a way to buy some time for the two parties. The Turks would use this opportunity to harvest their crops.

Chapter 13

1st National Congress

The ceasefire began on May 30th and the Turks went to the surrounding farms and fields. Some even met Armenians and expressed their complaints about the war that had destroyed their brotherhood. People emerged from trenches and started to talk. Some Turks even promised not to shoot Armenians again.

Critical Days and a Critical Decision – No Surrender to the Turks

All this was good. However, the worst was yet to come for the Armenians of Aintab.

The Military Body forbade any contacts between Armenian and Turkish fighters. The French were trying to prepare the ground for an agreement with the Turks. Not a single arrangement had been made for the Armenians. The latter eventually felt abandoned and questioned their well-being in the future.

The National Union had a meeting with Colonel Abady on May 30th during which he made the following announcement:

> According to the Armistice signed between General Gouraud and Mustafa Kemal, the French will withdraw their forces to the College and Chitji Kharaf. This operation will be completed by June 8th. The Armenian streets will be taken over by the Turkish authorities and Turks will be able to enter the Armenian quarter peacefully. Although I am deeply affected by these terms, yet, as a soldier, I am forced to comply with my superiors' orders. I therefore wait for your response on this issue.

The convention began on May 31st, at 9:30 p.m. All community leaders in the city were present, about 66 people, who gathered in the church vestry. The chairman was Father Nerses Tavoukjian. All the attendees were silent, thinking about the prospect of a turbulent situation. They fixed their sad looks upon the black gown of the priest. Poor people, how many times had you spent sleepless nights trying to find a solution to your malignant destiny? This time, the fate of thousands of children, orphans, men and women would be sealed. One wrong step would have led to the curses of the elderly, the rape of women, and the heartbreaking cries of the children. An expression of despair prevailed on the ghastly faces of the attendees. Finally, the silence was broken by the priest:

> Today, Colonel Abady informed the National Union of the terms of the Armistice, which were the following: according to the agreement signed between General Gouraud and Mustafa Kemal, the French will withdraw from Mardin, Ghourban Baba, the Yellow Hospital, the Beyaz Ahmed Hotel, and the Latin Church and will remain in defensive positions at the College and Chitji Kharaf. Similarly, the Armenians must remove all the barricades and surrender to the Turkish authorities, because the Armenian quarter now belongs to the Turks. The mosques and guard houses have to be returned to their rightful owners and the city will return to its pre-April 1st status. The Turks have tried to convince the French to withdraw from the College, but the latter have refused. The Colonel waits for our response regarding the issues pertinent to us, the Armenians, and he assures us that the Turks will not harm any Armenian.

It was for this reason that the Armenian intelligentsia of Aintab had gathered: to decide whether the Armenians should surrender to the Turks, remove the barricades, and return all the mosques captured with great sacrifices.

After a long silence, many started speaking, of whom we recall, in particular, Dr. Shepard, Hovh. Levonian, H. Karamanougian, T. Kupelian, Dr. H. Misirian, Dr. K. Arslanian, N. Fesdekjian, H. Melkonian, among others.

Hours passed. It was as if a court had been convened to try to find a solution during the night. Finally, the ring of a bell silenced everyone. Various solutions were suggested, and the following decision was adopted by majority vote:

1. We demand the preservation of the status quo.
2. We will remain in our positions, armed, and will not accept the entry of the Turks into our quarter.
3. We demand the protection of our supplies.
4. If our demands are not met, we will leave Aintab in three convoys.

These demands had to be delivered to Colonel Abady first thing in the morning by four delegates. The convention ended late at night.

The following days were to be the most decisive for the Armenians of Aintab, unparalleled even before the dark days of the 1915 deportations.

The desperate people started making preparations for their departure. Around 12,000 barefoot people were to go to Kilis, taking with them bread sufficient for two to three days. Deprived of all means of transport, they would not be able to carry any of their furniture. Acknowledging this, some even started to burn, or break up the furniture they had, denying the Turks any prospective booty.

The Colonel was very affected when he heard about the nervous situation of the Armenians. And when the Armenian delegates presented him with their adopted resolutions, the Colonel responded:

> I do not recommend a mass exodus. There are many dangers and it would be fatal for you.
>
> Only those committees, such as the National Union and the Military Body that were vulnerable to direct reprisals by the Turks, should leave the city. Given that the armistice is already signed, we are obliged to abide by its terms.
>
> I do not think that the Turks will commit a mass slaughter, because that would infringe the terms of the armistice. Therefore, the best solution for the notables, soldiers and their families is for their departure.

Father Nerses Tavoukjian replied:

> There are no political culprits for the Turkish government. As far as it is concerned, all the Armenians are the same: children or adults, all are equally dangerous to its existence and their annihilation is one of its primary objectives. As to the departure of the national committees, that is an impossibility, since we would be deserting our people after urging them to fight. Even if we agreed to do such a thing, the people would kill us first. Therefore, we cannot leave our people.

These were heartbreaking words for the Colonel. What could he do? He was obliged to obey his superiors' commands. When no solution was found, after long hours of deliberation, the priest said: "We still have time to think about it. We will let you know the final decision after meeting with the representatives of the people."

That day, the convoy from Kilis arrived in Aintab. It had brought large amounts of supplies and filled the 5-6,000 Armenians who were in

Aintab with a spirit of optimism. Surrendering to the Turks, after 60 days of victorious battle, was as bitter as death. The people went mad. They lost their minds. They had just discovered that the first convoy that had left for Kilis was said to have enjoyed a comfortable journey. Those remaining behind were suffering from a heartbreaking state. Where should they go? Surrendering and dying at the Turks' hands was dishonorable.

During those dark days, when all hope was gone, the Armenians found a French friend who really felt their anguish and made every effort to exhort them to find a solution to their deadlocked situation. This was Captain Reno, whose words inspired hope and optimism for the National Union and Military Body. *

> I am surprised about your situation. Why are you willing to leave? Who forces you to remove your barricades? Act and agree with the Turks in a way you find the most beneficial for you. We will not deprive you of our assistance. It is our duty to protect the local Armenians against Turkish attacks. As to the terms of the armistice, I do not understand a single thing. I hope it fails.

2nd National Congress

On the night of May 31st/June 1st, a meeting convened at the Church vestry at 8:30 with 120 participants.

This meeting was also like the one before, except that the attendees had grown old in 24 hours. All had suffered from nightmares. The same question plagued their minds: should we surrender to the Turks? Finally, the chairman of the National Union, Father Nerses Tavoukjian, stood up and announced the opening of the conference. His face seemed pale and his eyes radiated the flames of hatred and vengeance. With a sad voice, he uttered the following words:

> Dear guests, we, the members of the National Union, met the Colonel today and presented him with our decisions and clarified our stance on the Franco-Turkish armistice. The Colonel responded by saying, "I assure you that the Turks will do no harm to you, not because they are gentle, but rather because of their political and national interests. They will be forced to behave

* This captain enjoyed a good reputation among the Armenians. He had protected them against the calumnies of some of the French officers. The Armenians of Aintab owe many things to this captain, who was a brave man.

> gently and kindly with you." We replied by stating, "The Turks will disarm us carefully and eventually annihilate us. They will realize this in a way that the French would remain unaware of. Even if you found out, you would be unable to stop it." The Colonel could not say anything against our arguments. He only suggested that those individuals who were deemed dangerous by the Turks should leave the city. We also vetoed this proposal and added that we could not leave our people behind (followed by a round of applause).
>
> The Colonel's fury then reached its zenith and he said, angrily, "Then go, all of you!"
>
> Therefore, dear sirs, we bring the issue back to you, since we could not conclude it in our meeting with the Colonel. Let us all deliberate and decide the fate of the Armenians of Aintab.*

Taking into consideration the aforementioned issues, the members of the National Union, Military Body, and the various other committees spoke and expressed their points of view. Additionally, some information and details were provided concerning the meetings between General de La Motte, Colonel Abady, and some Turkish officers in the previous few days.

According to the Colonel this agreement was nothing more than an extension of the Mudros Armistice signed with the Turkish government a year and a half earlier. Therefore, according to the terms of this armistice, the French were obliged to withdraw and maintain the peace of the city. The Turks would therefore have the right to possess the Armenian quarter of the city without using any weapons or attacking it, otherwise the French reserved the right to intervene. By June 8th, the guns had ceased to fire, and if they continued to remain silent until June 20th, the ceasefire would continue.

After this, the attendees started discussing the issue of the Turkish and Armenians military forces. The Armenians were in a stronger position than they had been before and were able to defend themselves by occupying the abandoned French positions.

According to the political disposition that the French, Armenians and Turks had been displaying, the meeting adopted the following decisions:

* The man who uttered these words was this author.

1. Remain in our positions even more vigilantly and never permit the Turks to encroach on our barricades.
2. Accept a graceful death under any conditions.
3. Allow the departure of those whose absence would not hinder our self-defense and provisioning.
4. Draft a general letter explaining our critical situation to General Gouraud.

These decisions were reported to the people. However, their moral vigor had dissipated, trade had stopped, men were desperate and sleepless, and the fighters remained anxiously in their positions.

This was the general picture as people asked

> "Are you leaving?"
>
> "We don't know."
>
> "Are you?"
>
> "Yes! Dying on the street is better than surrendering to the Turks."

The cost of renting one cart had reached 50 gold liras. Some, having put part of their families on carts, were getting ready to leave on foot. Many appealed to the Americans to place their furniture inside their institutions but were refused. Some sold their food. A bag of flour worth 100 kurush was sold for three or four. There were two choices left for the Armenians of Aintab: the first was death by deportation, the second death through fighting. However, the French would not allow the fighting to continue, since this wouldn't be a defensive effort against the Turks but a rebellion against the Entente powers. Therefore, there was no option but to leave.

The decisions of the 2nd National Congress were delivered to the Colonel on June 1st, a Tuesday morning, on behalf of the National Union by Lieutenant Adour Levonian, to whom the Colonel replied:

> I have written to General De La Motte, demanding the introduction of reforms in the armistice terms and the removal of the point stipulating the entry of the Turks into the Armenian quarters. The Turkish delegate, Irfan Bey, left for Kilis today, to proceed with the negotiations about the armistice terms. Hopefully, my proposal and your points of view will be accepted. However, I repeat that this is only a wish, and we cannot act according to wishes. Therefore, acknowledging the disastrous prospects of a mass exodus and the Turkish entry into Armenian

> streets, I reiterate that the most reasonable solution is the departure of Armenian notables and soldiers with their families with tomorrow's convoy.

This proposal was again refused on behalf of our delegates and it was further stated that if the soldiers and notables left, all the people would follow them. However, such discrimination was impossible. The people would have even attacked us and stopped our departure. Therefore, we decided to stay and oppose the Turks' entry into the Armenian quarter. Despite the Colonel's insistence, his proposals were deemed impractical. However, the final "yes" or "no" was to be delivered in the afternoon.

The National Union then invited everyone to the church courtyard to deliberate because the Union was not able to decide the fate of its people all by itself at such a critical time. It was best for the people to decide their own fate.

Armenian orphans, Aintab, 1919.

Chapter 14

The 3rd National Congress of June 1st and the Referendum by Which the Armenian People Decided Their Fate

It wasn't even midday when a large crowd had filled the church courtyard. 2,500 people were present, among whom we recall the members of the National Union, the Military Body, intellectuals, party members, workers and craftsmen among others. All had come to find a solution to the critical situation, trying to look for the slightest hope. Their hearts were beating fast, and the will of the people swung like a pendulum on its past, present and future. The past was dark, the present terrible and the future precarious. Finally, it was 12 o'clock.

The president, Father Tavoukjian, took the floor and presented the situation as follows:

> My dear people. You are invited here to decide on a very critical issue. This crowd presents the will of the Armenian people of the city. You are all free to express your points of view because this issue pertains to your lives. Not a single organization or a national committee will be held responsible for the decisions adopted in this meeting. The people will decide its fate and act accordingly. We will act according to the majority's will. The issue is the following: during yesterday's meeting we decided to stay here, but in the morning we saw that some people opposed this. Some have told us that it was only the soldiers who had expressed their position during our previous gathering. Now, we should be cautious to use our minds and reason more than our emotions. Thus, we give you a chance to think rationally. Here is the problem: during the last two months, the volatile situation of our city made us aware of an imminent danger. In view of what we have previously experienced and witnessed, we tried to be vigilant and resorted to precautionary methods, including leaving our homes and shops despite the French wishes. We gathered together and acted according to our conscience, dictated by our previous experiences with the Turks, thereby remaining safe and satisfied until the April 1st events. The Turks attacked us and we defended ourselves and retaliated through our quick arrangements and

preparations. Thanks to God and our fighters, we realized victory during those 61 days without appealing to the French for advice. Then one day we heard that an armistice had been signed. A similar armistice was signed more than a year ago, yet the finalization of that peace agreement has not yet arrived. For various reasons, this armistice has been postponed and now General Gouraud and Mustafa Kemal have finally agreed to restore the old armistice and bring it back to life.

General De La Motte arrived to conduct negotiations about the Armistice terms, and when we met him, he said the following:

"Some changes have occurred in circumstances and an armistice has been agreed with the Turks. I had previously ordered the departure of 2,000 people from the city to conserve rations. We don't need to do that any more. Hopefully, the doors to peace for this city will be opened. * As for my proposal to the Turks, I pointed out the question of procurement of supplies to the Armenians and the acceptance of Transversal Street as the Franco-Turkish demarcation line."

General De La Motte met with the Turks. However, due to a misunderstanding, the meeting was stopped on the condition that the French and the Turks would appeal to General Gouraud and Mustafa Kemal respectively.

Then we met with Colonel Abady who told us the following:

"According to the Armistice terms agreed with the Turks, we will withdraw from the city and surrender the Yellow Hospital, the Hotel, Monastir and the whole Armenian quarter to the Turkish authorities."

We asked the Colonel, "When the Turks enter the Armenian quarter and inevitably slaughter all the Armenians, thus realizing their plan to annihilate the whole Armenian population, will you be able to interfere?"

The Colonel answered by stating: "Of Course not! I cannot do anything in case of common events." †

Thus, we decided to continue the fight without removing our barricades. This infuriated the Colonel, who proposed the

* These doors were opened a year later, after Cilicia was emptied of Armenians.

> departure of those who were involved in the organizational, national and military committees. As for the rest, he stated nothing would happen to them, since this would be against the national interests of the Turks. We remained firm on our decisions and explained that the Turks did not discriminate between the Armenians. For the Turks, it was enough to be born Armenian to be considered dangerous. Moreover, we explained that the people wouldn't tolerate the departure of their leaders at such a critical time. The Colonel replied angrily: "Go! All of you!" As you see, we and the colonel talk of the same issues. Therefore, we have organized this referendum in order to deliver your wish to the Colonel.

There was a moment of silence as the people felt the difficult situation they were in. Their decision would seal their fate. Whichever way they turned, there was death. Was it worth leaving everything to the caprice of time? It was imperative to find a solution and act accordingly.

Someone then stood up from among the crowd and requested further clarification from the president. Then another followed him and the president abruptly stated, "There is no need for explanations! We do not have much time. We should come to a final decision. There are two options, either to leave or not!" Again a moment of silence, decision time, to leave or stay?

The unfortunate people, blinded by their tears and almost losing their minds, wriggled like ghosts. Deportation, surrender to the Turks, or fight. After remaining silent for a few more minutes, a young man stood up and uttered the following words:*

> When in 1915 the Turks deported us, the conditions were relatively favorable for the Armenians of Aintab. During that time, the Turks provided us with means for transportation. We were able to save a part of our furniture and sell the rest. Despite that, we know the terrors and misery we witnessed. Thousands of us fell in the deserts of Arabia; our fathers, mothers, brothers and

† The capture and execution of some Armenians by the Turks was seen as a common occurrence. What would have been an uncommon situation would have been a war between the Armenians and the Turks. However, the Armenians would not be able to fight, since the Turks would have occupied all the positions essential for their self-defense effort.

* This young man was the present author.

> sisters remain buried there; it is now impossible to even find their bones or graves. Now, we, the survivors, have barely survived and are able to continue our lives here. Today, succumbing to French pressure, we would take the deportation road again. This time, we would leave under unfavorable conditions, on foot, having barely anything to eat. Refugees will always be a deportees. They will always be reviled, persecuted, and exist by begging from one place to another. Let each of you recall the horrific scenes you witnessed during the deportation. You will say that, that was the Turks' deportation. This will be even worse. The foreigner is always a foreigner and with respect to the interests of our nation, I prefer neither one, nor the other. They are both the same.
>
> Do you remember how we used to repeat, "Dying on the streets of our birthplace is much better than the life of the deportee, where we taste death at every turn?" How many times have we repeated, "We wish we had died honorably like the Armenians of Yetesia, rather than living in such conditions?" Look at our history. Do we want to learn from our previous experience? Do we want to have regrets again? This is our chance. Let us die honorably, rather than perish disgracefully on the road to deportation.

A round of applause followed. It was the wish of the young man's heart that echoed through his words. Despite the applause, the problem was not yet settled. People were still anxious.

A man from the crowd stood up and stated the following: "Let us speak to those who will protect us. If the Military Body, the National Union, and other governing committees are willing to stay here and die, we will stay by their side too."

Nazareth Fesdekjian then stated on behalf of the National Union:

> There is no third option for us. It is either one or the other. Letters from Kilis describe the misery in which the refugees from Aintab have been living there. If we leave, we will die. We will die here too. Why do we avoid an honorable death? Do we want to live, just for the sake of consuming these few boxes of supplies? Wretched is he who wants to give up this victory for the sake of such superficial things. Departure means death, whereas if we stay here, we will live through death (a round of applause).

One of the young fighters took the floor:

> We, the soldiers, are willing to fight until our last breath. If we resist and war erupts, France will be forced to intervene. Maybe you will blame me for ignoring the provisions we still have. However, who knows? Time is full of surprises. Often in the midst of the most desperate situations, a light has appeared. Maybe it will appear this time too. Time will fix everything. Wherever we may go, we will still find the French adopting the same policy towards us.

The soldiers decided to die fighting and there was a round of applause.

Then an Armenian for Suediya started speaking, and after talking about the rebellion of Suedia, he said the following:

> It was often the decision to fight that saved us during critical situations, rather than a willingness to surrender to the enemy. On the mountains of Suedia, when the smallest beam of hope had vanished and we were desperate, it was the French cruisers that saved us. Such events can happen again.

Next, Father Tavoukjian took the floor and presented the situation, drawing people's attention to some critical points.

One of the members of the Military Body provided some details concerning the arsenal and ammunition, and asserted that the Armenians, in that respect, were in a much more stable position than they were before. Others expressed their points of view on this matter. The president re-took the floor and said:

> I don't see any opposition. However, I do believe there are still people who prefer departure but remain silent. Therefore, I will speak on their behalf. If the French withdraw from Manastir, the Beyaz Ahmed Hotel and the Yellow Hospital, the Armenian front will expand and our positions will become weaker. If the Turks succeed in penetrating our lines at any point, what will we do then? You would regret not having left and would curse those who stopped you. You will have remorse for having lost a golden opportunity. Therefore, think carefully and examine every aspect of the issue, and then decide accordingly.

When some asked about the arrival of the next convoy, the president replied: "At least in 30 days and a maximum of 60." This point was also taken into consideration and the pros and cons were discussed in detail. In the end, a young man stood up and spoke:

> I have served in the army for eight years. I have seen war, hunger and much bereavement. Our positions can be defended with revolvers or even hunting guns. As for the problem of supplies, we can address it by forming mobile groups that could go to Turkish villages and procure them, forcibly if necessary. If we decide to leave, we will lay down our weapons and thus hunger and misery will haunt us in Kilis as well as Aleppo, thus making our situation worse. A refugee is always derided and weak, so let us keep the strength we have here.

Here, the president spoke again and provided some details about the meetings with the French and their amiable disposition towards the Armenians. Concerning the question of allowing 6–7,000 people to leave with that day's convoy, the President stated:

> I believe there is some exaggeration in that number. Although several people registered their names with the previous convoy, many did not leave. It is this issue that this meeting will hopefully settle. Will we allow them to leave? Is their departure allowed?

One of the attendants stood up and said:

> The key to our victory is our unity. Our force is dependent upon our solidarity. If some left, that force will be lost and a lot of disputes will arise to the extent that fathers and sons will rise up against one another. Since we are already organized and united, let us stay and win.

A fighter from Giurin provided the contrast and said: "Let those who wish to leave, go. This way they won't hinder the morale of the fighters with their presence."

The president asked Dr. Shepard to make some recommendations in this respect. The latter stood up and said the following:

> I cannot recommend anything. You know the Turks better than I do and there are veterans among you who can give better recommendations. You should decide your fate. The Armenians have often relied on foreign nations. The past 61 days have shown that by relying on your own forces, you were able to triumph. Let me say one last thing. Had the Americans been in your place, they would not have moved. Why should the Armenians be different? As you have done before, you should stay and resist.

The president read a letter according to which the Tashnagtsoutioun (Armenian Revolutionary Federation) had decided to stay.

Father Karekin Bogharian said:

> Our situation isn't hopeless. We have survived much harsher and darker periods in our history. We saw the defense of Zeitun. The Armenians there fought and struck, and when all hope was gone, the foreign consuls came to their rescue. We still have supplies for one month. A lot can happen in a month. Let us not despair. Let us be patient and fight, and rest assured that victory will be on our side.

On behalf of the Military Body, Adour Levonian referred to all the past events that the Armenians of Aintab had gone through and concluded by saying, "Our strength has quadrupled, whereas the enemy is relatively weaker. Let us trust in our forces. The Military Body will not leave. Those who wish to stay here, let them raise their hands."

Then the crowd asserted its decision to stay in Aintab. Hands were raised. Then the fighters returned to their positions, shouting "Victory is ours!" *

The Last Convoy Only Took the Orphans

The final decision to stay in Aintab was transmitted to the Colonel, who, satisfied, stated that this step was very favorable to the Armenians of Aintab, rather than the previous decision to depart. "We will always support you" he said.

Dr. Shepard was present at the public vote, as a witness. "What a huge difference between yesterday and today," he commented.

The market had changed. The prices returned to their previous levels. It seemed that the three day crisis had gone. Peace was restored. The National Union allowed the departure of foreigners or those whose family members were not in Aintab. These people would accompany the caravan of orphans and would set off at night.

It was a starry summer night. The moon was shining in the sky. This centuries old witness of the Armenian massacres was again watching the town, villages and the departure of the orphans.

The furniture belonging to the orphanage was loaded on the military vehicles. Young orphans would carry their belongings on their backs and follow the caravan on foot.

---

* The "*hurraa*!" calls of the Armenians scared the Turks away. Many left their positions fearing a general Armenian attack.

The Armenian orphan, deprived of parental love and the pleasures of this life, having blood, tears and grief as a friend, was once again forced to walk the endless road to Golgotha. I still see them before my eyes, all dusty, each wearing a small woolen jacket and carrying a small bag that barely contained a few things to eat.

They left, their eyes fixed on those they were leaving behind, carrying in their hearts the mourning and anguish of the Armenians of Aintab.

June 2nd–13th

The 3rd, 4th and 5th of June were appointed as days of prayer and fasting. The Armenian nation has always remained loyal to the Church, and during such critical moments, has prayed to God with greater fervor and faith. Today, during such a critical situation, the Armenians did not forget God. All prayed for strength and success. Dr. Shepard gave a lecture and said that "God always helps those who are innocent and fight for their rights". Some other people spoke too and hymns were chanted. The brave Armenian fighters were now lamenting and recalling the loved ones and compatriots whom they lost during the fighting.

On the 3rd June, the National Union decided to arm the policemen with revolvers. It also decided to establish two guard houses on Akyol and Pasha Sokaghuh streets. Additionally, two detectives were appointed to work against Turkish espionage. It also appealed to the Colonel and requested permission to harvest the Turkish fields, instead of the Armenians ones that were behind the Turkish lines. A political committee was formed, whose task was to arrange the necessary measures in case of political complications and conduct foreign policy during the armistice, negotiations, etc... Besides the representatives of the National Union and the Military Body, the following people were summoned for this task: H. Levonian, Dr. H. Bezjian, H. Karamanougian, H. Kendirjian, T. Kupelian, K. Sarkissian, H. Arakelian, Prof. N. Balyozian, and S. Karamanougian.

At this time, the following notice, issued by the National Union, was placed on the wall:

> 1. All men aged between 18 and 60 are obliged to work, except those who already hold political or military responsibilities. The sick are exempted from this regulation, and those who do not wish to work have to pay a fine of half to one mejidiye based on their financial means.

> 2. The Military Body requires 40 men who know how to use rifles and four others who can use machine guns. The non-fighters who possess cartridges must bring them to headquarters and receive a receipt for them.
>
> 3. Those who have crops outside the city should inform the National Union.
>
> 4. Those who possess animals must register them at the headquarters of the military police.
>
> 3rd June, 1920
>
> Military Body

On June 8th, the Turks and French finalized their negotiations. The terms of the armistice were set, according to which the French would withdraw from Manastir, the Beyaz Ahmed Hotel and the Yellow Hospital. The National Union met with the colonel for the last time. He proposed Armeno-Turkish negotiation and stated that he had already spoken to the Turks about this matter. Upon their return, the National Union appointed several men who, in the afternoon, met with the Turkish delegates at the Y.M.C.A * Apart from this, Dr. Shepard personally met with the Turkish delegates. After hearing the Turkish side, the National Union invited 200 intellectuals to the church courtyard for consultations. The meeting had not yet begun when a crowd entered the courtyard, stating their willingness to hear the decisions made.

The president, Father Nerses Tavoukjian stood, up and made the following announcement:

> The situation has changed again. Today is the date by which the terms of the Franco-Turkish agreement were to have been fulfilled. According to the terms agreed upon, the French have withdrawn from the three positions they had previously occupied which compels us to remove our barricades. We met the colonel this morning, who uttered these exact words:
>
> "You will occupy our abandoned positions. You will destroy your barricades and, according to the Franco-Turkish agreement, you will become Ottoman subjects starting from 5 o'clock. Thus the Turks will govern you and will establish guard houses wherever they wish. If you do not comply with these terms, I will not

* The Turkish delegates were Irfan Bey, mutasarrif Jelalettin, a commissioner, Bulbul Hoja (leader of Hiyeti Islamiyeh), Seyfullah among others.

> interfere in any way. I have already written to the Turks and it would be good if you agree with them."
>
> When we met with the Turks earlier today, they reiterated the exact same words that the French had told us: that we are their subjects, that all hostilities must stop and that peace would be restored in this city. In this respect, we requested further time to consult with the people and adopt a unanimous position. The Turks at first refused our request but in the end they accepted and said, "We will place soldiers in the three positions that the French have abandoned according to our armistice terms." The meeting ended on the condition that we would meet again today, at 4 o'clock. So, that is the problem. Due to time constraints, let us quickly finalize our decision.

Some people expressed their opinions and stated:

> The situation has been completely changed. Hereafter, the French will not help us and we are on our own. We are hopeless in terms of supplies and the food we have barely suffices us for 15 days. If we continue the battle, our fight will not be against the Turks, but rather the Entente powers. The French leave us with no choice. Therefore, we should choose the lesser evil and have an honorable death or sign a treaty.

During this time, Dr. Shepard, who had recently returned from his meeting with the Turks, announced, "The Turks will place soldiers on the aforementioned three positions, after 4 o'clock."

The people who realized the difficulty of coming up with a unanimous decision decided to elect a group made up of 28 members (The Convention of the 28) who would settle the issue in the best possible way.

The Convention of 28 succeeded in postponing the deadline by 24 hours.

The Turks displayed a very friendly and benevolent attitude towards the Armenians, puzzling the latter.

Chapter 15

Armistice Negotiations Between the Turks and Armenians

On June 9th, at 7:30, one of the last but historically most decisive meetings took place in the church courtyard in Aintab. A dense crowd of 2,500 people filled it. The President, Father Nerses Tavoukjian, explained the situation in detail, followed by Dr. Shepard. Referring to some letters received from abroad, Dr. Shepard considered some aspects of the current political situation and commented on the shameful policy of the Entente powers. He heartbreakingly stated that, henceforth, the Armenians would not receive any relief from either the Entente powers or from the Americans. He ended his speech, concluding, "We are forced to agree with the Turks. There is no other way."

Many of the attendees expressed their points of view. Some suggested fighting until the end and some preferred agreement with the Turks. The president took the floor and said, "Until now, the key to our success was our solidarity. And hereafter, we will stay united and act unanimously." Finally, to facilitate this task, the people re-elected the 28 members and confirmed their responsibility. At the same moment, a lieutenant named Charles arrived and said, "The French will try to evacuate some more people and make the necessary arrangements." He also presented an order that had been issued, according to which the Armenians would have to lower the French flags flying from their roofs, despite the fact that they had decided, many times, to serve and die under them. The Armenians, naturally, were infuriated and started questioning French honor. The crowd dispersed in despair and started lowering the French flags from their roofs and the minarets of the mosques.

During those days, people were in a bewildered state. Many young men, about 1,000 of them, decided to resort to brigandage, which was opposed since it implied sealing the tragic fate of the hundreds of widows, children and women. The best way was to either die or live together.

The 28 delegates convened, and after meeting with the Turkish representatives, proposed the following terms:

1. Arab and American consuls should come from Aleppo as a conciliatory delegation.
2. The barricades should not be removed until the finalization of the terms.

3. Armenians should be provided with the necessary supplies.
4. If the conciliatory delegation cannot come from Aleppo, Dr. Shepard or another American should be accepted as a substitute.

The Turks accepted these terms and assured the Armenians that their agreement was honest. They stated that their national interests had compelled them to cooperate with the Armenians.

After these negotiations, the Armenians guided the Turkish gendarmes to the three positions abandoned by the French.

The Convention of 28 gathered the people in the church courtyard in the evening and explained the friendly behavior of the Turks. The people, although partly satisfied, left the courtyard somewhat suspicious. An Executive Court was established in the Turkish quarter that would govern the city harmoniously.

On June 10th, the leadership of the Armenian military forces convened and presented the Convention of 28 with the following note:

1. No material reparation should be requested for the destruction of Turkish houses.
2. Political prisoners, old or new, will be set free. Similarly, after the armistice, no one will be dragged to the court under the pretext of political issues.
3. The boycott will be lifted.
4. Free traffic will be permitted in the city.
5. There will be no searches for weapons.

Other recommendations:

1. The organization of meetings to bolster Armeno-Turkish brotherhood
2. There should be Armenian gendarmes in guard houses.

After lengthy deliberations, the Convention of the 28 considered the demands stipulated by the military leadership and presented the Turks with our demands under the following terms:

1. No one will be held responsible for the recent fighting.
2. The boycott will be lifted once and for all.
3. Free traffic will be permitted in the city.
4. Besides existing guard houses, no new ones will be established.

The authorities will not demand the surrender of weapons.

The Turks accepted these terms and continued their friendly behavior.

Chinarli Mosque damaged during fighting.

To clearly understand the Turks' behavior, we refer here to a notice placed on walls on June 11th.

> The absurd events that occurred between us have ended. Everything will be forgotten. No one will be held responsible for any damage and destruction, and no one will be legally prosecuted. Everyone must maintain the peace and return to his work. Everyone must keep their weapons in their house. No one will have the right to carry weapons, except those appointed by the government. Every Ottoman subject will obey the commands of the government.
>
> The mutasarrif office of Aintab
>
> Mehmed Jelaleddin

Eventually, the Armenians went to the market and started buying goods.

The Convention of 28 sent a telegraph to Mustafa Kemal, whereby the Armenians accepted Ottoman citizenship and maintained their willingness to participate in the Nationalist Government (Milli Hukumeti).

On June 13th, at 3 o'clock, the people gathered in the church courtyard, where the mutasarrif bey, the commander of the Nationalist forces, Seyfullah and Jelal Kadri were invited to speak. The Mutasarrif spoke first and said that the reason for hostilities between the Armenian and Turkish nations had supposedly been the Europeans, who resurrected enmity between the two peoples. The Turks did not intend to kill the Armenians, but rather expel the French from the Turkish fatherland. Based on these words, it was understood that 20,000 Turkish chetes had attacked the Armenian quarters, but they have not occupied it, since they considered the Armenians as their brothers. And for this reason – not to harm the Armenians – they had taken the fight outside the city and defeated the French. The mutasarrif's speech was nothing other than an attempt to manipulate everything that we had hitherto said.

The floor was then given to Jelal Kadri, as a lieutenant to the commander of the Nationalist forces, Seyfullah. Kadri expressed his satisfaction regarding the honesty of the Armeno-Turkish agreement. He guaranteed that this step would open a new page in the history of Aintab. After his speech, Reverend Y. Hadidian and Father Nerses Tavoukjian stated: "After we have asserted the honesty of these speeches, we will not content ourselves with words, but bring life to them through our work."

After Father Tavoukjian, the mutasarrif took the floor again and provided some political information: The Nationalist Government was based in Enguri [Ankara], a new Franco-German war had begun, and the Nationalists wished to occupy Constantinople and dominate the whole of Turkey. He claimed to have received information from Kilis, according to which the Armenian refugees wished to return to Aintab. "Let those who wish to leave, go. As for the rest, let them stay here. I can assure you that those who leave will regret it and return to this city, yearning for its peace and harmony." The mutasarrif reiterated that the Turks were sincere in their agreement and that, as brothers of the same fatherland, we should expel the enemy together.

The mutasarrif told many lies in his speech. However, there was one thing, at least, in which the Turks were sincere: to gain the support of the Armenians and use them to expel the French.

The crowd dispersed. After 70 days of bloody fighting, peace was finally restored in the city.

Martyrs and Wounded from April 1 Until May 30:

April 1st: Hagop Arslanian (martyr), from Adana, from the orphanage. Kevork Sarejoghluian (martyr). Khacher Apovian, wounded. Azniv Oroullouian, wounded.

April 2nd: Yacoub Badvelian, (martyr).

April 3rd: Haroutiun Naneian, (martyr). Movses Matossian, wounded. Nerses Der-Haroutiunian, wounded.

April 4th: Soghomon Alabashian, (martyr). Yacoub Allekian, wounded and then martyred on April 7th.

April 10th: Krikor Kazekjian, (martyr).

April 11th: Kevork Sabounjian, (martyr).

April 12th: Kevork Aghaian, (martyr). Hovsep Haserjian, (martyr). Manuel Sabounjian, (martyred while working).

April 15th: Ovsannah Stanbolian (martyr, one of the maids in the orphanage).

April 20th: Mihran Terzibashian (a building collapsed on him).

April 22nd : Movses Kilejian (martyr). Avedis Khejvajian, wounded. Kirkor Oroullouian, wounded.

April 29th: Nazar Gumushian, wounded by a cannon shell. A woman and a girl wounded in the church. 6-7 people wounded in the 6th and 7th areas.

May 1st: Krikor Meskheian, (martyr); accidentally shot by the French.

May 2nd May: Kevork D. Balian, wounded.

May 5th: Avedis Demirjian, wounded. Roupen Hagopian, wounded.

May 7th: Misak Hekimian's wife is killed by Loutfi Chavoush. Kristineh Libarian, (martyr, killed by Sa'at Chavoush). Nectar Libarian, wounded. Eliza Libarian, wounded. Emilia Kouyoumjian, wounded. Bedros Kouyoumjian, wounded. Sarkis Kouyoumjian, wounded. Yussef (tailor), wounded.

May 8th: Roupen Davoian's daughter killed by cannon shell. His son, wounded.

May 9th: Kohar Abajian, wounded by cannon shell. Topal Nazar's wife, Meriyeh, wounded by cannon.

May 10th: Aram Odabashian, (martyr from Sepasdia). Mihran Karababaian, (martyr).

May 16th: Hmayag Krajian, (martyr). Aram Vezvezian, (wounded - from Sepasdia). Hrant Hekimian, wounded. Sarkis Keoleian, wounded. Magar Magarian, wounded.

May 17th: Nerses Kelejian, wounded.

May 19th: Toros Hamalian, wounded (accidentally shot by a friend from Marash).

May 22nd: Kevork K. Seteian accidentally killed by a friend from Zeitun.

May 23rd: Mayis Drtad Guleserian, wounded. Artin Avakian, wounded.

Chapter 16

The Armistice Period

June 13th–July 29th

Our position was stalemated during the armistice period since all contact with the French had been broken off. Thanks to the latter, the western side of the Armenian quarter was occupied by the Turks, and hence all the positions were completely surrounded by them. For strategic reasons, the Turks were reluctant to stir up the Armenians, but still tried to annihilate the Armenians through every covert way possible. The Armenians, however, were very cautious and watchful and never fell into their political traps. Therefore, we've named this period the "Armeno-Turkish diplomatic period." The Armenians started buying supplies from the Turkish quarter and, naturally, bought extra quantities to fill their warehouses. Additionally, Turks and Armenians started harvesting their crops in the surrounding fields and reestablished trade relations.

On June 28th, the commander of the Turkish nationalist forces, Rejib Bey, invited the chairman of the National Union to a meeting and suggested writing a letter of complaint in the name of the Armenians to Mustafa Kemal Pasha with the following content:

> We, the Armenians, are against the French occupation that has disrupted the peace of the city. Currently, they have withdrawn from their camps, and our relations with the noble Turkish people are very good. We therefore request the French to withdraw from the city.

Upon receiving this suggestion, the National Union invited the following people to a consultative meeting: H. Levonian, H. Karamanougian, Dr. H. Bezjian, H. Jebejian, B. Milletbashian, Dr. K. Khalfasian, T. Kupelian, K. Baghdassarian, S. B. Nazarian, M. Araradian, A. Kalemkerian, A. Levonian and S. Karamanougian. They decided the following:

> 1. The content of the letter must reflect the reality of the situation as far as possible.
>
> 2. This proposal should be postponed until Rejib Bey's second suggestion.

June 30th. The Turks started returning furniture and items belonging to Armenians. Similarly, the latter returned property belonging to the Turks that had been stored in the headquarters of the "Emlaki-Metruke."

July 7th. The Turkish governor demanded, through an official letter, the disbandment of the National Union. However, the latter refused this demand and decided to maintain its existence to govern the internal affairs of the Armenians in the city.

July 13th. The Turks sent a brigade to the Eyyoub Oghlu mosque, claiming to have chosen it as a military station. However, the Turks' real intention was the occupation of the city through a gradual deployment of soldiers at strategic points. The Armenian military leadership and fighters, who realised this, immediately surrounded the mosque and ordered the Turks to withdraw, since this was a violation of the armistice terms. To avoid any damage in case of a sudden attack, the Armenians rebuilt their barricades in 17 minutes. The Turkish military leaders, Irfan Bey, the commander of the nationalist forces Rejeb Bey and Jelal Kadri Effendi, were completely taken by surprise when they saw that the barricades that had been built and destroyed in one month had been fully restored by the time they got there. The latter, noticing the imminent danger of fighting breaking out, attempted to pacify the situation, claiming that they had never given such an order, and that it was all a misunderstanding. They pulled the Turkish soldiers out of the mosque and requested the destruction of the barricades by the Armenians. The latter complied with their demands and the situation was thus calmed. The Turks promised to make no such moves again.

July 14th. The National Union expressed its regrets about this incident, by visiting the government offices.

July 15th. The National Union was summoned to the government building, where the Turks suggested that the Armenians rebuild the devastated Turkish houses and return them to their rightful owners. The Armenians argued that the Turkish houses were damaged by the French and denied responsibility. Irfan Bey was skeptical of this answer. After a heated discussion, Irfan Bey asked Father Nerses Tavoukjian, "Why are you silent? Is this true?" The latter responded: "It is partially true. The Armenians and French destroyed these houses during the war and it is our duty to restore and return them to their rightful owners. You have the right to demand that. However, I believe that the restoration of each house costs at least 20 gold liras. To restore 2,000 houses, we need 40,000 gold liras, which we currently do not possess. How do you demand 40,000 gold liras from a people just returned from exile? This is what I have been thinking about." Irfan Bey replied, "You see? This man just explained everything in a very clear manner. Why the 'we are not responsible for the damage' talk? The man accepted that you should restore them, but claims to have no money!!"

Father Tavoukjian then added, "Since there are devastated Armenian houses in the Turkish quarter too, let those whose houses have been destroyed by us find temporary shelter at the Armenian homes in your quarter at the government's expense. Once the war is over, we will restore the damaged ones and they will have the right to return." Satisfied by the priest's suggestion, it was decided to establish two committees – "Inshaat Komisionu" (Committee for Restoration) – and "Iskan Komisionu" (Committee for Settlement) comprising of Turkish and Armenians members, whose task would be the settlement of the housing issue by restoring those houses whose renovation could be achieved with minimum expenditure to make them habitable for families.

July 19th. The governor proposed to the leaders of the three sects (the Turkish government recognized the three leaders as the head of the Armenian community) that they prepare a list of Armenians who wished to leave Aintab, so that permission could be granted by Mustafa Kemal Pasha. Only a few Armenians agreed to leave the city and go to Aleppo via Berejik.

That afternoon, the Turkish governor invited Father Nerses Tavoukjian and some of the other Armenian notables for a discussion of a particular issue.

Fesdekjian was sent on behalf of the Armenians, to whom the governor said the following: "Irfan Bey has been appointed commander of the Aintab region. He has requested the abandonment and surrender of the houses located on the western side of a line to be drawn from north to south – including Dr. Hovsep Bezjian's house – in order to safeguard the retreat of the Turkish soldiers in case of a Turco-French conflict. Please consider this issue and let me know what your final decision is."

After deliberating on this matter, the National Union refused this proposal on the following grounds:

1. It would be impossible to resettle the 4-500 families that would be left homeless because of such an occupation.

2. After handing over the houses demanded, it would be impossible to settle the people required to leave in the neighboring homes.

Father Nerses Tavoukjian and a few others were entrusted with the task of transmitting this decision to the Turks.

When, on July 20th, the aforesaid position was explained to Irfan Bey, he promised to concede some points after an investigation of the places mentioned. On July 23rd, the Turks invited the Armenians to their national celebration.*

After an investigation, Irfan Bey modified his request. He now demanded possession of only 17 houses that would be used as military stations. Most of the houses requested were already on the previous list and would jeopardize the Armenian position in case of an attack. The National Union also refused this proposal but promised to hand over the houses located on the eastern side of the avenue that passed in front of Sahag-Mesrobian College.

July 26th. Armenian notables gathered at Dr. Hovsepian's house and decided the following, since the Turks demanded all the houses located on the eastern side of the avenue that passed next to Shaban's house and stretched to the south:

1. The Armenians, who have recently returned from deportation and suffered moral as well as physical damage, cannot withstand the terror of a second war.

2. The conversion of the aforementioned houses into military stations implies the transformation of the Armenian quarter into a battlefield, something that is undesirable for the Muslim and Christian populations. If a war is imminent, let it be at the outskirts, preserving the city itself.

3. If a war does occur in the city, the whole Christian population should be allowed to go to a safer place.

---

* To cement the basis for good Armeno-Turkish relations, the commanders of the Turkish "lightning battalion" (Yildirim Taburi) organized a feast in Adour Niziblian's house in honor of the Military Body and the National Union. The Armenians did the same at the Y.M.C.A. building. These was much discussions about Armeno-Turkish reconciliation, cooperation and union.

> 4. Send copies of this letter to army commander Salaheddin Bey, to the central body of the Committee of National Defense, and if our proposal is rejected, send it to Mustafa Kemal Pasha.

Here we must recall the meeting between Father Tavoukjian and Chitji Ferid Effendi that was instrumental in delaying the fighting. Father Tavoukjian went to the Saboun Khan alone, where he found Chitji Zadeh Ferid Effendi. The city was filled with numerous chetes, to the extent that it was almost impossible to pass through the streets. During their meeting, Father Tavoukjian said the following to Ferid Effendi:

> According to what I have heard, your father was a very noble and magnanimous man, whereas your mother is said to have been the epitome of mercifulness and tenderness in the Muslim population. Let their souls rest in peace. Assuming that the child of such parents would not have a very different personality, I have come to you with a proposal which I believe you will not refuse. I have heard that you will begin to fight the French. I suggest that you do this outside the city. You are aware that fighting in the city will claim the lives of innocent Armenians and Turks. A war in the city is barbarity.

Ferid Effendi, whose eyes were filled with tears, promised to endorse this viewpoint during the conference of the Turkish general staff due to be held in Sam Keoy. We were later informed that serious discussions had taken place there. Although Ferid Effendi's arguments were refused, any attack was postponed for a few days.

July 27th. The members of the National Union and the Convention of the 28 held a conference and heard the details of the previous day's meeting between father Tavoukjian, N. Fesdekjian, Irfan Bey, Major Bekir Sidki Bey and the president of the Committee for National Defense, Ferid Effendi. Following the rejection of the Turkish proposal – about the surrender of the houses – the Armenians avoided going to the market and anxiously waited for a solution. It was decided that if there was a conflict between members of these two communities, a notice would be posted on the walls after the respective representatives met and discussed the issues at hand. Moreover, the Mutasarrif asked Armenians for a signed note, guaranteeing the non-participation of Armenians in any pro-French movements and displaying the concessions made by Irfan Bey with respect to his demand of the houses. Our delegates were ready to sign any agreement that stipulated Armenian relief for Turkish soldiers and the connection of the Yellow Hospital to the Beyaz Ahmed Hotel using a trench, on the condition that the Turks would renounce any demands for houses in the Armenian quarters.

The content of this note would be the following:

> 1. Reference to the loyalty of the Armenians towards the Ottoman government and their reluctance to participate in the pursuit of any political goal.
>
> 2. The duty of all Ottoman subjects towards their fatherland; however, due to their miserable status resulting from deportation, acknowledgment that the Armenians were not in a state to provide services for the fatherland.
>
> 3. The Armenians' resort to weapons during the events of the 1st April was merely a measure of self-defense.
>
> 4. The absence of Armenians in any pro-French or anti-Turkish movements.
>
> 5. If the city became a battlefield, the Armenians would provide free passage to Turkish troops through Pasha street and Sounbourjeh avenue.

The terms of this agreement were approved by the attendees.

July 28th. The National Union and the Convention of the 28 held a meeting to discuss the following event:

During the preceding night, around 3:30, a Turkish officer came to Ali Bey's house and loudly gave instructions regarding the position of the Armenian fighters during the Turco-French fighting. The Turkish soldiers had fortified their positions at Akyol Mosque, the Keorkuji House, the Nigoghosian College and the Chinarli Mosque. When the Armenians wanted to know the reason for their fortifications, the Turks replied that they had received orders to fortify them. Eventually, the Armenians had also fortified their positions but had left the ones at the three avenues of Soubourjou, Balekleh, and Pasha Street open. Seeing this, the Turks had refused to sell supplies to the Armenians in the morning. An invitation was received from the governor at the beginning of the meeting and, as the president, Father Nerses Tavoukjian had met the mutasarrif and present him with the Armenian note of July 26th, in which it was written that the Armenians would not demand any houses and that a mixed police force (Inzibat) should be formed to maintain peace in the city.

Upon receiving the governor's invitation around 8:00 p.m. that day, Father Nerses Tavoukjian and a delegation had gone to Irfan Bey's office once more. Ferid Effendi was present too. During the meeting, the Turks stated that they had nothing against the Armenians. Irfan Bey said that they had decided to make some houses into military stations but, as the Armenians had regarded this act as a threat to their security, the Turks renounced their decision. He concluded that this should serve as proof of Turkish honesty and an indication of the Turks' friendly attitude towards Armenians.

The Turks were wrong in their efforts to build their barricades at night. A war with the French was imminent, so Commander Salaheddin Bey's proposed mixed police force was necessary. Its task was to pacify and solve all the problems that may have arisen between Turkish and Armenian fighters and maintain peace in the city. The number of police available depended on the number of soldiers the Armenians were ready to provide. The settlement of the housing issue was satisfactory. It was suggested that the task of the mixed police should be confined to the Armenian streets alone, using a force of 40 men (20 Armenians, and 20 Turks). As for the Turkish quarter, its peace could be maintained by the Turkish government. Another point: it would be better to keep the secondary barricades that had been well built by the Armenians in order to prevent any problems that might have arisen during military movements. Finally, the Soubourjou and Pasha streets had to be opened for military movements, giving access to the unarmed soldiers who would provide supplies and food to the fighting soldiers on Balekleh Eyyoub Oghlu Avenue. This route would also provide a communications channel. The Armistice with the Turks lasted until July 29th. The Turks did not start fighting after the deadline passed. This was supposedly due to the French retreat towards Kilis and the departure of Armenians with them. Filled with great expectations, the Turks were waiting for the convoy, positioned on the hills of Kizil Hisar. Such Turkish speculation accelerated the retreat of the French troops from Teyabiad, Gul Tepeh, Arap Pounari, Birejik and Jarablus. The French were retreating from these areas in order to occupy the more important Syrian cities, such as Aleppo, which they entered without any resistance. They did not retreat from Akcha Koyoun, so they could maintain the connection with Aintab.

The Turks made many attempts to capture this town from the French but failed. Rejeb Bey, an opponent of fighting for the city, was dismissed and Irfan Bey appointed commander. But suspicious of him too, the Turkish high command dismissed him and appointed Ozdemir, who began the attack on the French on July 29th, on Mustafa Kemal's orders.

Chapter 17

The Turks Violate the Terms of the Armistice

July 29th–August 11th

During the armistice period, the Turks had made their preparations in accordance with their plan to destroy the small French force located in the college and Chitji Kharaf with a single attack. It is exactly for this reason that during the "peace" they did not want to enrage the Armenians, thus adding another enemy that was against their forces. Their strategy was to keep the Armenians neutral and only fight the French.

The French army bases – the college and Chitji Kharaf – were surrounded by the Turks. Cannons and soldiers secretly positioned on the northern and north-western hills were waiting for the attack signal. Despite the fact that Ghourban Baba and the Mardin orphanage were in the neutral zone, the Turks had occupied them, along with Boz Tepeh, on the western and southern sides of the college and were ready to assault it with a large force. As for the eastern side of the college, the Turks were positioned around the Muslim Hospital, the Beyaz Ahmed Hotel and in some Armenian houses between the two that the Armenians had abandoned as a result of the Franco-Turkish agreement. Thus, the French army was completely surrounded. At their military conference at Sam Keoy, the Turks agreed that Salaheddin Bey was to first occupy Chitji Kharaf and then assault the college from every direction. This is why they had pointed their 7.8cm cannons towards Kharaf.

The attack began at 6 am on July 29th. Kharaf was surrounded during the armistice period. A small force of Senegalese soldiers, with its commander, Lieutenant Bars, was located there. It is through the courage and bravery of this man that the Armenians of Aintab were saved. The Turkish 10.5cm cannons started bombarding the Kharaf buildings. The French were taken by surprise, since the Senegalese soldiers had left for a military exercise and now had to rush back to their positions.

The French 7.5cm cannons started bombarding the Turkish positions around the Beyaz Ahmed Hotel and the hospital. The noise of cannon and machine gun fire filled the air for 15 minutes. The Turks continually attacked Chitji Kharaf from three sides. The French were forced to send some of their troops, positioned in the college, against the regular and irregulars troops attacking Chitji Kharaf. During these critical moments, previously unseen in the history of Aintab, a French 7.5cm cannon was blown up as the shell in the barrel exploded. Meanwhile, French machine-guns, positioned on the second floor of the college, annihilated the Turkish troops around Kharaf in a few minutes. We observed these operations from our tall buildings. 10 to 12 cannon shells fell per minute on the area surrounding Kharaf and the college. Suddenly, the Turks started advancing from the southern hill behind Chitji Kharaf. Advancing from the Jamgochian fields, they moved forward quickly. Many soldiers were camouflaged. They advanced as far as the barbed wire around the farm building and started to cut it. A small group of wounded Senegalese soldiers, at the exhortation of their commander, were able to regain their vigor and strength and opened continuous fire using their machine gun. The Turks, thinking they had fallen into a trap, started retreating, leaving many dead. They found shelter in the old buildings from where Kharaf was impossible to see.

The French in a Difficult Situation

The Turks did not stop the bombardment. They did not even spare the military hospital located on the western side of the college building, despite the fact that the Red Cross flag was raised on its roof. The wounded were therefore moved to the lower floors. This is how events unfolded on the first day of fighting. The French, who were surrounded, had no means of communicating with their troops in Kilis and Akcha Koyoun. Their telegraph facility had been damaged and they were unable to inform their superiors about the attack. It was restored that night. No airplane had flown over. Thus the French were in a very difficult situation.

July 30th passed calmly. However, that night, at about 9 or 10 o'clock, the French started heavily bombardment of the Turkish hospital with the only 7.5cm cannon they had left. Guided by the moonlight, the French destroyed many Turkish barricades, burying many chetes under the ruins. Similarly, the Turkish ammunition dump at Beyaz Ahmed Hotel was destroyed and left in ruins.

On that first day, the French cannons succeeded in destroying the wall that linked the Turkish hospital and Beyaz Ahmed Hotel, cutting off the connection between the two.

The fighting lasted until August 11th. The French were in a difficult situation. To compensate for the loss of their cannon and prevent the Turks from knowing about it, they moved the remaining one from one place to another. The Turks attacked from every direction, particularly at night. The French had requested Armenian assistance by ringing the college bell, particularly during the attack on Kertenkelleh (Lizard) Pasha, when the Turks had arrived at the outer gates. We did not hear the French alarm because of the noise made by the cannons and machine guns. They used flashlights at night to make their situation understandable.

The Armenians, as we have noted, were in a neutral position and observed the clash between these two forces. We communicated with the Turks using the Y.M.C.A. barricade alley. Although there were no obstacles, very few Armenians went to the Turkish quarter. They helped the Turks by grinding wheat at the only undamaged mill that was located in the Armenian quarter.

The French suffered greatly until August 11th. Here, we should recall an event that an unbiased historian ought to write, describing what really happened.

The Turks had high hopes of success. However, when all their attacks on Kharaf, the college and other French positions failed, they could do nothing else except to continue their attacks more cautiously. Yet, all their efforts were pushed back by the sacrifice and bravery of the French troops. The Armenians noticed the difficult situation the French were in and understood that they were in need of Armenian assistance. During the attacks, the French had tried to call for help using every means at their disposal, but we had not understood or heard them. Finally, the chairman of the Military Body found a way of understanding the French situation. The Aintab water supply came from a nearby village called Panjarluh, located on the western side of the city. A tunnel had been built to ensure the flow of this clean water to Aintab. This tunnel, passing under the Giligian Jemaran (college), arrived at the Armenian quarter and then continued to the Turkish one. The width and height of the tunnel was enough to enable a man to stand up and walk through it. It was hollowed out of rock and its depth reached 40-50 meters below ground level when passing under the hills of the city. It stretched from west to east and reached every house through its numerous side channels. As we have previously noted, the city was built on three hills. The inhabitants of these hills had water cisterns, while those who lived in the valleys and lower streets had ponds in front of their houses.

The chairman of the Military Body wanted to get in touch with the French troops in the college through this water tunnel. Father Tavoukjian disapproved of this proposal, the reasons for which will be clarified below. That night, the chairman of the Military Body appointed two men to go through the tunnel. They dived into the Arejians' water cistern and entered it. After they had gone some distance, they were forced to return as the water level was too high, making their further advance impossible. This attempt was made in utmost secrecy. On the following day, Father Tavoukjian was summoned as the Turks had acquired information about this Armenian attempt. * No one dared to accompany him and he went all by himself.

Several Turkish generals and the director of the Turkish Intelligence Bureau were in Irfan Bey's office and the latter referred to the tunnel episode. Father Tavoukjian gave the following answer:

> I believe this is an accusation by traitors who wish to undermine the brotherhood of two newly reconciled peoples. I am surprised by your thoughts. Why would the Armenians do such a thing? Can we help the French? No. Can they help us? No. Therefore, as we are living in peaceful conditions, what would compel us to go to the French? You are suspicious that we will betray you by providing information to the French. But, what do we know of you? Do we know how many soldiers you have? No. Where have you placed them? We do not know, since we have not left the city. Therefore your doubts and suspicions are groundless. I suggest you destroy those people who provide such information, because they will resurrect the enmity between our nations.

Irfan Bey, in the end, told the priest that whatever happened, the Armenians have always been pro-French and have always worked in their favor. The past events confirmed this and they have served as the basis of Turkish doubts. For example, when the French came to Aintab two months earlier, and Armenians welcomed the French entry while the

* Some accused Armenian traitors of leaking this information to the Turks. However, I believe that the Turks had already some doubts about this tunnel, since the water was stirred up, because no rain had fallen and naturally the two men who went down it had caused the muddiness of the water.

Turks did not. Armenians greeted them with flags and cheering, and guided them into the city.

At this, the priest stated the following:

> Irfan Bey, if you beat a man and let him die under the burning sun, what would be his first job after receiving some water from a person passing by? To thank him! Do you think he would ask if that benevolent person was a Jew, Muslim or Kurd? We have always been like that beaten person. You have deported us, but the French returned us to our lands. You have killed our fathers and mothers, but they have cared for the widows and orphans. Are we worse than dogs not to express our gratitude with simple cheering and respect? My effendi, had you done what they have done, we would have shown the same respect to you. You consider our self-defense an act of treason and cooperation with the French. There is no such thing. I was deported with 15-20 people but returned with only a few. Every Armenian in this city has suffered the same fate. One person barely survived from each family and they are again in danger. No Irfan Bey. No, we will not die this time! We will live in peace if you do not touch us, otherwise, we will fight until the last Armenian and die with honor.

Moved by the priest's words, Irfan Bey said with a soft voice, "My Effendi, you have signed a peace agreement with us, and moreover, promised to help us. What have you done until now? Let your craftsmen build bombs for us. Won't you at least help us in that way?"

The priest replied:

> You must establish the basis of honest and real cooperation now. Prove your honesty by respecting the terms of the armistice and our neutrality. God knows, maybe with your good conduct, our future generations would fight for this fatherland even more fervently than we did. How is it possible to convince our community to help you after yesterday's terrors? Despite everything, we suggested providing 2-3,000 Armenian workers to open a trench from the Hospital to Beyaz Ahmed Hotel. But you refused that too. Instead, you have built a wall that obstructed our communications during the first day of fighting. Who should have made this suggestion, me as a religious man, or you, an experienced military commander?

Father Tavoukjian returned to the Armenian quarter, after a discussion that lasted for three to four hours.

The National Union was occupied during this time with purely military affairs. It elected a new Military Body, whose chairman acted as the military commander. After discussing this issue with the political parties, the National Union elected the Military Body comprising the following members: Adour Levonian, A. Kalemkerian, M. Araradian, R. Yaghsezian, S. Jemelian. They elected A. Levonian as its chairman.

The Convention of the 28 was maintained for civil affairs, working in the meantime with the National Union and the Military Body.

On August 9th, the mutasarrif summoned Mr. N. Fesdekjian of the National Union to investigate the issue of the communications made between the Armenians and the French using flashlights. After debunking the accusation, Fesdekjian demanded the punishment of those people who were responsible for such accusations. However, the mutasarrif requested the moving of the mixed police force located at Ali Bey's house to a place near the battlefront. This last point was refused by the National Union.

Here we cannot ignore a fact that surprised the Armenians. During the armistice period, the Armenians bought large amounts of weapons and ammunitions from Turkish soldiers who had been fighting against them. Even the commander of the Muslim Hospital allowed his colleague to go to the college and sell food supplies to the French in order to distribute the money that was collected. That same commander sold a rifle to the Armenians for 18 Ottoman gold liras. We could thus see the extent of the ideas of Nation and Fatherland among the Turks. For many, these ideas meant nothing. This barbaric people not only refused the French presence in its fatherland but also the presence of all infidels.

I witnessed the beheading of a Turkish hospital guard by a French cannon shell when the man, wrapped in green, was still firing at the general staff building.

His brave and audacious movements mainly reflected his religious fanaticism rather than patriotism. This is why the fighting at Aintab was very violent, even more than battles fought on some European battlefields.

On August 8th, the French received a telegraphic message, saying that French troops under the command of Lieutenant-Colonel Andrea were on their way to Aintab. Their goal was to break the siege and clear Aintab of any Turkish chetes. French troops thereafter wanted to occupy Ghourban Baba and Mardin on August 10th to facilitate Lieutenant Colonel Andrea's entrance into the city. At 2:45, the French attacked Azis Yokushu, located on the southern side of the college. The Turks, after resisting for an hour, withdrew to Ghourban Baba. The French continued their advance and occupied Ghourban Baba, from where the Turks fled, sheltering at Mardin orphanage. The occupation of Ghourban Baba was completed at 1:00. The French once more found their comrades' graves destroyed. That evening Colonel Andrea's battalion held the eastern hills of the city. It left Akcha Koyoun on August 8th and arrived in Aintab on the 10th. Colonel Andrea brought two 15.5cm cannons and 4 vehicles with him.

August 11th

A detachment of Colonel Andrea's battalion, which was camped in the Nourzana Gardens located on the eastern side of the city, started advancing in the morning after coming under heavy attack from the chetes in the Sheikh house. Well fortified in the Sheikh's house, the Turks conducted stubborn resistance against the French. The latter started bombarding the building with their 7.5cm cannons. The building was strong and the Turks were located in special trenches and were thus able to withstand the bombardment.

The French eventually brought in their 15.5cm cannons and pulverized the Turkish soldiers. The latter lost many men when some of the 15.5cm shells fell on the building. This was the first time the French had used it against the Turks. Unable to withstand the bombardment, the Turks fled, leaving the dead and large amounts of ammunition behind. The retreating soldiers were shot down and suffered badly after a machine gun opened fire on them. Once the Sheikh's house was occupied, the only remaining place where numerous Turkish soldiers were still concentrated was the Mardin orphanage.

The Chivalry of the Armenians

The first bomb fell on a machine gun positioned on the eastern wall of the Mardin orphanage. We saw the ensuing slaughter from our tall buildings. When the next few shells hit, the Turks started to retreat towards the Armenian quarter. Since the Turks were surrounded on three sides, the only alternative route open to them was the Armenian quarter that held a neutral stance. Here, the Armenians displayed real chivalry towards their hangmen, who thanked them through letters of gratitude. Had the Armenians been as vicious as the Turks, 600 to 700 Turkish soldiers would have been captured or executed that day. The Armenians not only respected the armistice terms, but also guided the Turks towards the Turkish quarter by carrying the wounded on their backs. The Turkish community was greatly moved by this act and confessed its guilt in stirring up enmity.

Turkish soldiers also started withdrawing from the Muslim Hospital, the Beyaz Ahmed Hotel and the Akyol Mosque.

The French confiscated 18 rifles, many boxes of ammunition and food supplies during the occupation of Mardin. The right flank of Andrea's battalion advanced towards Duluk Hill (on the northern side of the city). 200 chetes, taken by surprise, started fleeing towards the village of Duluk. When the French reached the peak of the hill, they noticed a group of Turkish artillerymen retreating towards Karahuyik. They started bombarding them with their 6.5cm artillery and forced them to flee northwards. They also saw two brigades of Turkish regular soldiers who were retreating towards the village of Sam. The French confronted the Turkish soldiers, who fled to the north leaving behind many dead, a cannon, nine mules and supplies. All the confiscated supplies and ammunition were transported to the college in convoys.

After the Turks abandoned the western side of the Armenian quarter, the Armenians occupied them and recovered their pre-armistice position. Nevertheless, they kept their neutrality.

Colonel Andrea had come to Aintab with the following orders:

> To bombard the city when the need arose, to assert his control. To choose the targets carefully, aiming, for example, at the houses of Kemalist sheikhs and key positions occupied by the enemy. The bombardment of humanitarian centers, mosques and religious institution was banned. To present an ultimatum after every bombardment. To always keep the French pacifying mission in mind.

At about noon, the French presented the Turks with an ultimatum signed by Colonels Andrea and Abady. The ultimatum was carried by a Turkish villager under a while flag from Shrekustu to the city:

1. The peace treaty signed with Turkey puts Aintab under the French mandate.

2. As a sign of respect, the mutasarrif of Aintab, the Turkish notables and the commander of the Nationalist forces were invited to the general staff building before 5 p.m. on that day, August 11th, to demonstrate their subjection.

3. If they refused, the city would be heavily bombarded with larger caliber cannons.

This ultimatum was signed by Colonels Andrea and Abady. The French also demanded a war indemnity worth 1.5 million gold liras and the surrender of the fighters in the city (policemen, soldiers and gendarmes).

At 4:00, the Turks sent the following reply:

1. I received your ultimatum at 3 p.m.

2. I did not know that Aintab was to become part of the French mandate according to the Peace Conference. Therefore, you should extend your deadline until I receive an official order. It is only after that that I will approve your request.

3. We are sure that French civilization will not permit the bombardment of women and children. The declaration made by Mr. Milran clarifies the matter, because he believes that the French won't use cannons in their operations in the East.

Signed by

Sabri Bey, Mutasarrif

The Turks obviously wanted to gain some time. The French started bombarding the city at 6:00, particularly the municipal building (Belediyeh Khanuh) and Heyyeti Merkeziyeh (Saben Khan). The Turks, however, under Ozdemir's command, resisted the French and did not show any signs of surrender. A fire started in the city that claimed many Turkish lives.

The Armenians remained neutral during this bombardment and maintained their relations with the French as well as the Turks. However, a decision had to be made concerning this issue. Captain Reno, during his meeting with the Armenian National Union, stated that the French had decided to occupy the city and restore peace. The newly arrived battalion would not leave without realizing these objectives. However, the National Union, in consideration of the latest conditions, made the following decision:

> Given that there is no significant change in the situation, we do not see the necessity to change our stance. We only allow the National Union to develop official relations with the French and the settlement of the issue of Ilian's house with the Turks. Moreover, the National Union only allows individuals to communicate with the French with the consent of the Union.

August 12th–15th

After the beginning of the French bombardment, the Turks became organized and divided the city into two sections: Muharrem Bey (commander of the regular troops) took charge of the northern part and Arslan Bey, the southern. Ozdemir was appointed as commander-in-chief, and Ferid Bey as the leader of the Nationalist party.

After the first few bombs fell, all men in city capable of bearing arms were conscripted, and they decided to resist the enemy at all costs. The second bombardment began on the morning of August 12th and lasted until nightfall. This time, the French used 7.5cm and 15.5cm cannons. A Turk describing the devastation of this bombardment commented, "The city took on a horrible appearance, the like of which cannot be imagined." The 15.5cm artillery pieces caused a lot of damage. The green, black, yellow and red smoke from the explosions of 50 kg shells filled the streets with a suffocating odor and killed any living being where they fell. The sudden appearance of the 15.5cm cannons forced the population to take shelter on the lower floors of their stone-built buildings. However, this did not protect the poor people. One shell would devastate two buildings and bury all those sheltering in the lower floors.

In a city where thousands of bombs may fall, men, women, and children need shelter. Similarly, the dead need to be buried and the wounded transported to a hospital. In such circumstances, mounting a successful resistance is very hard. The Muslim people, about 60,000 souls, could not come out of their hiding places. Those who dared to do so were either killed or wounded and did not return home.

On August 13th, the French sent a second ultimatum with the following message:

> We confirm our previous ultimatum. If you surrender by nightfall, we might modify our terms. Otherwise, we will continue the bombardment and attack with additional vigor. As a token of your acceptance of our terms, you must raise a white flag on the western tower of the old fortress. Do not waste your lives and properties in vain. Submit to the French authorities who will guarantee a comfortable and prosperous life.
>
> Signed by Andrea & Abady

The Turks, however, replied by raising a red flag on the tower. The French restarted the bombardment of the important Turkish positions and barricades.

August 15th – 19th

The National Union revived the civil committees disbanded during the armistice period. It formed a municipality, with H. Bezjian as its chairman, to control the city's hygiene. A police force was formed under the auspices of the previous chief, S. Karamanougian, to maintain peace in the city. He would have policemen at his disposal, and the gendarmes would obey the commands of these men. Ali Jenani Bey's building was chosen as their headquarters.

A court was established in this same building, comprising H. Karamanougian, T. Kupelian, and Y. Beian.

The Turks still ground wheat using the Armenians' mill. The Armenians still held to their neutrality, even after Colonel Andrea's entry into Aintab and against the will of the French, because the latter had surrendered the Armenians to the Turks and made them sign a conciliatory agreement. As a result we, the Armenians, had established peace and maintained the status quo.

Through a letter sent to the National Union, the mutasarrif pointed out that Armenian soldiers had obstructed the construction of a barricade at a Turkish position located on the right side of the Transversal and prevented the entry of some Turks into the Armenian quarter. As a response, the National Union wrote that these issues were due to misunderstandings and that the appropriate measures would be taken.

The National Union demanded some explanation from Adour Levonian regarding his meeting with the French. The latter stated that the meeting was of a personal nature and not a political one. The National Union then made it clear that if the French wanted to have political meetings, they should only meet with the National Union.

Chapter 18

French Efforts to Break Armenian Neutrality

On August 16th, Captain Reno requested that all the Turks who had entered the Armenian quarter be guided to the general staff building. This proposal was for personal reasons and did not have any hostile overtones. During discussion of this issue, he sent another letter demanding the cessation of all Armenian relations with the Turks and the detention of Turks who had entered the Armenian quarter. These acts were the beginning of a French policy that tended to pull the Armenians into the conflict and hence end their neutrality. The French were suspicious about the Armenians' position, especially since they heard that Father Nerses Tavoukjian had met with Chitji Ferid Effendi and other Turkish generals at the Kurkjians' house. Father Tavoukjian had recommended the following:

> Resistance is futile, since the Entente powers decided to make Aintab part of the French mandate and it is impossible to make the French reverse their decision. Your national interests require an understanding with the occupying armies. A futile fight will only destroy your young people and add more bloodshed. Had the liberation of this land been possible through fighting, I would have recommended resistance until the last man. However, when all hope is gone, why do you still kill your young men? Submit yourselves to the occupying army, grow and develop, establish schools, and who knows, maybe one day you will realize your dreams and liberate these lands again. I reiterate that stubbornness will only lead to futile death.

The Turks found the priest's words very reasonable. However, the actual circumstances had placed them in a situation where surrender to the French was not possible since all the Turkish notables, commanders and government employees had convened at Kara Tarla Mosque on that Friday and concluded that they were not able to resist a Franco-Armenian alliance.

Some had suggested that it was better to agree with the French and surrender, otherwise the latter would continue the devastation of the city. In other words, the Turkish notables displayed a willingness to surrender, given that the enemy was undefeatable. However, the fanatical Turkish youth and the military had rejected this proposal, considered these men as traitors to the nation, and had decided to continue fighting, fearing that in case of a surrender, the Armenians would be the slaughterers.

The Turks had two choices: either to fight until the last soldier and surrender the city in ruins or break the siege and leave the city. They did not even reply to the French ultimatum, since they were able to resort to either one of these choices whenever it was possible. Thus the Turkish notables left the Kurkjians' house without even concluding anything. As the reader may have noticed, this meeting did not have an anti-French character and neutrality was always favorable for the Armenians. However, some people, who had "Sold their honor for a few gold liras" had stirred up some suspicions among the French, saying that the Armenians were involved in anti-French movements and were helping the Turks. The common usage of the flour mill in the Armenian quarter was presented as proof of this accusation. We, the Armenians, could barely import food supplies, and that with great difficulty; whereas we were able to buy large quantities of wheat, at good prices, through an opening in the Balekluh barricade. We acted according to our national interests. Then, one day, a French machine gun opened fire on the Armenian street of Kastel Bashi from Mardin that left a woman and a boy wounded, and a man dead. The National Union appealed to the French and demanded an explanation for this. The reply was that the soldiers at Mardin had been replaced and were still unaware as to which direction to shoot. They had accidentally fired at the Armenian street, mistaking it for a Turkish position.

Another day, a French 15.5cm shell fell on Soulahians' building, destroyed its walls and sent 200 fragments onto the surrounding rooftops and street. The National Union appealed to the French once more, since the Armenian quarter was under bombardment. The reply was that the gunner, named Eyyoub Oghlu, had accidentally fired at the left side of the tower, instead of the right. The Armenians soon noted that similar mistakes would increase in the future and they decided to meet with the French command.

The supply efforts of the French army were also poor. Their supplies would only last for a couple of days – until August 19th – and bringing fresh supplies from Akcha Koyoun would take at least five days. The French were forced to withdraw some of their troops to deal with this situation and thus weakened the siege lines. It was deemed best to bring the French troops withdrawn from Duluk Baba to the hills of Haji Baba. The Turks immediately occupied Duluk Baba and fired 30 shells at the French troops holding the Aleppo road. The French knew that the Turks had chosen Bedir Keoy (16 km to the north) as a center for their outside forces. A squad of cavalry was sent there on scouting duties and the Turks opened fire on them from Sbateren. They always attacked when a French convoy was leaving Aintab.

The French sent a third ultimatum on August 17th. However, the Turks had already received good news and ammunition from the outside, and they replied in the usual manner. The French then started a bombardment for the third time. Hundreds of Turkish houses were destroyed and countless lives were lost. This was why the Turks hid their families in underground caves and basements. The people squashed in those caves started to suffer from epidemics a few days later. Typhus claimed the lives of many people. Furthermore, there was a shortage of doctors and medicine and they began to suffer from hunger. Two Mosques were overflowing with wounded and others suffered on the sidewalks and streets. There was a lack of chloroform and tendirdion, forcing the doctors to amputate the limbs of the wounded with terrible suffering.

During the fighting, the wounded of the Turkish army were treated by Shehabeddin, Fakhreddin, and Mejid. The latter operated on 50 patients daily. We can infer that the Turks were losing a great many men. At noon, when the bombardment was reduced, the commander of the police force, Talat, summoned a large crowd around him and went to the Hiyyeti Merkeziyeh, where he shouted:

> Brothers, have mercy! You have turned the city into a slaughter house. This situation has become unbearable. The people will revolt. What will the end be? There is no hope from the outside. It would be stupid to think about anything other than an agreement. Give us the order, and we will raise the white flag.

Ozdemir and the Hiyyeti Merkeziyeh dismissed these people and expelled them from the city. On the same day, another incident occurred at Dabbagh Khaneh Street. The people there secretly decided to prepare a white flag and raise it on the fortress. The Hiyyeti Merkezieh discovered this plan too and punished 20 of the collaborators.

When these events were occurring in the city, one could also see movements in the Turkish army outside. They were preparing a plan of attack. The night was dark. The Turks exploited this opportunity and mounted a violent attack. They had already bombarded the college and Chitji Kharaf with their 10.5cm artillery by the evening. They started the attack at night and moved north. Other fighters started harassing the French from inside the city, who were badly weakened by the convoy's departure. 40-50 men managed to penetrate the French positions and bolster the Turks' morale.

Seeing this success, the inhabitants of the city celebrated victory with drums and trumpets until morning, coming as far as the Armenian quarter. The Turkish people, willing to surrender, had "been transformed into a lion" as a result of a minor victory.

The representatives of the National Union, in accordance with their decision, went to the general staff building, where they welcomed the Colonel and explained the Armenians' situation. The Colonel gave the following reply:

> The hour of welcoming us has not yet arrived. I had information about your situation and have given the appropriate orders. You were about to break off relations with the Turks a few days ago. From now on, you will not communicate with the Turks and will capture any Turks that come into the Armenian quarter. These captives will be exchanged for the French prisoners detained by the Turks. We will defend the Latin Church and Pasha Sokaguh. The defense of the Transversal is your responsibility. If you don't want to do that, we can defend that too.

The National Union was satisfied with this proposal and, in order to avoid any mistaken bombardment of the Armenian quarter, decided to raise white flags on the Armenian positions on the Transversal.

The Turks positioned on Haji Baba Hill started bombarding the college and Chitji Kharaf on August 18th. A rocket signaled the attack at night. A squad of Senegalese soldiers, who were defending Haji Baba Hill, were attacked, but resisted. On the following day – August 19th – the French noticed that the aforementioned squad was not able to withstand any further fighting, so they were forced to pull them back, covering their retreat using cannon fire. The Turks were thus able to break the French lines and establish a connection with their interior forces.

The Turks raised the Ottoman flag on Haji Baba Hill and celebrated their victory with great festivities. They had come from Marash, Ourfa, Sourouj, Bazarjek, Behesni, Berejik and Nizib. During the evening, some French troops left Aintab to hold the Sazgin hills in order to facilitate the passage of the convoy through Nafak Boghazuh (200 chetes had opened fire on the convoy around Jurum Evrek). When the French convoy that was leaving Nafak Boghazuh reached Aintab's gardens, the Turks attacked it again. Nevertheless, French cannons and machine guns pushed the enemy back. When the convoy arrived at Ghourban Baba, the Turks started bombarding it with their 10.5cm cannons, resulting in a few dead animals and soldiers.

August 20th–September 8th

A battalion was formed on August 21st under Colonel Andrea's leadership, whose mission was the annihilation of the chetes located in the northern part of the city. Sam Keoy was the center of the Turkish command at that time. The battalion eventually engaged in several fierce battles around Ibrahimli, the Esbadren hills (lasting about 2 hours), and Duluk Baba. The enemy always fled, leaving behind many dead. Finally, the French army entered Sam Keoy, where it confiscated 10.5cm cannon shells, about 12,000 cartridges, carts and 40 tons of wheat and barley. The battalion lost 30 men during those days. It then returned to Aintab. The Turkish losses were greater, since they were always taken by surprise.

Colonel Abady declared to the National Union, through a note numbered 22 and 360/A, that besides the Latin Church, where the French had placed Senegalese soldiers on August 17th, all the Armenian positions and Mr. Levonian should only respond to the military commands of the French authorities.

The National Union responded to this note with following letter:

> We are satisfied with this arrangement and believe it is exactly for this reason that the French decided to include the Armenian quarter within their remit. Due to recent events, the people have been impoverished and are starving. Without your support, our situation would be worse.
>
> The Armenians trust their lives and honor to French protection. Moreover, given the defective nature of the police force, we request that the new organization be compatible with French law.

August 23rd. The Turks once more refused the ultimatum sent by the French.

August 24th. The National Union summoned the Armenian military leaders to a meeting at the Prelacy, where it provided details of the policy to be adopted by the Armenian community.

The Armenians Strive to Adopt a Position

> The nub of the Armenian position should be the elaboration of friendly relations with the French and the avoidance of any hostilities with the Turks. The National Union has frequently pointed this out during its meetings with the French command, which has approved our point of view. Our national interests require that we avoid being complaisant concerning foreign powers and reserve our sacrifices for that purpose. The city has been made part of the French mandate. Therefore, we cannot pursue any national goals here. We don't have any reason to stimulate the hatred of the French nor the enmity of the Turks. The Military Body and the National Union have approved this position.

This position was unanimously approved by the military leaders.

August 26th. Another battalion left Aintab for the north-west to pursue the Turkish chetes. It reached as far as Kizil Hisar, where the villagers expressed their loyalty. The French troops fought against the Turkish chetes around Balluh Kara and Nafak Boghazuh, pushed the enemy back towards Nizib, then returned to Aintab. During their absence, the Turks bombarded the college, Ghourban Baba, and Mardin on August 27th with their 10.5cm cannons. The Turks always fired their cannon in the morning, so as not to show their locations, since muzzle flashes at night would let the French know their position and distance. It was only in late November when the Turks started night-time bombardments. The Turks initiated a large night attack against the hill located 2,500 meters to the west of the college. After wasting large quantities of ammunition, they finally occupied the hill, where there hadn't been a French force. On the morning of August 28th, the French pushed the Turks back using their 7.5cm cannons. Another attack was stopped and then repulsed by the French when some Turks located in the city tried to assault Mardin.

Chapter 19

The "Color" of the Franco-Armenian Relationship

This is the description of the meeting between the National Union and the Chairman of the Military Body on the one side and Colonel Abady and Captain Reno on the other. This description is essential for an understanding of the nature of the Franco-Armenian relationship. It occurred on the afternoon of Tuesday, August 26th. Colonel Andrea first welcomed those present and stated that he truly wanted to meet with the delegates of the National Union.

> From April 1st until the signing of the Armistice, the Armenians exhibited a very friendly attitude towards the French. We expected to see a similar reception this time, yet the reality turned out to be different. We hoped for your assistance. Relief does not imply enmity against the Turks. It's a moral act. You could have met with the Turks and told them about the French, pointing out that our mandate would be beneficial for them, and that their city would prosper and develop according to European standards. Moreover, the French would not violate your honor, rights and religion but rather respect them. This is what we had been expecting from you. It is true that we abandoned you during the armistice and became the cause of your current misery, but you should also know that it was the turcophile policy of the moment that forced us to act in the way we did. Currently, the situation has changed. At that time, the leader of this country was unknown. Now, the Peace Conference has placed Kilis, Aintab, Hromgala, Yetesia and Mardin under French mandate. This decision is irreversible and the French will forcefully take possession of these cities. It is therefore your duty to re-establish your friendly attitude to us, given the current political situation of the region. Moreover, let it be known that during the Armistice period, the French as well as the Armenians made mistakes.

Father Nerses Tavoukjian responded to these words with the following words:

> It is true that the policy you adopted during the armistice period deeply affected and vexed us. However, it is equally true that that policy was not decided by the generals located here but emanated from your government's national interests. As proof, Colonel

> Abady and Captain Reno told us, on July 10th, that we should surrender to the Turks by July 11th. Although they [the Colonel and Captain] were in tears and tormented, they could change nothing. These developments do not mean that our regard for France has changed. We owe our education to France, and nothing can change our sympathy towards you. We have been impatiently waiting for your arrival and when you entered Aintab on August 11th, our eyes filled with tears of joy. You demand our moral support. Since the first day of your arrival, we have provided much assistance and spread your good name. We have already told you about our meeting with the mutasarrif and Ferid Effendi. Unfortunately, Colonel Abady banned every contact with the Turks and we have complied with his orders. If you wish, we can still be of help to you.

Colonel Andrea noted that the cessation of relations was a mistake.

> You are able to receive information on the city from the Turks since you still have some kind of relationship with them. You can convince the non-Kemalists about the hellish conspiracy of the Kemalists, and thus help us. We do not wish for enmity between you and the Turks, but rather seek your moral support.

The priest pointed out that it was difficult to obtain supplies and that French support was needed. He wished for a quick solution to this conflict and the recovery of the Armenians. At that time 6,000 people were receiving supplies from the Directorate for Provisions. The French promised to write to General De La Motte, asking him to make the necessary arrangements for the transportation of supplies.

August 27th. Some people interrupted a meeting discussing the departure of some people using French carts. The people protested and were finally dispersed after the Military Body interceded.

August 30th. The French convoy from Akcha Koyoun arrived in Aintab.

As we have previously mentioned, the French were also in a difficult situation as far as supplies were concerned. They needed 10 tons of barley daily to feed their 2,000 horses and mules. Thus the need was seen, on August 31st, to send a battalion to Nizib. The aim was to punish all the rebels located in the eastern part of the city and gather supplies for the army between September 1st–7th. Large quantities of cereal were located around Nizib. The battalion marched out on September 1st at 3 o'clock and was attacked by Turkish chetes barely two kilometers from the city.

After 30 minutes of fierce fighting, the Turks retreated to the east, when they noticed that the French troops had occupied Ouroum Evlegi Hill. The Turks left large amounts of ammunition behind during this battle which the French confiscated and loaded onto their carts. The French arrived at Sinan and then the village of Giavour, where they camped that night. The French knew from two Turkish captives that they had been fighting against a force of 1,000 men composed of regular soldiers, cavalry and artillery.

The French continued their mission on September 2nd and arrived at Oroul. The inhabitants prepared a welcoming reception for them and expressed their gratitude for the French mandate. They requested the stationing of an army brigade at Oroul, as protection against chete raids. The French replied that they were unable to provide every village with a separate brigade. They suggested that the villagers organize themselves and resist the chetes, thus also helping the French authorities in their struggle against the Kemalist forces. The villagers argued that to do that they required weapons, ammunition and a leader, which they lacked. All these developments seemed normal to the Colonel.

September 3rd. The French arrived at Nizib. They surrounded the city but found a welcoming reception. They were invited to the government building. There, the Turks reiterated the same idea: that the Kemalist had left before their arrival and that the villagers were dissatisfied with their government and wished to see French authority in the region. On the following day (September 4th), the French sent a small detachment to Berejik and Rum Kaleh, where no large Kemalist forces were present. The French established a new government in Nizib and continued their journey to Oroul. On 5th they bought large quantities of supplies from Nizib and paid high prices for them.

September 6th. The French entered Tel Bashar and Sadek Effendi's village which had been a source of great misfortune for them since the first day of fighting. Before their entrance into Tel Bashar, the French had a fierce battle with the Turks, who avoided being routed by fleeing northwards. Many of them were followed by French cavalrymen and were killed or captured. The French camped that night at Tel Bashar, Mezereh and Zramba and confiscated 60 tons of barley, 100 oxen and 500 sheep that belonged to Sadik Effendi. They told the few remaining old men that the property was confiscated as punishment for their effendi's rebellion.

September 7th. The battalion returned to Aintab after a minor clash with Turkish chetes at the Nurzana gardens.

The following developments took place in Aintab during these military operations. After the departure of the Nizib battalion, the Turks, who thought the French had left permanently, attacked Chitji Kharaf and the Sheikh's house (Samsak Tepeh). The Turks bombarded the aforementioned places with their 7.5cm cannons on the morning of September 1st. They started using their 10.5cm cannons in the afternoon, bombarding Chitji Kharaf once more, but were silenced by a heavy retaliatory bombardment from the French. Readers already know that the French did not have the troops necessary for a complete siege of the city, imported supplies from Akcha Koyoun, and only pursued the chetes in areas around the city. The last two military operations were vital to the French, which is why they did not have the necessary number of soldiers in the city. As we have previously said, the French had withdrawn from Haji Baba and had completely abandoned their northern and eastern positions since July 19th. The Turks exploited the moment to move troops, supplies and ammunition into the city. They had, moreover, evacuated a total of 40,000 people out of the city over several nights.

These developments led to dissatisfaction among the Turkish fighters, since most of the people departing belonged to the rich class. The fighters insisted that they were poor people and had nothing left in Aintab. They refused to die protecting the lands and properties of the rich. The Kemalists were finally able to persuade them that the departure of one part of the population was essential, since there was not enough supplies for all. As a result, the Kemalists decided to exact a departure fee from every family leaving, according to each family's financial abilities. There were cases where 800 Ottoman gold liras were taken from a single family. The departing families passed through the Dabbagh Khaneh Street and left the city through the eastern and south-eastern valleys. They were often caught in clashes and suffered many losses. The French troops, positioned particularly at the Sheikh's house (Samsak Tepeh), harassed them a great deal. On September 2nd, the Turks attacked the Samsak Tepeh from two directions to obliterate the French threat. Due to the darkness of the night, the Turks missed the enemy and started killing each other. When the French also began shooting, part of the Turkish forces returned to the city and the rest fled, leaving behind many dead. Despite this, however, many Turkish civilians left the city that night and went to Marash, Nizib, Berejik, Rum Kaleh, Ourfa, Malatia, Harput and Behesni among other places. 20,000 people remained in the city.

After the Nizib battalion returned to the city on September 7th, the French sent the 5th ultimatum to the Turks. The Turks then replied that the city could not surrender as long as the people could see the bombardment of the French positions by the Nationalist forces. But Kemalist forces were absent. As a response, the French sent the following letter:

> 1. According to the peace treaty signed with Turkey, Aintab is placed under French mandate, and every Turk should be aware of this. Whoever opposes the terms of the Armistice, whether a military man or a civilian, is a rebel.
>
> 2. It is with great pain that we bombard a city where there are lots of innocent people. However, the commander of the Turkish forces, Ozdemir, and the majority of the Turkish troops are still in the city. Let him leave with his soldiers and choose open warfare, rather than hide his fighters inside mosques and Red Crescent buildings.
>
> 3. The bombardment will not stop until all shooting has ceased.
>
> Colonel Abady and Colonel Andrea

The Turks wrote the following response on September 9th.

> To the French command of Aintab,
>
> We do not hide behind the Red Crescent and neither do the honorable civilians of Aintab. Our lionhearted soldiers are not assailants, but protectors, whereas, you, the embodiment of civilization, perpetrate an unprecedented crime. You bombard our mosques and hospital with your cannons, but we don't fire at the wounded in the Red Cross center. Had you had mercy for the innocent, the blood of the children would not have been shed. I have already proposed the idea of open warfare to Mr. Boyd. So, to avoid the insertion of a shameful chapter in the pages of your history, I am ready to negotiate with you and wait for your reply.
>
> Ozdemir

We can fully prove the falseness of these statements since the Turks were not able to leave the city and resort to open warfare. Their outside forces were always defeated. How could one expect a Turkish soldier to leave his position in an impregnable city like Aintab and resort to open warfare? It was obvious that Ozdemir wanted to gain some time and delay any bombardment through such correspondence. The French did not respond to this letter and intensified the bombardment.

September 8th–October 1st

From what we have described so far, the reader might ask why the French did not occupy the city with a single general attack. The French command discussed such a plan with the chairman of the Military Body but it was rejected for the following reasons:

1. The lack of a sufficient numbers of soldiers required for the general occupation of the city.

2. Even if the required number of soldiers were present, the Turks had fortified the city in such a way that its occupation would have cost the French many lives. It was not worth it. The French command always opposed the loss of lives.

What should have been done? The best plan was to eventually arm the inhabitants, intensify the siege, and hinder the movement of the Turkish convoys transporting supplies into the city.

The Turks were already unable to transport supplies into the city because of the French siege line in the morning. They moved supplies at night but had little success during the day as the French cannons controlled the siege line. For these reasons, the Turks were not able to provide their population with the necessary quantity of supplies.

Although the Armenians of Aintab always prepared their winter provisions during summer, the war had disrupted their annual tradition this time. The Turks were using their remaining supplies which were sufficient for two to three months. Once their provisions were finished, the city would have to surrender. This was the adopted plan: to starve the city into submission rather than occupy it through a general attack.

On the other hand, the French supply efforts were also in difficulties. 6,000 French troops and 2,000 transport animals were stationed in Aintab. Therefore, it was decided to send a convoy to Akcha Koyoun once every week. Seven-ninths of the supplies that the convoys brought would be used directly by the troops, and the remaining two-ninths would be stored in the warehouses. Armenian convoys would accompany those of the French in the future, thus bringing supplies for the Armenian population too.

Aintab in ruins.

Greater importance was given to the supply efforts starting from September 8th. On that day, the Turks bombarded the French position with their 10.5cm and 7.5cm cannons. The French organized an attack on the following day on the northern Turkish positions to capture their cannons. The French arrived at Sam Koy but could not achieve much because the Turks had brought their cannons close to the city and were firing at the French troops. Whenever the Turks spotted a French convoy, they would notify their artillerymen, who moved the cannons northwards. Pursuing Turkish artillery was impossible and the Turks always had two hours to hide their cannons.

After fierce fighting around Nurzana, the French supply convoy entered Aintab on September 13th. The Turks lost 30 men and suffered many wounded.

On September 16th, a convoy left Aintab and was attacked by Turkish chetes near Nurzana. The French killed countless chetes, one of whom was a general. The convoy returned to Aintab on September 20th, after defeating the Turks at Nurzana.

September 20th. There was a clash between the Armenians and the Turks at Dardaghlian. As a result, the National Union, Dr. H. Bezjian and some other notables met with Ozdemir (the mutasarrif had returned). The latter complained that the Armenians were always acting in favor of the French, despite the neutral position they had adopted. After receiving clarification, and the rejection of the accusations made, Ozdemir finally decided to contact the command at Ibrahimli and establish a neutral zone, restricting the movement of the two parties beyond their limits.

The French bombarded the city ceaselessly from September 9th to the 23rd. Every shell caused the death of many Turkish civilians in the city. The hospitals and mosques were replete with the wounded. Others were treated inside their houses by old ladies since the shortage of doctors had made the situation very difficult. Everyone was hiding in their basements and no one dared to come out. Often, families were unaware of the deaths of their neighbors. The Turks were unable to report the exact number of their casualties under such conditions, since those entrusted with this task would often not return. People were either lost in a street or buried under the ruins.

In such circumstances, the Turks threatened the Turkish notables of Aintab who had sheltered at Aleppo. They considered them traitors. During the one-week ultimatum, Ozdemir begged them to return to Aintab, otherwise their property would have been confiscated and their houses burnt down. Moreover, the Turkish commander ordered the execution of many Turks accused of betrayal.

The 5th convoy left Aintab on September 24th and was attacked by 4-5,000 Turkish chetes near Ouroum Evleg. The Turkish gunners fired 40-50 shells at the convoy, but the French successfully cleared the area of chetes and continued their journey.

Chapter 20

Correspondence Between Ozdemir and Colonel Andrea

This chapter looks as some of the correspondence between Ozdemir and Colonel Andrea. This correspondence began on September 23rd and lasted until the 28th. Its aim was, as we have previously said, the cessation of the bombardment and to gain some time.

Colonel Andrea to Ozdemir, September 23rd (number 23):

> The responsibility for our bombardment is yours, since you have decided to resist, whereas the interests of the people requires you to surrender and cooperate with us for the well-being of this country. Every man will be free and each man's religion and family will be inviolable. The French have a respectful attitude towards you, as they have for the Muslim population of Algeria, Tunis and Morocco.

Ozdemir to Colonel Andrea, September 23rd:

> You preach about the freedom of people and of French chivalry, yet I do not believe your lies. I wonder why such a powerful nation like France does not recognize the independence of a weak Turkey and attempts to give the Armenians the upper hand. The Armenians have been the hangmen of the Turks. Thus, I wish to "carry on" with this conflict outside Aintab. For this reason I wish to meet the French commander alone (without the microbe next to him – the Armenian interpreter). I will be accompanied by a Turkish doctor, fluent in French.
>
> Ozdemir

It was obvious, in the aforementioned letter, that Ozdemir demanded a private meeting with the French commander. On September 25th, the French replied by stating their willingness to meet the Turks at around 2 o'clock that night. The meeting would take place at the Mardin orphanage where the French were located and the Turkish commander would remain unnoticed by the Armenians.

First, Ozdemir approved the French suggestion, but later presented the French with another proposal. The Turkish commander claimed that the Turks had supposedly obstructed the entrance to his office and blocked his way to the Mardin orphanage. He therefore suggested that the French commander should come to a Turkish position near the Armenian quarter, where the Turkish crowd would welcome him with a good reception. The French refused this proposal, assuming that Ozdemir would invite the French commander to his office and then send him back after refusing his proposals. Such a scenario would encourage the Turkish crowd and boost Ozdemir's standing. The French warned the Turks that if they did not accept their proposal by 5 o'clock, they would continue the bombardment. The Turks did not reply and the French continued the bombardment. As we have noted, the Turks gained some time through this correspondence and fortified their barricades. On the other hand, the French received some information concerning the Turkish positions in the city:

1. Around 500 regular and irregular soldiers were stationed near Ferkah and Musullu Street. They had built underground tunnels for communication purposes.
2. Barricades destroyed by the French bombardment in the morning were restored by Turkish workers at night.
3. The French scouted the important Turkish positions and pinpointed the defensive buildings.
4. Such information was provided to the French artillery and soldiers.

Clashes occurred between the Turks and Armenians on September 27th at Yokaruh Beyligi. When an explanation was demanded, the Turks claimed that some French soldiers had been seen among the Armenian soldiers. This claim was refuted.

The French were waiting for their convoy that was due to arrive on September 28th. Noticing that the convoys always had clashes with Turkish chetes around Urum Evleg and the fact that supplies were getting into the city from Nizib, the French decided to hold the Nizib road and make it part of their siege line in order to protect the convoy's entry into Aintab. Thus, the French got rid of the chetes hiding around Nurzana. On the same night, the French confiscated a Turkish supply caravan near Nizib.

The Turks attempted to push the French back from their newly occupied positions on September 29th with a heavy bombardment. 200 Turkish fighters also attacked the French siege line but were pushed back by French machine guns. The Turks returned to the city before dawn, leaving behind many dead.

Chapter 21

The French Oblige the Armenians to End Their Neutrality

Adour Levonian met with Colonel Andrea on September 29th and was told that the French had decided to station soldiers on the Transversal and attack the Turkish positions. Levonian gave this information to the National Union and, although they approved this plan, warned the French command about repercussions, such as the bombardment of the Armenian quarter by the Turks and the worsening of the situation with regard to supplies.

At 5 o'clock in the evening, a conference was held comprising the members of the National Union, the Military Body, delegates of the political parties and the Convention of 28.

28 people discussed the repercussions that the French attack could lead to in the Armenian quarter and the situation it would create. Some of the attendees, opposed to the ending of neutrality, insisted that the Armenians should not take part in the conflict. The debate ended when news arrived that French soldiers were spreading out inside the Armenian positions. They had emptied the Barsoumian College and transformed it into the general staff building. Similarly, some Senegalese soldiers were placed inside the Y.M.C.A, the Red Cross buildings and Bulbul Hoja's house. There was thus no need for further debate. It was a fait accompli. So, it was decided to end neutrality and take part in the conflict alongside the French. After fighting for 70 days, lowering the French flags, reconciliation with the Turks and adopting various precautionary measures not to fall into Turkish traps, it was the French troops besieging the city who demanded that the Armenians end their neutrality and get involved in the conflict once more. We did not have the freedom to choose our position. We were not the masters of our situation, either in wartime or peace. We could not operate freely. This was why, if the Armenians decided to continue their fight against the Turks, they would have violated the armistice terms. Had we not violated the armistice terms, the French artillery would have bombarded our positions. The success of the armistice required a sacrifice, and nothing would have served it better than the Armenians of Aintab. However, we did not become the victim. It was clear that the French authorities had compelled

us to sign a treaty with the Turks and had lost all hope in us. However, we could also say that the cleverness and experience of the Armenians of Aintab saved them from disaster. We did not succumb to the Turks: we defended ourselves and survived.

After the stationing of French soldiers in some Armenian positions, the latter were eventually drawn into the war and fought bravely at the side of the French until the fall of the city.

When the Turks saw this change on Transversal Street, an ultimatum was sent to the Armenians. They demanded the maintenance of neutrality and a refusal to permit the stationing of French soldiers, otherwise the Turks would bombard the Armenian positions. Due to the circumstances, no reply was sent to the Turks since, on September 30th, the French forces at the Transversal started a heavy bombardment of the Turkish positions, thus making the Armenians take part in a renewal of the Armeno-Turkish conflict.

Then, about noon on the same day, September 30th, the Turks started bombarding the eastern hills of the city that had just been occupied by the French as part of their operation to hold the Nizib road. The bombardment lasted until 3:45 in the morning. The Turks attacked a French position previously assaulted many times (the nearest position to the city), and the French pushed the enemy back. After an hour, another attack – the third – began from the southern side of the road to Nizib, which also ended in defeat for the Turks. After a couple of minutes, a squad of Nationalist soldiers consisting of 150 fighters approached the French positions and prepared to assault them. The night was dark and the French had withdrawn from their positions. Nevertheless, the French commander summoned reserve troops for assistance and commenced a sudden attack on the Turks, pursuing them as far as the city. In the morning, 35 dead bodies were counted near the French positions. The Turkish casualties were greater.

The *Anaforji* Army

The Armenians of Aintab started using the term "anaforji" during the war. The term was previously unknown to them. "Anforji" meant a man who appropriated the belongings of others. During the war in Aintab, the difficulties in finding supplies and the threatening famine had compelled some people to use this "art". Eventually this "art" was systematized and regularized under the protection of the Armenian gendarmerie with

French consent. As it is known to the reader, the city of Aintab was surrounded, yet fields and vegetable-gardens were located in areas defended by French machine guns and cannons beyond the siege lines. It was therefore decided that every man should go and bring supplies in, thus supporting their own supply efforts, as well as supplying the French with the necessary vegetables. Thanks to these "anaforjis," every kind of vegetable was found in the Armenian market and was sold at low prices.

Such people formed an army. They would gather before dawn at a safe place on Mardin Hill and later return, many carrying bags or baskets. They numbered around 5-600 people. When the gendarmes arrived, the commander of the "anaforji" army would signal the time for departure, and all of them, armed with knives or hoes, would go to Turkish or Armenian fields and reap different kinds of vegetables. When the baskets were full, they returned to the city. Some sold more than the amount they needed. The Armenian municipality began buying supplies for the Armenian fighters. Some people made fortunes through this "business." During the vintage season, there were some people who carried baskets on their backs and transported them into the city on foot. This army of ants supplied the city until winter, yet their lives was always in danger, since people would cross the French line of defense and mix with Turkish "anaforjis." This often ended with fighting between the Armenian and Turkish guards who accompanied the "anaforjis". On one occasion, a 15 year old boy and the onions he was carrying in a bag were both hit by enemy bullets. Armenian "anaforjis" did not suffer any losses, yet Turkish "anaforji" casualties were significant, since the latter often went near the French positions.

One day I was wandering through the fields when I witnessed a strange debate. "Anaforjis" were dispersed throughout the field. An Armenian came to his field and saw that some "anaforjis" were already harvesting the crops. He told them to leave the field, but the latter refused. They explained to the owner that the system of private ownership had been stopped and that they had the right to collect crops from wherever they wanted. Moreover, they told him that if his vineyard did contain 500 liters of grapes, he was still able to collect 10 times more by going to the unattended Turkish vineyards. In the end, the owner left, went to a

Turkish field and loaded his mules with large amounts of grapes before returning to the city. The difficult situation created by the war had created this temporary system.

Five to six clashes occurred during these three or four months because of the “anaforjis” but fortunately nobody was killed.

October 1st–November 1st

The Armenians Reveal the True Nature of Their Policy.

A delegation met with Colonels Abady and Andrea and Captain Reno on the 1st October, at 4: 30, and stated the following:

> We have entered a new phase since yesterday. The friendly attitude of the Armenians towards the French and the hatred towards the Turks is already known to you. We fought by your side from April 1st, until June 8th. Your policy changed after that. We were forced to adopt a new policy since we were left on our own against the Turks. As you know, we declared our neutrality in this conflict. You are also well aware that our neutrality is not stipulated by international law. Our neutrality is hostile to the Turks and friendly towards you. On July 21st, when the Turks attempted to occupy our positions in order to expand their front against you, we resisted by resorting to arms, whereas when you occupied our positions yesterday, we only presented our protests and arguments, which were ignored. We kept our neutrality, as long as it did not hamper your military operations. Thus, when you felt the need to occupy our positions to facilitate your military expeditions, we were ready to give them to you. You occupied our positions yesterday and the Turks started firing at us. We could not stay silent and indifferent of course. We were forcibly drawn into the war again and end our neutrality. Therefore, the Armenian National Union places all its resources and men at your service. We wait for your orders.

Colonel Andrea was very satisfied by this statement and praised the policy hitherto adopted by the Armenians. He also apologised for the French policy change. He declared that the current policy of the French was unchangeable and that Aintab belonged to the French. So, he asked the Armenians to maintain their policy, since the French were about to take possession of the city by force.

In response, the Armenians said that their previous policy was also structured to accommodate French demands and that the latter had replied to our countless appeals by praising our neutrality and only requested our moral support.

Besides expressing their gratitude, the Armenians demanded an increase in French relief. They argued that they were sympathetic to the French until now, but they had now become their military ally.

It was pointed out that in order to develop successful cooperation, representatives of both sides ought to enjoy mutual trust.

Colonel Andrea promised to deliver the necessary assistance. Moreover Colonel Andrea and Adour Levonian would decide the role and responsibility of the Armenian fighters in this new situation.

October 2nd. The National Union re-established the Fuel Committee, since winter was near and the people needed wood. The members of this committee were T. Kupelian, H. Ferejian, M. Ammiyan, H. Piranian, G. Apanian, K. Karamanougian, Kh. Kabakian, N. Kharajian, Yacoub Danielian, M. Haserjian, and M. Karamanougian. Thanks to their systematic activity, the mulberry and walnut trees in the city's southern gardens had been cut down and brought into the city. Hence, we had large amounts of combustible material.

Educational efforts were not ignored. A new trusteeship was formed and all the children were invited to go to school. The two important school buildings of the city were filled with students. When a bombardment started, they were dispersed and resumed their work once it was over. The Armenian quarter resumed its normal life. Stores were opened, artisans began working, and hundreds of shops transformed Akyol Street into a grand market.

While the Armenian soldier was fighting in his position under bombardment, the barber was shaving, the shoe-maker was repairing shoes, weavers were weaving and others were entertaining themselves in coffee houses. Some bathhouses started operating and the Armenian quarter turned into a lucrative neighborhood, with French soldiers and Armenians as customers.

This situation became normal for everyone. Many merchants made fortunes, as artisans worked day and night, such as jewelers and tailors. They were not bothered by the shelling. One day I came across a blacksmith who was working. Suddenly, a shell fell and damaged one of the iron bars located next to him. After uttering a few insults, he continued his work. At the Eyyoub Oghlu market some people were playing chess. When a shell destroyed the roof of a nearby house, the chess players cleaned the dust off their clothes and continued their game. When a Turkish shell hit one of the National Union (Kastel Bashi, Kiulhan Damuh) meeting houses, the delegates soon resumed their conference.

October 2nd. A few French soldiers in Ghourban Baba were wounded by shots fired from a minaret. The Iki Sherifeli Mosque minaret was used as a firing point. On the following day, the French destroyed the minaret with one cannon shot and sent the following letter to the mutasarrif:

> I have often referred to occurrences of sniper fire from mosque minarets. I must inform you that if any such event is repeated in the future, I will bombard the mosques without hesitation. I was recently informed that shots had been fired from the minaret of Iki Sherifeyi Mosque. Our cannons destroyed it today.
>
> I assure you that your other positions will face the same fate.
>
> Please accept…etc.

October 4th. The French fired 200 shells at the Turkish streets.

1. Attack on the Nigoghosian College (October 5th)

Two important military operations were carried out against the Nigoghosian College that ended in failure. To understand the details of these operations clearly, one has to describe a map of this position.

The avenue on the northern side of the city extended from the west to the east and included the Latin Church, Tufah Hamamen, and the Akyol Mosque that were under Armenian and French control. These presented the demarcation line between Turkish and Armenian fighters, starting from the Nigoghosian College and extending as far as Kezeljeh Oba. The Turkish positions therefore ended at the Chinarli Mosque and Nigoghosian College that were connected through underground tunnels.

The road running south from the Latin Church, west of the Chinarli Mosque, led to Kiulhan Damuh. The Latin Church and the Ketechejian mill located at its northern end were occupied by the French. The city ended beyond that. Similarly, the area on the western side of the Latin Church was open. Feraga's house was located on the eastern side, which the Armenians had connected to their positions with a safe-corridor between two parallel walls, despite it being a street away. The street on the southern side of Nigoghosian College and Chinarli Mosque was filled with Armenian positions (Kala Aghasi, Leylegians' house etc…).

The wheat fields and gardens of Sajouri were located on the northern side of the aforementioned mosque and the college. The college and the Chinarli Mosque faced the Latin Church on the western side and the Armenian positions on the eastern.

Nigoghos Agha's house was one of the most affluent ones in the city. It was a duplex building along European lines. The south side of the building was square, although when one entered, one would find themselves in a corridor with numerous rooms opening to the left and right. A staircase at the northern end of this corridor led to the lower level. One thing that helped the Turkish resistance was the tunnel located at this lower level which remained intact after 15.5cm artillery pieces bombarded the house, since the ruins of the building provided an extra layer (2-3 meters deep) of protection above it. The Turks had also dug deep trenches that ran to the four corners of the courtyard walls. They had made loopholes in the Latin Church's wall along its whole length. Secondary holes were created for air and light. These too would also serve as loopholes if the enemy entered the courtyard. The French placed their 15.5cm cannon at Kavaklek in the afternoon. The dexterity of the French gunners was much evident here.

They had to bombard the Nigoghosian College from a distance of 1,000 meters. A slight mistake would kill their soldiers located in the Latin Church. The 15.5cm cannons first destroyed the building in 15 minutes. Then, the 7.5cm and 3.5cm cannons destroyed the street's western wall. Thousands of shells were being fired from the Armenian positions at Chinarli Mosque and Nigoghosian College. The huge trees in front of the college were pulverized by a single cannon shot. When the bombardment stopped, the French and Armenian fighters entered the courtyard without any difficulty, but they could not proceed from the side of Chinarli Mosque, since any advance would have meant many casualties.

Losing two men dead and 10 wounded, they retreated towards Kala Aghasi's house. Thanks to the wall that the Armenians had built on the street at the main entrance of Nigoghosian College, the machine-guns at Chinarli Mosque were neutralized in 15 minutes.

The bombardment continued from October 6th until the 14th. During this period, nobody was allowed to leave the city. The Turks used cannons inside the city but did not damage anything.

2. Second attack on Nigoghosian College (Aruh Bornou, October 14th)

A second attempt to occupy Chinarli Mosque and the Nigoghosian College was made at this time. The attack was from two flanks: the first through the narrow street between the Latin Church and the Bogharian's house, and the other through Kol Aghasi's house.

The 15.5cm cannon bombarded the aforementioned buildings again. The second attack was fiercer than the first one. Once the bombardment had stopped, French and Armenian fighters entered the courtyard. One section got into Nigoghosian College while the other entered the Chinarli Mosque. The audacity of the French officers was admirable. They started moving ammunition to the college, ignoring thousands of bullets coming from the Alleben woods. The Turkish connection with Chinarli Mosque was lost (the ruins had obstructed their tunnel). In order to block the retreat of Turkish fighters, the French placed a machine gun covering their line of retreat. The soldiers who entered the building stood on ruins. The building had become unrecognizable, just a pile of rubble. The soldiers could not see each other, since the smoke of the shells had impaired their vision. In such a situation, it was easy to fire at them from underground firing pits.

Some Turks left their positions. A French officer killed the first with his revolver, and the second with his sword. The blood was still dripping from its edge when the officer returned to the Latin Church to summon fresh troops.

Panicking, the Turks started abandoning their positions. Some had even forgotten how to use their rifles and picked up stones to throw at the enemy. They were forced to either kill or die; retreat was impossible, since the machine-gun threatened them. However, the French had entered the building and that meant death too. Thus, they were forced to fight. A French 15.5cm cannon shell fell on the building at that precise moment, so their soldiers could not wait in the ruins, since the shells had destroyed everything and their position was open to attack. The Turks coming out of the tunnel were bayoneted. When the shell hit, the French were forced to retreat after losing four men and 10 wounded. Nigoghosian College remained under Turkish occupation, so holding positions at Chinarli Mosque was impossible. The French withdrew from there too. An Armenian fighter brought a hoe and a basket from the Mosque. There was nothing else. Once the bombardment stopped, it was the noise of gunfire that deafened ears. It was a hellish scene, the mere memory of which horrifies human beings. Some of the attacking soldiers fell at the college entrance, while others were transported to the hospital. Their grief and pain appalled the people in the market. During this time, a heroic act was carried out by an Armenian:

> One of the wounded soldiers had fallen under the south-western corner of the wall of the College. He was shouting for help. The French and Armenians ceased firing, yet the Turks continued their heavy fire at the soldiers who were desperately trying to save their comrade. The wounded soldier had fallen beneath a wall, thus any rescue mission had to cross an area under enemy fire. No French officer or soldier dared go forward. It was at that moment that one of our Armenian gunners, S. Chakmajian, volunteered for this rescue mission. He started crawling past the entrance of the Kol Aghasi, beneath the wall of the cross street. The Turks started firing their machine guns. The crawling soldier arrived at the wall of the college that was on that side of the street, from where he continued towards its western corner. Thousands of bullets were flying over his head and missing him by a few inches. Given the way the Turks had constructed their loopholes, they were unable to point the barrels of their guns low enough to hit the crawling soldier. They shouted "Infidel, why are you rescuing that French dog?"
>
> "That is none of your business, you Muslim dog," replied the soldier and advanced towards his wounded comrade, who was lying around the corner of the wall. The Armenian soldier shouted, so that the wounded man would move forward. However, the latter thought him a Turk (he saw the crawling soldier's hat) and did not move. Chakmajian returned to the French position, took one of the French officers' hats and a long

> pole. After returning to the wounded soldier, he pulled him to him, using the pole, and then managed to carry him to Kol Aghasi's house with great difficulty. One can imagine how hundreds of fighters breathlessly observed this scene.
>
> The French embraced the hero soldier and promised him a medal as a token of their gratitude, as well as an Ottoman gold lira. The Armenian soldier refused the reward, claiming that he had not endangered his life for money but the heartbreaking cries and grief of the wounded soldier.

The primary reason for our failure was the strength of the Turkish positions. Moreover, while the Turks had placed their best fighters there, the French had dispatched a squad of Algerian soldiers who, as fellow Muslims, were reluctant to fight against the Turks. During the fighting most of the deserters were Algerians. Some two or three soldiers had tried to desert from their position at Mardin and go over to the Turkish side, but they were caught by Armenian fighters and brought to the church. Thinking it was a mosque, they had confessed that they were reluctant to shoot their fellow Muslims. In the end, the Colonel was informed by telephone, and he sent a captain who got them transferred to the College. As an objective writer, I should clearly state that, had the occupation of Nigoghosian College been carried out by the Armenian fighters, they would undoubtedly have succeeded. The Algerians were disloyal to the French. They would steal many ammunition boxes from the convoys and bury them. They would mark these places using piles of cartridges, so that after the convoy left, the Turks could come and pick them up. The Armenian fighters, who transported these boxes, often discovered them and informed the French commanders who were unable to identify the culprits. On one occasion the Armenians discovered 16 bags of flour and five or six boxes of cartridges, and informed the French officer present. Another time, they found six or seven boxes of 7.5cm cannon shells and transported them to the armory so that their gunpowder could be used for the production of new cartridges. The Algerian soldiers carried out these operations at night, when all the others were resting in their tents. Many even sold them to the villagers. You cannot expect anything different from a mercenary.

The overall loss to the French, during these two attacks, was six dead and 20-22 wounded. The Turkish casualties on the other hand were innumerable, since many were killed by the 15.5cm cannon shells that fell around Chinarli Mosque. The Turks vented their rage on the following day by spitting on the carcass of a Senegalese soldier and dragging his body through the streets. They dumped the unrecognizable body in a sewer.

These two attacks once again showed that the occupation of the city through a general attack would lead to numerous casualties.

October 15th. The Armenian government declared martial law since some protesters had denigrated the National Union. These men were beaten and imprisoned.

Saturday, October 18th. A scheduled meeting was postponed until Sunday due to enemy shelling. This meeting was called because, when some Armenian notables were severely punished by the Idariyeh Orfi for disobeying the commands of the Armenian government, they attempted to stir up the community against the National Union. During such critical hours, a popular protest could lead to serious consequences. Therefore, on Sunday, October 19th, a general meeting was organized in order to dispel any misunderstandings. Captain Reno personally participated in this meeting and expressed, on behalf of the French command, their satisfaction with the position that Armenians had adopted. He reiterated that the National Union was the embodiment of the general will and was the representative national body. Any disobedience to it would be considered defiance to the French authorities and would lead to severe punishment.

Certain people present spoke on behalf of the National Union about maintaining discipline. After the crowd dispersed, 120 notables elected a committee of auditors – seven members – whose task was to investigate and audit the accounts of the National Union. These people went to the National Union office on Monday at 11 o'clock and demanded that the National Union opens its accounts for investigation in order to dispel any misunderstandings. The Union replied that the committee did not have the necessary authority. Eventually, the chairman of the National Union, Dr. H. Bezjian announced that the Union was willing to open its accounts for investigation by those who wished to examine them, whether they were individuals or a committee. The members of this committee were chosen from among the experienced merchants of the city: they were H. Levonian, K. Sarkissian, R. Yegavian, R. Soulahian, H. Bakkalian, H. Shnorhokian, H. Barsoumian, and Y. Matossian.

On the 20th October, the National Union formed a committee that would settle the issue of homeless families by sending them to Kurd Mahallesi. The city police force would assist the committee.

The 8th convoy arrived in Aintab that night, after being shelled at Fak Boghazuh. The Turks had placed their cannons on Belli Kaya Mountain and had forced the convoy to remain in the Fak Boghazuh gorge. Once the convoy was at Fak Boghazuh, the Turks fired 200 shells. The Turkish artillery was inaccurate. Only three French soldiers, two Arabs, one Armenian carter and 15 animals were killed, with four soldiers and four civilians wounded. Had there been a panic, the casualties would have been greater.

Turkish Orgnization

We can divide the soldiers fighting at Aintab into three categories: 1. Regular troops, 2. Volunteers, and 3. Chetes.

1. The regular troops consisted the 9th Army Corps, whose "Yildirim Battalion" operated in Aintab; the Marash battalion, made up of Nuri Bey's 300 fighters and Kenan Bey's battalion. They operated in the area around Aintab and were entrusted with harassing the French convoys as well as attacking the French troops in the city from time to time. These soldiers had always evaded a regular war and were occupied with brigandage. They possessed a 7.5cm mountain gun and two 7.5cm Russian cannons, as well as one Shneider howitzer. Kenan Bey's battalion possessed six 7.5cm cannons and one Russian Obusieh. The ammunition for these cannons was very scarce and most of the 7.5 cannon shells did not explode.

2. Some military officers were volunteers. These volunteers, blinded by religious fanaticism, would return home after the first skirmish. One day the deputy of Malatia, Haji Bedir Agha, came to Aintab with his 300 volunteers. After suffering heavy casualties, they returned to Malatia. Most of these men had come to Aintab with the hope of plundering Christian honor and property. Since the first days of the fighting, many volunteers came and returned home after witnessing a reality much different from what they had expected. After the war, the Turks told the

story of an incident that was the result of a strange coincidence. Two chieftains were brought to Aintab with their tribesmen as volunteers. They took the men to the barricades and the firing points established at Abdy Effendi's house to show them the Armenian positions. Suddenly, a bullet killed two men who were standing behind one another. All these tribesmen left Aintab the next day.

3. Chetes. These were irregulars, commanded by civilian officers and had come from the surrounding villages. They fought until the end at Aintab as well as its surrounding areas since they could not abandon their birthplaces. The famous chete leaders were Sadik Effendi (from Tilbashar), Habesh Effendi (from Nizib), and Fayad Effendi (from Mezereh) whose father – Omer – had been a chete leader himself. They all operated under the command of Husni Bey.

The commanders of the regular and irregular troops operating within the city were Ozdemir and Arslan Bey among others. Their internal affairs were administered by Chitji Ferid Effendi, under the supervision of the directorate of the National Defense Committee, composed of 10 members. The mutasarrif complied with their orders.

As we have said, their overall number – within and outside the city – had reached 20-23,000 men, yet they usually numbered about 9-10,000.

The French troops fighting against these forces reached 6,000. Some of these men, however, were deployed for convoy protection or other tasks. Thus the number of soldiers who remained in the city was between 2-3,000. There had been instances when this number was reduced to 3-400.

The number of Armenian troops had, relative to the number of rifles, increased.

The number of men deployed for military purposes reached 1,500. Only 500 of them were regular fighters who were stationed at different positions. During the last period, the quantity of Armenian weapons had increased to such an extent that the Armenians were able to deploy 2,000 fighters. As for ammunition, there was sufficient rounds for two years.

To bolster the morale of their soldiers, the Turks used propaganda announcements as follows:

> 1. A large communist force was on its way to help them. That Enver Pasha had formed two armies – a red army (Kizil Ordu) and a green one (Yeshil Ordu) – ready to save Izmir and Aintab.
>
> 2. The French were not able to dispatch more than 3,000 soldiers to the east, and that their numbers was slowly decreasing. Thus victory was imminent.
>
> 3. If the French occupied Aintab, they would indiscriminately kill every one of its inhabitants, whether he had fought against them or not.

October 23rd. A detachment of soldiers left Aintab and occupied the positions from which the Turks have been constantly firing.

Two hours after leaving Aintab it captured 21 chetes, 100 oxen, 80 sheep and eight boxes of corn. The captives stated that Turkish soldiers commanded by Kenan Bey and armed with cannons were about to attack the column. As a precaution, they were divided into two groups. The French left for Ekiz Keoy on October 25th and arrived on the 26th. On their way back to Aintab on October 27th, the convoy clashed with Kenan Bey's soldiers, who lost 12 dead. The French 15.5cm cannons never stopped bombarding the city during this time.

October 29th. The French exchanged a Turkish agha for a Senegalese soldier captured on the August 17th. He informed the French command about several deaths in the Turkish hospital that had occurred due to a lack of medical supplies.

October 31st. A battalion left for Beyler Bey but did not encounter any chetes on its way. It returned to Aintab after cutting some telegraph wires.

November 1st–20th

The Turks attacked the Latin Church on November 2nd but were pushed back. On the following day, they bombarded the Armenian quarter. They then sent the following letter to the Armenians:

> I can inform you that Kars was occupied by our soldiers on October 30th. The Armenian army was defeated and a minister, high ranking officials, three generals (one of whom was General

> Piret), 50 officers and 500 soldiers were captured. The brilliant attack by our troops made the Armenian army incapable of defence.
>
> Ozdemir

This letter did not really affect the Armenians of Aintab since their connection with the outside world had been lost. Moreover, the truthfulness of the events cited in the letter was dubious.

The convoy left Aintab again on October 23rd and successfully returned on November 3rd.

In order to incite the Algerian and Tunisian soldiers against the French, the Kemalists sent the following letter:

> Fellow-Muslims, how can your conscience be clear when you turn your weapons against other Muslim soldiers who are protecting the Caliphate?
>
> Does your devotion allow you to attack your brothers when they pity you?
>
> Brothers, if you help our enemy, you will exterminate Islam. This will be your greatest sin against God and the Prophet.
>
> God loves those who fight for him. If you act otherwise, how will you justify yourselves on Judgment Day?
>
> God has not ordered a jihad in favor of the French. The latter are trying to occupy our cities and obliterate our faith. We recommend you to turn your weapons away from your Muslim brothers and unite with us. We impatiently wait for you. Your lives will be secured and you will live comfortably with us.
>
> Do not trust the enemies of our faith. Do not believe their lies. Our cause is just; our goal is to secure happiness in our lives, whereas yours will lead you to loss and error.
>
> We will welcome you if you come over to our side. Then we will work together for the protection and security of our country and our Muslim brothers.
>
> Islamic Association (Cemiyetti Islamiyeh)

Such an appeal had some effect. As we previously said, mercenary Muslim soldiers stole ammunition boxes from convoys and buried them for the Turks. There were several deserters too.

On November 13th, the convoy left Aintab accompanied by 1,000 soldiers. They surprisingly found all the villages empty as far as Akcha Koyoun, which aroused their suspicions.

At Ekiz Keoy, the mukhtar said that the Kemalists had used oxen to pull their cannons.

That night, a Francophile Arab chieftain, who had expressed his loyalty to the French, arrived from Telbashar and informed them about the Kemalists' plans, including an ambush of the convoy on its way back by 1,500 regular and 3,000 irregular troops, as well as dozens of cannons, all commanded by Kenan Bey. Turkish cannons had been stationed on the Karaburunu and Zramba hills and the villagers had been forcibly employed to dig trenches. After destroying the convoy, this force was to assault Aintab and end the siege.

The convoy arrived at Sajour safely on November 14th, where a chete confirmed the aforementioned information. The convoy commander reported this to Aleppo and Aintab. To avoid enemy cannons, the convoy marched on the morning of November 16th. The commander and 700 soldiers attacked the Karaburunu Mountains. The convoy consisted of 500 carts and 800 camels, and that of the Armenians comprised 40 carts and 40 camels. There were other Armenian coachmen, who transported provisions to Aintab at their own expense. They were proceeding along the usual road. A force was dispatched from Aintab at the same time to outflank the enemy by arriving at Ekiz Keoy on November 16th.

The convoy started at 5 o'clock. Its right and left flanks were guarded by soldiers. The cavalry secured the road ahead and reserve troops defended the rear.

At 8 o'clock, the fighting began on the eastern side of Tuleli Chour Mountains, which the French occupied and captured two cannons (with their shells), a machine gun and a seriously wounded captain. The French planned an attack from the eastern side of Kilegib to occupy the northern hill but decided against this strategy due to bombardment and machine gun fire from the aforementioned hill. The 6.5cm cannons covered the French retreat and the troops turned left when the last carts of the convoy had crossed Tuleli Chour, and the Turks were harassing it from the left side of the hills near Yona village. The 7.5cm cannons started bombarding the aforementioned position heavily, where the Turks had dug trenches. This last position was occupied by Senegalese soldiers who captured two wounded Turkish captains, three machine guns, ammunition and other materials abandoned by the fleeing soldiers. The convoy proceeded to Ekiz Keoy.

At midnight on November 16th, the French battalion that had left Aintab arrived safely on the northern hills of Ekiz Keoy. On the following day, the Turks, who had sheltered inside their trenches, attempted to obstruct the convoy's advance by attacking it. However, they started fleeing east and west upon the sudden appearance of the French. Thus, a united French force, after defeating the Turks, entered the Nafak gorge, and then moved on to Aintab, without leaving a single cart behind. The French casualties were six dead, 37 wounded and 30 dead animals. According to the confessions of a captive Turkish soldier, their casualties were in hundreds. He confessed that until his capture, their division had suffered 40 losses. The French brought 25 captives to Aintab.

The captured Turkish officers confirmed that the Turkish force attacking the convoy comprised more than 4,000 regular and irregular troops and was personally commanded by Kenan Bey and his assistant, Hilmi Bey. The chetes were commanded by Sadik Effendi (from Tilbashar), Habesh Effendi (from Nizib), and Boyno Oghlu Memig Agha (from Marash). The Turks had been planning this attack since October 10th and had high hopes for its success. Although the attack failed, the Turks attempted to avoid any panic by firing a few shots at 1 o'clock at night, on November 17th. The Turkish forces in and outside the city often communicated using gunshots.

At 2 o'clock, the Turks attacked the French force that was holding the Nizib road from the north-western and eastern flanks. However, they were dispersed by French shelling and machine-gun fire. At dawn there was no one was left in the Turkish positions.

November 20th–December 18th

Noticing that the occupation of the city required a comprehensive siege, the French command decided, notwithstanding the various chete bands that had been keeping them busy, to finalize the occupation of Aintab. For this reason it ordered the dispatch of the majority of the soldiers stationed in Alexandretta (Iskanderoun) to Aintab, where they arrived on November 20th, under the command of General Goubeau.

General Goubeau assumed overall command of the 12,000 French troops in Aintab, including coachmen, nurses, and logistical support personnel. The latter totalled 6,000 men. After receiving details of the situation in Aintab, the General decided to surround the city completely. For this purpose, he prepared six battalions, two squadrons of 7.5cm cannons and a brigade of cavalry. He decided to attack the Kemalist troops with the remaining forces and expel them from the French borders.

Chapter 22

The Final Siege of Aintab

The French front lines were divided into four sections:

1. The north-western section. This stretched from the Marash road as far as the road to Rum Kale. The area between these two roads were held by two battalions.

2. The north-eastern section. From the road to Rum Kale as far as Sajour, including the area between them. This area was held by two battalions and a squadron of 6.5cm cannons.

3. The southern section. From Sajour as far as Ghourban Baba, was held by one battalion of Senegalese soldiers, and one and a half companies of machine gunners.

4. The western section. From Ghourban Baba as far as the road to Marash, and all the areas between them, including the Armenian quarter, Chitji Kharaf, the American College, and the general staff building. This was held by a battalion of Senegalese soldiers and one and a half companies of colonial soldiers.

All the mortars deployed in this section, including the 6.5s of the north-eastern section and the 7.5cms of the College, were located in Ghourban Baba and its surrounding area and, stationed to bombard the interior of the city as well as the areas outside it. The French double line was deployed in a way to fight against both internal and external forces. The Turkish quarter's lines of communication were thus broken. The besieging military forces communicated with each other using telephone lines, with their headquarters being at the College. Barricades were established everywhere and flags were raised. Nothing could leave or enter the city.

The General Union welcomed General Goubeau on November 21st, at 4 o'clock and wished him success in his future operations. They also thanked him for all the services that the French troops had provided for the Armenians.

The General thanked the Union for his reception and promised to end the difficult situation. Colonel Andrea had praised the Armenians who had defended the Transversal very well. The General wished for the continuation of the loyalty shown by the Armenians to the French.

After fulfilling its duties on the battlefield, France now turned its attention to the small nations. They did not intend to obliterate any nation, but rather promote justice and equality in countries that were under its mandate. This was their slogan in the refugee camps.

After asking a few questions concerning the overall number of Armenians and details of the schools, the General thanked the General Union once more. The Union representatives left his office with good impressions.

The complete siege of Aintab troubled the Turkish officials, and particularly the Turkish elite, who were disappointed. The following classified letter, which was sent by the commander of the 9th Army Corps, Kheyri Bey, was the main cause for the failure of the attack by the Turkish forces on the French convoy on November 16th-17th.

> Do not hope for any relief by the 5th Army Corps, since our troops are dispersed and supplies are scarce. We are unable to help you with the number of troops at our disposal. For the sake of avoiding slaughter by the Armenians, you will not be held responsible for any surrender to the French authorities. The fate of Aintab will be sealed by its defenders (This implies that you are free to surrender or continue fighting).

November 23rd. The Turks prepared to attack the western flank of the French line and fired hundreds of 7.5cm and 10.5cm shells towards the College and the Central Telephone building in the afternoon. French scouts spotted Turkish movements trying to concentrate in a valley located three kilometers from the French line at 1 o'clock. A fierce battle started at the north-western positions at 10 o'clock that night. Then they started attacking from Beyler Bey at midnight. They were pushed back by the French soldiers and reserve troops protecting the outer line.

Shooting continued until morning without an attack being mounted.

The Turks attacked again from the same direction on November 27th but failed. The French disposed of the Turkish corpses that were located near their positions. The Turks were thus convinced that it was impossible to breach the French besieging line and help the troops inside the city.

General Gouraud formed several light brigades and left the city on the night of November 23rd on a military expedition to push the Turkish forces back towards Su-Boghaz and Nezib. By dawn, his forces had already pushed the entrenched Turkish regular troops back towards Su

Boghaz and Bedir Keoy, which was the headquarters of the Turkish command.

General Goubeau was informed at nightfall that significant Turkish forces were located at Geollu. His forces set off before dawn and encountered the Turkish soldiers on the northern and southern flanks. The latter were resisting fiercely, but when they saw that additional French troops were approaching, they abandoned their positions and fled. The army camped at Oroul that night. On the following day – November 26th – the French arrived at Nizib and witnessed the last Turkish forces crossing the Euphrates River. An artillery battle ensued, but the Turks, unable to resist the French shelling, fled. The detachment entered Nizib on the 27th and established a governing body there.

The Turks, hampered by the scarcity of ammunition and supplies, sent the following letter to Mustafa Kemal Pasha.

> 1. I have requested ammunition and supplies for the heroes of Aintab from Husni Bey, but he did not send them. My request for Kenan Bey's 50 ammunition boxes also was ignored.
>
> 2. I have attempted to establish a warehouse in the city and collect supplies from the outside, but not only did he not assist, but he also confiscated the provisions destined for Aintab.
>
> 3. I have sent many requests for artillery, but he has only sent one useless cannon.
>
> 4. Currently 20,000 men, women and children are threatened. I have assumed the task of defending them.
>
> 5. If I die or even remain alive, Husni Bey will be held responsible for the bombardment and fall of this city.
>
> 6. Aintab must not have a tragic end after resisting for so long. I therefore request that a trial be held to determine full responsibility for these developments.
>
> I fulfill my duties, and thus my conscience is clear towards mankind and God. I only demand the punishment of those responsible.
>
> I am Ozdemir who is unfortunate enough to write these lines to you. The people of Aintab send you their regards.
>
> Ozdemir

This letter demonstrated that the Turks of Aintab considered that their days were numbered. However, they still had to resist and sacrifice soldiers, since the blood of the thousands of Armenians killed at Deir-ez Zor had not yet been atoned.

The National Union settled the issue of the police and gendarmerie on November 29th during a meeting with the Military Body and the Police Administration.

It was decided that the Police Administration would be handed over to the head of the gendarmerie, H. Momjian, who would be accountable to the National Union. The military police would serve as gendarmes under his command. As chief of police, he would be subordinate to the military commander. He would be accountable to the National Union for all the issues pertinent to peace and discipline in the city and would receive his orders from the latter.

The military command would not be able to issue orders and make arrangements for issues regarding peace and order in the city.

A military court would be established at the Military Body's office to adjudicate on issues pertaining to the soldiers. The civilians would be tried in the Civil Court, but if a problem arose between a soldier and a civilian, the case would be examined in the prosecutor's court. In case the positions of the two parties were unclear, the issue would be settled by the primary aggressor.

With this issue settled, there was no further need for policemen, and the chief of police would announce the disbandment of the police force, starting from December 1st. Thus the military and civilian police were united, which was very beneficial in terms of finance.

General Goubeau returned to Aintab on November 30th and began a military operation at Geollujeh on the following day, December 1st. He pushed back the few enemy troops positioned there and returned to Aintab on the 2nd. General de La Motte also arrived in Aintab.

Chapter 23

Correspondence for Surrender

General Goubeau sent the following ultimatum to the Turks:

> I have come to Aintab with the responsibility of implementing the terms agreed upon by France and Turkey at the Treaty of Sevres.
>
> I have pushed Kenan Bey and his armies operating east of Aintab beyond the Euphrates River. Your reinforcements coming from Marash suffered the same fate. Therefore, you do not have any choice other than to choose one of these two options: 1) Accept the terms previously presented by Colonels Abady and Andrea, of which I will modify only one – I will not collect the war indemnity. 2) Suffer a heavy bombardment. My terms are the following:
>
> a) Recognition of the French mandate over Aintab and its surroundings.
> b) The surrender of your gendarmes and soldiers, along with their weapons, as prisoners of war.
> c) The surrender of weapons and ammunition located in Aintab.
> d) The demolition of barricades established in the Turkish quarter within 24 hours.
> e) The return of government safes to French officials (these were to be returned to their owners).
> f) The detention of criminals, a list of whom we will prepare and send you.
> g) The return of the sum taken from the Public Debt Administration.
>
> I will wait for your reply until 12 noon on December 2nd. If you wish for a private meeting either at our general staff building or at Mardin orphanage, I am ready to see you. Your arrival and departure to these places will be secured.
>
> If you refuse our terms, I will have no other choice than to resort to battle.
>
> Commander of the 4th Army Corps, Goubeau

The Turks decided to keep the French busy through such correspondence to gain time. Their reply to the aforementioned ultimatum was the following:

> Just as you have defended your fatherland against your enemies, so we too protect our country. We are surprised that you have chosen Aintab as your center among all the other places under your mandate. You have also asserted your authority over Ourfa and Marash. Why have you not chosen one of them? If you accept the following terms, we will not turn our weapons against you:
>
> 1. You should occupy all the other cities so that the defenders would understand that their resistance is futile.
>
> 2. Life has no meaning to me. I am not scared of fighting, dying or being captured. My only fear is that I will not be able to fulfill my duties towards my fatherland, which is the protection of this city.
>
> 3. I want to draw your attention on two points mentioned in your ultimatum. a) You demand the surrender of our soldiers and gendarmes. Here, there is no one other than fathers and sons defending their families. All of them are natives of Aintab, so how do you want to separate them from their families and take them as prisoners of war? b) You demand the surrender of criminals according to a list you have. There are no criminals here. All the people on the list are protectors of the fatherland and therefore, according to your ultimatum, you want to arrest the whole population. This is impossible. Finally, there are some contentious points in the ultimatum, the clarification of which can be done through correspondence. The end of hostilities is essential for this reason.
>
> If you refuse our terms and demand prisoners of war, we will not have any other alternative than to fight and die like soldiers. Please accept our terms…
>
> Ozdemir

The French lessened the bombardment and sent a reply to Ozdemir as follows:

> I do not have time for lengthy correspondence. I'd rather end this issue through a personal meeting. I therefore promise, upon my military honor, that you will not be harmed. Therefore, I will be waiting for you tomorrow, December 3rd, at 2 o'clock at the general staff building. The hostilities will cease at 1 o'clock and will resume an hour after your departure. You may come to Chinarli Mosque, from where my officers will lead you here. You

> are allowed to bring a translator with you and a few officers. I request your reply by tomorrow, before 9 o'clock.
>
> Commander of the 4th Army Corps, Goubeau

Ozdemir sent the following reply on December 3rd:

> Unfortunately, I received your letter rather late and will be forced to answer it tomorrow. I ask that you facilitate correspondence efforts.

As a response, General Goubeau wrote the following (December 3rd):

> I accept that my reply was late and I give you another deadline – tomorrow, December 4th, at 7th in the morning. I wait for your response. Our meeting is also scheduled at 2:00 in the afternoon, under the previously notified terms.
>
> Correspondence will be facilitated by the establishment of a post office.

The Turks were thus able to fortify Dabbagh Khaneh Street and turn the fortress into a secondary position. Moreover, they were able to establish contact with outside forces and to pacify the population for a while.

The Turks responded to Goubeau's last letter, based on Ozdemir's reply on December 1st. In other words, besides Aintab, the French would have to occupy all the other cities under the mandate. A deadline would be set for this too, so that the Turks could stop firing from inside the city.

The Turks made many such meaningless demands.

General Goubeau, who had understood the deceitful policies of the Turks, ordered the bombardment of the city to continue for three days.

During this period, the information received about the Turks was as follows:

1. The fighters inside the city, aged between 24-28, numbered 2,000 men, who were regular army troops. The second group (aged from 29-49) built the barricades. They had one million cartridges and supplies sufficient for a month.

2. Kenan Bey, who had escaped to the other side of the Euphrates River, had returned and was preparing to send reinforcements to Aintab. There was a high rate of desertion and the soldiers despaired, particularly after the fighting of November 16th-17th. The Marash battalion that was composed of 1,000 regulars had stopped fighting after the battle of November 23rd-27th. They had five artillery pieces and two 7.5cm

cannons. The officers' morale had been destroyed, as they were fighting under duress. This was shown by a telegraph discovered on one of the dead bodies. The telegraph said:

> To the Third Battalion,
>
> If you do not commence the attack, you will be held responsible. I order your troops to attack immediately.
>
> Signed by command of the 27th Army Corps.

This telegraph was found on the body of the commander's adjutant.

On December 4th, Ozdemir sent an ultimatum to the Armenians and informed them about the loss of the Armenian army on the Caucasian battlefield against the Kemalist forces. It demanded their surrender, and announced the imminent arrival of the triumphant Turkish armies at Aintab. On the one hand it stated that their fate was tragic but on the other requested relief from Turks in other areas.

As we have previously said, the Turks had succeeded in establishing contacts with the "outside" Turks during the time taken for correspondence between General Goubeau and Ozdemir and sent them their requests for relief. On December 5th, they received a response from the outside with the following message:

> 1. We have received a copy of General Goubeau's ultimatum. I thank the heroes of Aintab on behalf of our nation.
>
> 2. The reality of the facts about the annihilation of the 9th Army Corps and the 5th Army Corps crossing the Euphrates River, will soon be revealed.
>
> 3. During the resistance period, we will attempt many attacks. Do not despair because of our retreat as, after every withdrawal, we will strike again with more power. The next attack will take place in the next few days.
>
> Salaheddin

The French started to drop announcements from an airplane, trying to convince the Turks to surrender and save themselves from a meaningless death. However, these leaflets did not affect the Turkish people.

December 5th. The Turks sent another letter which read:

> We have not received a response to our previous letter. Send us ammunition by breaching the French line. Inform us about Kenan Bey's forces and other events occurring outside.
>
> Ozdemir

December 6th. The Turks received the response to their previous letter:

> We understand from General Goubeau's letters that the French intend to occupy the city through peaceful means. We therefore recommend that you obstruct their attempts. Moreover, try to gain some time, so that we can finalize the arrangements for your rescue.
>
> The appropriate orders have been sent to provide you with ammunition. If our rescue mission is delayed, do not cease the efforts to help the "criminals" wanted by General Goubeau to flee the city. I wish that you didn't need this support.
>
> Commander of 2nd Army Corps, Salaheddin

On the same day, the Aintab Turks received the following letter from Fevzi Pasha:

> General Goubeau's letters have been examined. The Ministry of Foreign Affairs will send protest notes to the appropriate places concerning this matter. The War Ministry expresses its gratitude to the heroes of Aintab.
>
> – War Minister, Ferik Fevzi

The Turks in Aintab replied to this letter, on December 11th, as follows:

> Despite the enemy's bombardment using heavy artillery, we took an oath to fight until the last soldier. We hope that the Grand National Congress will not forget us and will strive to find a solution to our situation. May God grant us success.
>
> Ozdemir

December 6th. The Turks fired a few shells at the French positions. The latter retaliated with a heavy bombardment.

December 7th. The Turks received a letter from the commander of the 9th Army Corps, Kheyri Bey, stating that the Armenian army, defeated on the Caucasian battlefield, had accepted Turkish terms.

December 8th. The French shelled Ahmed Chelebi, Maghara Bashuh and the government building, heavily. Despite this, the Turks of Aintab sent a letter to the Grand National Congress, signed by Dr. Fakhreddin, Ozdemir and 25-30 other notables:

> The situation of the city of Aintab, that has been resisting the enemy for nine months, is known to the civilized world. It is heartbreaking to see devastated houses and the bloodshed. Not

> one mosque or even a hamlet has remained standing in which one could find shelter and feel safe in Aintab. This is merely for refusing the French mandate.
>
> Why should this city, populated with Turks for centuries, capitulate to the French authorities? Why is the civilized world ignoring our efforts and disrespecting our struggle for national liberation and independence? We do not even accept the "m" in "mandate". An honorable death is more favorable to us. During the burials of our mothers and sisters, we hope that the world will intervene and stop the French atrocities. If they stay silent, we will fight and overturn this decision with our last drop of blood.
>
> We therefore request your assistance and action to end the massacre.

December 10th. Snow was falling on Aintab. The Turks shouted to the Armenians that their time had arrived, and that winter would finalize the Turkish victory. The French pounded Tutun Khan with their artillery. Some people who had sheltered in the lower levels of the building were asphyxiated due to the fumes of gunpowder and gas.

The Turkish quarter was suffering from famine at this time. The cries of women and children requesting bread was really heartbreaking. The Turks had lost all hope from the outside world. The heavy shelling resumed.

December 14th. The Turks received a heartening letter from Kazim Karabekir that bolstered the Turkish fighters' morale. Karabekir informed them of his victory over the Armenians on the Caucasian battlefield, praising his efforts and stating, "I have obliterated all the Armenians."

The Turks sent the following letter on December 15th:

> There is no one who recognizes this people who have devastated our prosperous cities and pillaged them for 40-50 years. Your victory has alleviated our suffering. With the help of God, the final blow against this barbarian race will be struck. The heroes of Aintab greet and embrace your arms of steel.

December 14th. A French battalion set off for Sam Keoy and Beyler Bey but encountered no chetes on its way. The French tightened their siege and the Turks fortified their positions even more.

Some of General Goubeau's soldiers withdrew to Kilis and Sajour due to the harsh winter, since feeding all these men and their transportation animals was impossible. The departure of the French soldiers gave the Turks a sense of optimism, even though the siege continued. The soldiers surrounding the city had built fortifications on the hills, with trenches and dugouts where the soldiers enjoyed the heat of the fires they had lit.

December 16th. The French bombarded Kurd Tepeh, Maghara Bashuh and Ferkah.

The Turks, who noticed that the famine was getting worse each day, bought all the nuts and raisins in the shops and stored them in a warehouse. They distributed 100 dirhem of raisins and nuts to their soldiers each day. The people would gather in front of the Hiyyeti Merkeziyyeh every day and shout "We are hungry!"

Chitji Ferid described the situation of the people in a letter to the outside forces:

> December 16/17. To the command of the Second Battalion,
>
> Misery, ruins, tragic scenes, dead bodies and ghastly looking people everywhere. The people of Aintab are confronting their misery tenderly, despite these heartbreaking scenes, for the sake of their aims. Our goal is Nation, Faith, Honor and Independence.
>
> To attain this goal, the people have sacrificed everything during these critical hours and have asked for God's help. By turning its tearful eyes to the east and north, it has asked for relief from their co-religionists. They have boosted each other by stating "Let us be patient, let us wait a little more." All have turned into giants and resisted the enemy attacks to the extent that they want to kill the enemy with their teeth. They have decided on "Independence or Death."
>
> These are people who embrace such torment and misfortune as happiness. They are facing yet another problem, the resistance to which is beyond human powers – famine. This is the problem hindering the bravery of our heroes. Our remaining supplies are sufficient for seven days and then there is nothing left to consume, all that will remain is a bunch of innocent children, orphans and unfortunate people praying and asking God for relief.
>
> Such despairing people, who consider death as an honor and who are keen to amputate body parts just to feed the hungry and the besieged, have one last request: We ask you to breach the French

line and deliver ammunition and supplies essential for the preservation of our national honor.

President of Hiyyeti Merkeziyeh, Ferid.

December 18th–February 9th

December 18th. General Goubeau set off south-west to Aleppo in order to deter any future clashes. His departure motivated the Turks to initiate new attacks.

The harsh cold of winter put the French soldiers in a difficult position, particularly the Senegalese soldiers, who had never seen snow in their lives and were terrorized by this cold, white substance. Some tried to taste it. They were the ones most hurt by it. To prevent any further injuries, the French ordered that all the soldiers should grease their bodies. Those who did not comply were punished.

December 18th. The Turks made preparations to assist an attack from the outside but, disappointed, returned to their positions. They were informed that a second attack would commence on the night of December 19th, but after waiting for two hours, they returned in despair. During this time, however, the outside forces, commanded by Kenan Bey, were waiting for the arrival of the French convoy.

December 18th. General Goubeau left Aintab. The Turks, who had been waiting for the French convoy since the night of December 19th, only heard the French cannons in the morning. Exploiting the darkness of the night, the Turks had approached the French positions near Beyler Bey and the Nizib Road, but retreated when they were hit by French artillery and machine gun fire. They fled north and north-east. The French captured eight soldiers, one of whom was an officer. The French scouts noticed some clashes on the Marash road and Ibrahimli Hill. From 2 until 4 o'clock, the Turks fired 300 shells at the north-western section. The French expected a night attack on Chitji Kharaf and Haji Baba, so sent reinforcements there. However, nothing occured except a few gunshots. The captured officer confessed that the man who had attacked the French positions was Kenan Bey, who had chosen Su Boghazuh as his headquarters.

The soldiers who attacked on December 20th were part of his cavalry force. The primary cause for the Turks' despair was now revealed. It was because the Marash army, that was on its way to Kenan Bey's assistance, was delayed for two days . The Turkish attack was therefore postponed until December 20th. Kenan Bey had 15,000 men, eight cannons and 18 vehicles under his command. The number of vehicles showed that the wounded soldiers located inside the hospitals had been wounded again by the French bombardment.

December 22nd. A French airplane announced that the Turks were occupying Duluk, Kara Hoyig, Etebeg and the area around Su Boghazi. It was therefore decided to plan an attack with the soldiers who had just arrived with the convoy. The force was divided into two groups: the first was to hold the Turkish line of retreat from Duluk, Kara Hoyig and Etebeg, while the second group was to obstruct the enemy's retreat from north-eastern Etebeg, Bedir Keoy, Su Boghaz and Goellujeyeh.

These two battlegroups were to meet at Etebeg. The first set off and, after a few skirmishes with Turkish regular troops, arrived at Etebeg, while the second one delayed its departure by two hours due to a Turkish bombardment from the southern hills of Su Boghazuh. So the two groups were not able to converge at Etebeg at the specified time. The Turks exploited this delay and avoided the French siege by fleeing to the north-east. The two battle groups returned to Aintab the following night.

The Armenians attempted to occupy the taverns and buildings around Simon Agha's mill, located on the southern edge of Transversal, on December 23rd. The French started bombarding these buildings as the Turks hid in underground tunnels. Terrorized by the heavy bombardment, some Turks attempted to escape through a narrow corridor. However, the Armenians noticed their shadows and killed some of these chetes who fell in the trenches. To prevent further desertions, the Turks put the corridor under machine-gun fire. Once the bombardment stopped, the Armenians went in. There was no cover to take up any positions. The rear of the building was completely demolished. The Turks came out of their trenches and started attacking. After killing a few chetes, the Armenians withdrew to their previous positions.

December 26th. The 17th convoy left Aintab with a few soldiers. The last carts had barely left Aintab when clashes began with the Turks in the vicinity of Duluk Baba and Beyler Bey.

The Turks made significant efforts to breach the French line on the 27th. They had been preparing this attack for a few days and had brought 15 cannons from Marash and positioned them on the road leading to it. The attack began from all sides. For the first time, the Turks attacked

Ghurban Baba and its environs from the southern side. It was the first time in the whole war they attacked from this direction. Since the French had felt safer on this front, they had not undertaken the necessary preparations. Moreover, with the departure of the convoy, the Turks anticipated the weakness of this flank. The worst thing was that most of the French mortars were located there and the Turkish artillery had them in their sights. The Turkish artillery bombarded the French mortars throughout the day and destroyed one cannon. Most of the soldiers necessary to defend the aforementioned positions had left with the convoy. The French tried to hold the siege line at all costs, since any breach in the final moment of their victory could have turned the tide of war against them with greater casualties. Therefore, all the remaining men, whether coachmen or cooks, were mobilized and sent to the various positions. The French defended themselves very well.

This was an unfortunate day for the Armenians as well as for the French; at 3:00 in the afternoon, the Armenians suffered a great loss from 15 cannon shells fired by the Turks.

This was the second occurrence, after the one that fell on the Zahatjians' house. But it was even more terrorizing.

Throughout the whole war, two Turkish shells had caused great damage to the Armenians; the first was the one that hit Saatjians' house and killed one person and wounded six others. The second one fell on the vicinity of Arejians' house in the Akyol market.

Previously, the Armenians had been cautious. For example, when the Turks started a bombardment, their first few shells would fall on the outskirts of the city. It was only after that, that their shells would hit the Armenian quarters. Thus the first shells falling outside the quarters would be the signal that a bombardment was about to hit them. The Armenians would then take shelter in the lower levels of their houses. Unfortunately, this time, despite warnings, the Armenians had not reacted and the shell claimed four lives and wounded 16 others. Among the dead were Soghomon Kabakian, Kasbar Andonian, a man called Sahag and a woman. The wounded were transported to a hospital and the dead were buried after a proper funeral.

After the capitulation of the city, the Turks mentioned three or four similar events that were really horrible. They recounted how people were buried alive under the ruins. Such events occurred frequently in the

Turkish quarter, yet the most horrifying incident was the French 15.5cm shell that had fallen on the fortress moat. As a result, the Turks had to carry 40 arms, feet, heads and other body parts to the cemetery to be buried. I have personally seen that place and it is incredible how accurately the French had bombarded it. The Turks had established a market in the eastern moat of the old fortress. One can imagine the damage that bomb did. The second 15.5cm shell has caused real slaughter in Bughda Bazar, exactly at the same place where an Armenian boy was executed on April 1st.

The bomb fell on a wheat pile, around which numerous people had congregated. They picked up their body parts from the market called Sabounjuh. A third one fell on the Iki Kapulu, killing five people and wounding many others who were sheltered in the stable. The fourth one fell on the supposedly safe Kurkji Khan killing many inside.

A Turkish bomb breached the southern wall of the American College and demolished an ammunition warehouse. The fire lasted until 6:30 and destroyed large numbers of cartridges and shells. The final bomb wounded five Senegalese soldiers and commander Geots, who died two days later.

At 7 o'clock, two Turkish attacks – one from the north, the other through the Sajour valley – were pushed back. The Turkish aim was to keep the French busy with minor attacks while breaching their weakest position. They failed, however, thanks to soldiers from the convoy who were summoned back by telegraph and travelled 70 km in 26 hours without rest. Their appearance put the Turks to flight. They fled 40 km. in four hours.

The Turks left 50 dead near the French positions and, according to certain sources, transported 400 wounded from Bedir Keoy over two days.

The French convoy left on December 30th and was able to return on January 3rd with great difficulty. 60 of the Senegalese soldiers, who arrived with the convoy, had frozen feet. The French suffered many difficulties.

During this time, the situation in the Turkish quarter remained awful. Despite everyone's frugality, the warehouses were empty. A special committee visited all the houses and, after buying scarce provisions, distributed very small quantities to the people. They were, however, continuing their efforts to obtain relief from the outside world. The bombardment of the city resumed.

Chapter 24

The Desperate Situation of the Turks and their Supplicant Letters

The Turks sent the following letter to Salaheddin, commander of the 2nd Army Corp on January 6th:

> By giving each individual five dirhems, and 10 to each soldier, our supplies are sufficient for five days. If, however, we consider nuts, raisins and meat of different animals, we are able to hold for 15 days. After that, it is impossible to defend ourselves for even one day. Therefore, we ask for relief supplies from you for the sake of Turkishness, Islam and patriotism.

Salaheddin Bey replied by letter as follows:

> We reconnoitered the enemy's forces and found that they are much stronger than we had imagined. Our attack from the Haji Baba direction, on December 27th, surprised them. This was their weakest point. However, the incompetence of our soldiers failed us. Thus, it is impossible to fight with such soldiers at our disposal. Now the enemy has turned its attention to the position against which any attack is destined to fail. Despite this, we have decided to carry on with our plan of attack, since the convoy has left Aintab and will not return for a few days.
>
> But we will try to send provisions through individuals who will carry the supplies on their backs. Nevertheless, I have to reiterate that with such soldiers, nothing is possible.
>
> I have thus explained our situation to you.
>
> Salaheddin.

January 8th. The National Union's budget was ratified as follows (in liras): military expenditure, 600 Ottoman gold liras; supplies for the poor 1,300, officials' salaries 100, educational needs 150 and 50 for miscellaneous items. Total 2,200 Ottoman gold liras.

I can provide the following information concerning financial accounts: between April 1st and February 8th, the National Union collected 40,000 Ottoman gold liras. Most of this amount was donated by the American Red Cross, the A.G.B.U., as well as some philanthropists and prelacies

Aintab Y.M.C.A. building, 5 January 1920.

close to Aintab. The French contribution was also significant. The details of these financial accounts are held by Karekin Bogharian.

January 10th. The Turks started mixing apricot grain with bread flour for distribution to the soldiers, so that they would survive for a few more days. Inedible bread was thus consumed by Turkish civilians and soldiers out of necessity. A few days later 50-60 people suffered food poisoning and died. Despite the fact that the doctors had forbidden it, the hopeless people continued consuming such bread. Thus, what shells and bullets had failed to do was achieved through food poisoning. However, by this time, the apricot grain had run out.

January 13th. A letter sent by Ozdemir to Salaheddin informed the latter of the following:

> I confirm what I have previously written. I am deeply troubled by the famine threatening our people. The daily gatherings of people in front of my office and shouting "We are hungry!" worry me. The bread made using flour and apricot grain has finished. It is impossible to describe the suffering and misery around.
>
> Dear commander, I pity the people who have been weakened so much. The soldiers still possess provisions sufficient for a week, but the people have nothing left.

> Any delay by you is a sin. Do what you need to do and realize your final attack plan. God will grant success.
>
> However, if you have not finalized your preparations, leave any supplies near the nearest French position and we will attempt to retrieve it under your covering artillery fire. Thus, either accept my proposal or begin the military operations. "Let me sacrifice my life for my nation." I am certain that God will protect those who work for a noble cause.
>
> Waiting any longer, due to the cold on the one hand, and the famine on the other, is impossible, since the arrival of French artillery and troops will delay your plans and eventually hinder them. In that case the city will capitulate, not through fighting, but rather because of the famine.
>
> Ozdemir.

Thus three Turks were informed, through this letter, that the outside forces would first attack the French convoy returning to Aintab from Akcha Koyoun and then proceed to a final attack on the city from the south.

A French airplane shelled the Turkish quarter on January 16th. The bombardment resumed on the 18th. Some artillery fire was heard from Akcha Koyoun in the afternoon.

On January 18th – 19th, 1921, there was an attack on the French convoy. The convoy had left Aintab on January 14th and arrived at Akcha Koyoun on the 17th, and then it had set off for Aintab on the 18th.

French cavalrymen arrived at Ekiz Keoy about noon. A French officer noticed some men were dressed in black and positioned in trenches on the opposite hills. The French did not have any information about a probable Turkish attack until this point. This time, the Turks were operating covertly and were well organized. The officer immediately enquired about the movement of these men by interrogating the villagers who had remained in the village. They responded by stating that the men on the hill were Turkish regular troops, divided into three units, each one comprising 200 soldiers. However, the Turkish forces were much greater than the number provided by the villagers. They numbered around 4-5,000 fighters. The vanguard of the French troops attacked this supposedly weak Turkish position but were forced to hold their positions when a Turkish machine-gun started firing at them. Moreover, the

Turkish mortars started bombarding the convoy, and the soldiers stationed in the Sajour valley attacked it. The French commander decided to concentrate all this troops and resist the enemy. He ordered the army's vanguard to halt the convoy and leave all the freight animals and carts on the western plain of Kuyu. He also positioned the soldiers in trenches. Furthermore, he sent couriers to Aintab and Sajour for help. However, during these preparations, the convoy suffered many losses due to the mud and enemy bombardment. The animals and the carts caused havoc with the traffic.

An attack by 400 Turkish fighters was pushed back to the north of the convoy. The few French soldiers to the east of the convoy mounted an admirable resistance against Turkish forces that numbered more than ten times those of the French. The convoy's center was left undefended but a small French detachment arrived just in time hindering the progress of the Kemalist forces by using machine-guns.

The French were able to resist until nightfall with great difficulties and sacrifices. At times the French stopped and killed the Turks with their bayonets.

At 10 o'clock that night, the Turks ceased all their military operations. The French commander, Knal Demar, summoned all his officers and decided to hold the position until morning since, according to information they received, it was impossible to move because of the large enemy force surrounding them.

The night passed calmly. The supplies were placed in the mud in a field west of Ekiz Keoy. To avoid the snow and cold, the 5-600 Armenian logistical workers sheltered inside Kuyu's small huts. Some passed the night in their carts. Despite the cold, they waited until morning. Fortunately, the thousands of Turkish shells that were falling would often not explode when they landed because of the water and mud where the provisions and soldiers were positioned. The unreliability of the Turkish bombs was also another of the main reasons for their not exploding. While these events were occurring, on January 19th, a French airplane informed us about the convoy's difficult situation near Ekiz Keoy. It did, however, provide inaccurate information concerning the number of Turkish forces – 600 fighters. Thus the French command at Aintab considered such a force to be harmless or innocuous. It decided to only hold the hills of the Nafak gorge in the morning. However, at midnight, the French commanders were notified by telegraph that the number of Turkish troops was greater than they had anticipated.

It was therefore decided to send reinforcements to the besieged soldiers of the convoy without seriously weakening the French siege line, since the capitulation of the city was a matter of days. At few soldiers were summoned from each position that night and a battalion was thus formed in the morning and set off at 10:30 and 2:00. This force arrived at Saghzen and noticed through binoculars three Turkish cannons and began firing at them. This battalion understood that the French convoy of soldiers was still resisting and thus rescuing them was easy. Upon seeing the advancing army, the Turks retreated. Their cavalry withdrew to the west, while their artillery and chetes went to the east. At 4:00, the forces converged and headed for Aintab, where they arrived at 8:30 at night.

Before returning to Aintab that night, the French attempted to distract the enemy by lighting camp-fires. The Turks, who thought that the French soldiers were gathered round them, opened heavy fire. The Turks continued firing even after the French departed.

The French suffered 32 dead and 109 wounded, of whom nine were officers. Moreover 193 animals were either killed or wounded and 42 cannons and carts were destroyed.

The Turks withdrew to Su Boghazuh, Beyi Keoy, Kara Huyugi, and Etebeg after their failure, even though calls for help were still coming from Aintab. The Turks decided to breach the French line and started organizing themselves.

The city was bombarded from January 21st until the 24th. On January 25th, the Turks fired 450 shells at the French positions around Haji Baba using heavy artillery. The French, who had learned that the Turks commenced their attacks after the bombardment ended, fortified their positions using reserve troops and expected an attack at night. Yet, nothing occurred, apart from a few gunshots, the means of communication adopted by Turkish fighters.

On January 30th, French vehicles attempted to cross their own lines in order to understand the condition of the besieged Turkish fighters and their forces. Before they set off, the French 15.5cm and 7.5cm cannons destroyed some of the Turkish fortifications, killing many people. The vehicles set off from Pasha Street and passed the trenches at Ferkah, where they destroyed some positions with their machine-guns. Afterwards, they turned towards the Transversal and started advancing.

After travelling for a few hours, they returned to the college. They had slaughtered the Turks with their 3.7cm shells. One of the vehicles had taken 400 hits by bullets, implying that the Turks still possessed a significant force inside the city. Five drivers were wounded, two of them seriously.

The Turks desperately attempted to breach the French siege line at Rum Kale on January 31st. Outside forces prepared to assist them.

Exploiting the darkness of the night, the Turks focused on the southern side of the Rum Kale hills, whose peaks were occupied by the French. That night, two divisions of Kemalist forces, each consisting of 200 men, attacked the French positions. The right flank of the Turkish troops failed against the French resistance after numerous attempts to breach their positions. The Turkish left flank, however, succeeded in occupying the French barricades, as the latter had withdrawn from these positions after the death of their officer and were afraid of getting captured. The Turks continued their advance towards the French command post by shouting "Ya Allah! Ya Allah!" A captain, who had assumed the command, mobilized the reserve troops and initiated a counterattack. The retreating soldiers accompanied him. However, the captain fell after being hit. Similarly, his lieutenant was killed, and the Turks wounded an Algerian officer who had replaced the fallen lieutenant. Hence, the counter-offensive failed and the French withdrew to their previous positions, where they tried to hinder the Turkish advance. The Turks rushed westwards towards Rum Kale gorge and 40 of their men succeeded in breaching the French line and escaped. The remaining men were forced to return to the city due to a subtle counterattack executed by the French soldiers from the north-west.

The French position at Akhr-Baba to the north-west also suffered an attack, but the Turkish fighters were repelled. In the morning, the French noticed that the Turks were still holding their positions on the Rum Kaleh road. They were very close to those of the French and some Turkish units were positioned at Rum Kaleh valley. At 8:00 in the morning, the French cleared the area of Turkish fighters and recovered their previously lost barricades. As a result, the Turkish mortars started bombarding the college, causing a lot of damage. A Turkish mortar bomb started a fire on the lower floor of the college, and another one burnt down a fuel warehouse established during the British period of occupation. The black smoke was seen from Sajour. The Turks also fired at the college to obstruct the efforts of the fire-fighters.

At 2:00, the French spotted a caravan of 300 camels loaded with supplies that the Turks had attempted to smuggle into Aintab. It was returning after its failure to cross the siege lines. During this battle, the French suffered 16 dead, one of whom was an officer, and 21 wounded. However, the enemy casualties were greater. 37 bodies were counted in front of the French barricades, and after the capitulation of the city, it was revealed that 102 wounded had been transported to Turkish hospitals. The French captured two soldiers.

The Turks corresponded with their outside forces as follows:

> January 31st, 1921
>
> To the Command of the Second Army Corps,
>
> We deployed our best troops to breach the French line as a token of gratitude for your promises of relief. Unfortunately, you have not kept your word and only sent 1/100th of the supplies promised, caused the death of our best fighters and undermined the morale of the people. Please make a final effort tonight or on Tuesday to bring us salvation and end the lamentation of the people. To inform us of your consent, fire three shots from Sumak Tepeh. Unfortunately the message was lost. Please make a final effort, and if it fails, we will try to save ourselves. Our troops achieved great success during the night and, had your forces helped us from the outside, our victory would have been complete. But you have not kept your word. I cannot describe the extent to which these 18,000 starved men hate you. This is the psychology of the people: since all of Anatolia and the Grand National Congress are unable to save a small city that has sacrificed a great deal, they should not have caused the death of thousands and the material damage that has been inflicted here. If fulfilling our duty is equivalent to cowardice and maliciousness, then we are proud of it. Shame on the Grand National Congress and its armies. We will unfortunately witness the fall of the Ottoman crescent. What can we do? It is God's will
>
> Ozdemir

As a response, they received the following despondent letter from Salaheddin:

> Your letter sent on January 29th greatly disappointed both Kenan and Khayir Bey. We are aware of your situation and have attempted to put into action all the means at our disposal for your salvation. Unfortunately, we have failed. I have referred to the incompetence of our forces from the beginning. However, troubled by your dire situation and moved by the spirit of sacrifice, we have attempted everything to rescue you. 40 of your fighters arrived at our headquarters. Unfortunately we have not been able to breach the enemy line, neither from the outside, nor the inside. We are truly aware of the situation. What can we do? Who can defy God's will?
>
> Commander of 2nd Army Corps, Salaheddin

The Turks dispatched a team to retrieve the six bodies and eight wounded left behind after the attack of February 1st. They succeeded in moving them to the hospitals by carrying them on their backs. Some of the wounded had lost their arms, feet, eyes, etc. and presented a gruesome scene in the courtyard of the hospital, where the cries and wailing of their relatives exacerbated the situation. At this, the Turkish notables decided to appeal one last time to the outside forces to save them before February 7th, otherwise the city would capitulate.

After receiving this ultimatum, the Turkish commander of the outside forces sent a letter to Ozdemir, stating that their troops were not sufficient to breach the French line. However, he wrote that they would continue their efforts, with the hope of bringing out some of the besieged civilians before February 7th. Finally, the letter stated that, if these final efforts failed, they should not hope for any outside relief and survive on their own.

At midnight on February 6th, the Turks attempted a last attack on the French line. Their target was the Sajour gorge. The Turks started from this point and bombarded the northern and southern flanks. A strong unit tried to breach the French line and managed to advance despite heavy French machine-gun fire. But they were repelled. Afterwards they turned towards the south and occupied a French post. The French recaptured the lost position by mounting a counterattack. During this time, however, many Turks got out of the city.

Armenian military command and its officers, Aintab, 1920.

Another attempt was made through the hills around the Sheikh House. However, strong resistance stopped their progress and the Turks retreated to the city.

The outside forces attacked the French positions at Sajour again at 3:00 on February 7th. They came from Urum Evleg but were reluctant to approach the French positions since the latter were firing their machine-guns and using their artillery. The situation was calm at dawn. The French noticed a caravan of mules leaving the city on the Nizib road. These were the supplies that the Turks had attempted to smuggle into the city during the night but had failed.

The morning of February 7th passed calmly. The French had previously decided to take the Turks by surprise. All the French positions and mortars would open fire at 8:00, aiming at the Turkish quarter.

The French would strike with all the machine-guns and artillery they possessed.

An awful explosion was heard at the specified time, the like of which had not been heard during the battle of Aintab. Everyone was petrified thinking that a nearby shell had exploded. The Turks, who thought that the French were advancing from every side, started firing randomly and continued for many hours. Consecutive explosions were heard and metal pieces burst everywhere. The hellish detonation of the 15.5cm shells gave the impression of the Day of the Apocalypse. The French surprise attack ceased after 45 minutes but the Turkish gunfire continued for a few hours, and then silence prevailed.

Chapter 25

The Capitulation of the City (February 8th)

On February 8th, two Turkish officials holding a white flag approached the Armenians at Kozanluh and asked the soldiers to guide them to the French command post. They carried a letter addressed to the French command. The Armenian soldiers blindfolded the officials and took them to the command post.

The letter stated:

> To the Command of the French Troops of Aintab,
>
> We ask you to inform us of a convenient time and place where we could meet in order to discuss the terms of the surrender of the city. We additionally request that you provide the necessary guards to guide us from the Kozanluh barricades to your office. Finally, please issue the necessary orders to cease all hostilities.
>
> Signed by the six delegates of the temporary government.

The French asked the couriers where Ozdemir and the mutasarrif were and about their situation. They replied that they had fled, but the Nationalists' Committee (*hiyyetti milliye*) was still in Aintab and willing to receive orders.

The French sent the following letter to the Turks:

> To the President of the Nationalist Committee of Aintab,
>
> A delegation arrived this morning at 10 o'clock and offered, on behalf of the population of Aintab, the capitulation of the city.
>
> We have the honor to inform you that negotiations on the terms of surrender will be held today at 3:00 in the afternoon (February 8th). The negotiators will come to the Kozanluh barricades, where they will be welcomed by an officer representing the French command, and a squad of soldiers will accompany them as far as the French command post.
>
> It is desirable for the sake of the Turkish people and the Nationalists' Committee that the delegates have the authority to accept our terms.
>
> We have ordered the cessation of all hostilities once the white flag is raised over the fortress by the Turks.
>
> Colonel Abady and Colonel Andrea

At the specified time, the Turkish delegation comprising Dr. Mejid, Dr. Ibrahim, Nuri Bey, Fakhreddin Hoja, Mejdeddin, and Kamil Kulekji arrived at the Kozanluh barricades and were escorted to the French command post.

The President – Dr. Mejid – explained that a revolution has started in the Turkish quarter and that the Nationalists' Committee did not now hold power in the city. Moreover, he stated that Colonel Ozdemir has fled and the remaining officers had lost their authority over the people, whom the delegates represented. They presented their authorization letter signed by the municipal officials and the notables of the city.

Each of the terms were examined carefully and accepted by the Turkish delegates. The conference ended at 6:00. The delegation asked for a chance to present the terms to the people before signing the final document. After getting the consent of the French command, the document stipulating the final capitulation of Aintab was signed on February 9th at 10:00.

This is the translation of that document:

> The Terms of the Surrender of Aintab to the French Authorities
>
> The members of the temporary government of Aintab, elected on behalf of the people, express their loyalty to the French authorities and accept the following terms:
>
> 1. The complete capitulation of the city as stipulated by the Treaty of Sevres signed on August 10th, 1920.
> 2. Turkish regular troops and policemen are prisoners of war and will be released once all the French prisoners captured by the Kemalist forces are set free. Moreover, the soldiers who are natives of Aintab will be set free, after full identity verification. It should be clearly understood that pardon will be granted only to regular soldiers and their officers.
> 3. All weapons, machine-guns, cannons and all kinds of ammunition will be surrendered to the French authorities. If all weapons are handed over, no investigation will be carried out. If the French authorities suspect that any remaining ammunition is being retained, investigations will occur in the presence of Turkish officials. If any weapon is discovered after February 20th, the owner will be severely punished. Turkish officers, however, may keep their weapons.

4. The main Turkish barricades will immediately be destroyed. These will be destroyed by February 20th as indicated by the French. All barricades should be destroyed by February 28th.
5. The French will not demand a war fine or reparations. The cost of damages will be assessed by a mixed committee.
6. Strategic points, deemed essential for the maintenance of order and peace, will be occupied by the French. For example, the fortress, the government building and the peaks of Kurd Tepeh.

   Not a single armed Armenian will enter the Turkish quarters and vice versa.
7. The officials of the Turkish government, operating under French patronage, will be chosen by the French.
8. A police unit will be formed for the maintenance of peace and order in the city.
9. If any of these terms is not implemented, the French will demand a fine, arrest the notables and cease supplying the city.
10. An amnesty will be granted to rebels and Nationalist leaders who are natives of Aintab. Each individual's faith and property will be respected and secured.
11. The terms of this treaty are valid as of today, February 9th, 1921.

– Commander of French Troops, Lieutenant-Colonel Andrea

– Temporary Governor of Aintab, Dr. Mejed

– Commander of the Aintab region, Lieutenant Colonel Abady

– Translator of the Sanjak of Aintab, Mejeddin

– Religious leader, Fakhreddin

– Notables: Dr. Ibrahim, Nuri Bey, Kamil Kulekji.

Once the treaty was signed, Colonel Abady invited the members of the National Union to visit him on the same day at 2:00 in the afternoon. He read them the terms of the capitulation and then discussed the formation of a police force comprising 200 men, 50 of whom would be Armenian.

The Armenians would also participate in governmental affairs, and there would be Armenian officials. The government would operate under

French patronage. The Armenians had to remain calm and peaceful because the French would rule justly and promote equality.

Father Tavoukjian, on behalf of the Armenian National Union, congratulated the French on this achievement and thanked them for all that they had hitherto done to serve the Armenian nation. Moreover, he stated that the Armenians were certain that the French government would take the devotion of the Armenian nation into consideration and protect their rights.

The Colonel thanked the Armenians for their loyalty and asked for their opinion on the following two issues:

1. The Turks demanded the inclusion of Aintab in the sanjak of Beirut, rather than Aleppo, as well as the authority to develop relations with the High Commissioner.
2. The status of Dr. Mejid, the appointed governor of Aintab.

The National Union promised to deliver its response after consultations.

On February 10th the National Union suggested the following names to the Colonel as candidates for offices: 1) Justices of the Peace: Haji Hanifi Zadeh Abdullah Effendi; 2) Mehmed Kheyri Effendi; 3) The appointment of an Armenian as the governor's assistant. The Union also suggested, verbally, the names of the following candidates to office: Nejati Effendi, former judge of the penal court, former governor Sabri, current governor Dr. Mejid and Nimet Effendi from Nizib.

The National Union agreed on the inclusion of Aintab in the Sanjak of Beirut, arguing that the latter possessed a port.

Colonel Andrea ordered the disbandment of the Armenian armed groups, but the Military Body, and the National Union decided to keep a unit of 100 men.

* * *

One of the first tasks of the French command was the provision of supplies to the city. Four tons of flour and one ton of salt were transported to the city square and distributed to the poorest and most starving civilians.

Second, the French formed a government for the city and it's surroundings, appointing Dr. Mejid Bey as its temporary mutasarrif. With the latter's assistance, the French tried to form a police force of natives and then implement the remaining terms of the peace treaty.

The surrender of weapons and ammunition started on February 9th and ended on the 26th. By then, 1,400 rifles, 10 machine-guns, a few handguns, and around 70,000 bullets had been confiscated. The quantity was so small that it was obvious that the Turks possessed a lot more, which was confirmed by Ozdemir's documents. Yet, the French were satisfied with this amount.

Workers started demolishing the barricades and other fortifications under the supervision of French officers. However, this task took longer than expected as the Turks had constructed numerous barricades.

Some workers were sent to neighboring villages to buy supplies for Aintab.

The exchange of prisoners of war was mediated by a special committee and certain Turkish officials. The captives wore red ribbons on their arms.

After the implementation of these terms, permission was granted to the people to start rebuilding their homes and revitalize the city.

During the prisoner exchange, the Turks acted deceitfully and did not surrender some of the high ranking prisoners. Instead, they surrendered a few idiots by forging their identity papers. However, the temporary government received information that these individuals were about to conspire and initiate hostilities anew. They were arrested immediately and handed over to the French. This happened on the night of February 13th.

The number of Turkish prisoners of war was 2,000, of whom only 100 had come from areas outside the Sanjak of Aintab.

On February 26th, 1921, investigations were carried out according to the 3rd article of the treaty, but did not achieve any results.

On the following day the siege was lifted. The formation of the government was very difficult, since all the competent or qualified people had left the city. Some had gone to the villages, others to Aleppo. Thus the French called upon the former officials to return to Aintab and form the administration of the new government. However, the return process went slowly due to the devastation and the harsh winter. One of the first to return was Abdo Effendi, who was called upon, on February 22nd, to accept the position of mutasarrif. He arrived on March 14th. Despite the lack of officials, the formation of the police force was vital. Thus, a group of policemen was formed, under the command of a Turkish officer, comprising 100 Turks and 50 Armenians. Additionally, a municipality was formed that was entrusted with supervising the city's hygiene and some other administrative tasks.

A Health Committee was formed for the treatment of the sick and wounded. Eventually other initiatives were taken to complement the efforts for the implementation of the surrender terms. The Armenians were represented in the new municipality in accordance with their numbers. Turkish and Armenian officials agreed to rule the city justly and maintain peace. However, there was a lack of money. The French command provided 1,000 Ottoman gold liras to contribute to expenditure. Eventually shops opened, trade restarted and villagers started coming to the city. The latter still felt threatened by the Kemalists. Aintab was an isolated region which had submitted to the French. Some of the village chiefs expressed their loyalty to the French, as a way to save those still held as captives, as stipulated by the 2nd article of the treaty. However, the only real loyalty shown to the French was that of the villagers located on the Aintab-Kilis road, since the French trade route passed along it. The capitulation of the city would have been complete once the clearance of chetes from the surrounding villages had been achieved.

On March 8th, 1921, Colonel Andrea's forces withdrew from Aintab and moved towards Kilis and Aleppo.

Lieutenant-Colonel Jay assumed command of the remaining troops in Aintab. The government was barely formed, but the movements of the Kemalist forces in the vicinity increased.

Chapter 26

The Treaty of London and the Evacuation of Aintab

This was the general situation when news about the Treaty of London, signed on March 15th, reached Aintab. According to this treaty, Aintab, Cilicia and Kilis would be evacuated and restored to the Turks.

This news was pasted on the walls and was a great shock to the Turks, who had come to terms with the Armenians and the French. The Armenians got ready for a mass exodus, while the French tried everything to dissuade them, claiming that a French consul would remain in Aintab to safeguard the security of the Armenians after the departure of French troops. They had two months to evacuate the city. However, the French did not grant passports to the Armenians. Then, the director of the American Red Cross in Syria came to Aintab and told the French:

> You do not have the right to obstruct the exodus of an endangered community that wishes to move to a safer place. We, the Americans, have spent millions of dollars to revive this people saved from deserts of Deir-ez Zor. And now it is unacceptable to hand them over to hangmen. We will therefore send our complaints to the American government. Forbidding their departure is a violation of human rights.

Finally, the French granted passports and allowed the departure of 5-6,000 Armenian families.

The evacuation from Aintab continued until January 2nd, 1922, when the last French unit withdrew from Aintab. The remaining Armenians suffered great difficulties after the departure of the French troops. The Turks started pillaging the Armenian quarter at night and murdering people. Their goal was to drive the Armenians out. Finally, after suffering a few losses, the remaining Armenians were transported to Aleppo on Turkish passports.

Francophile Turks left with the Armenians. One of them expressed himself to the French command in this way:

> We are surprised as to how a state can sign a treaty with a chete leader. Who is Kemal Pasha and what is his government? A chete leader and a band of bandits. By a government, we understand an

> organization that works for the welfare a community, whereas Kemal made forests of gallows. Don't you believe me? Talk to a Turk from Pontus or Trabzon and let him tell you of the horrendous slaughter that the Greeks suffered there. And after all this, you sign a treaty with such a government, ignoring the government at Constantinople. How can the Armenians stay here with bloodthirsty Turks? Bloodshed will occur again in this city after your departure. We, the Francophile Turks, decided to cooperate with you, since you encouraged justice and peace for this city. As a result we are looked upon as traitors. What will become of us?

The French commander provided a short reply by stating:

> I personally oppose these arrangements but am obliged to comply by my superiors' commands. We are aware of the situation here, whereas the signatories of this treaty view the entire world and make diplomatic decisions favorable to France and French interests. The Aintab question does not constitute a thousandth part of French policy. Therefore, as a military man, I obey the commands I receive. You are free to come with us to Aleppo.

During this period there was only one Frenchman who voiced his opposition to the French evacuation of Cilicia. He asserted that the officials stationed in France were not able to comprehend the relation between Syria and Cilicia. The latter was necessary for the protection of the former. Destroying it meant undermining French authority over Syria.

This soldier's speculation turned out to be real with the clashes that followed in Syria, causing much material damage and exhausting the French soldiers. We know that some French circles voiced their complaints about the French evacuation of Aintab.

The Damage Caused by the War

Material damage: assessing the material damage caused by the war is impossible. According to the French authorities, their expenses during the war amounted to two-milliard francs, which was a huge figure. Without considering the damage caused to individual moveable and immovable properties, the net amount spent by the National Union was 4,000,000 francs (40,000 Ottoman gold liras). On the other hand, assessing the damage that the Turks suffered is impossible.

5 Jan. 1920, Armenian orphans prior to evacuation.

Casualties: from April 1st, 1920 until February 8th, 1921, the Turks fired 3,898 7.75cm shells, 658 10.5cm shells, and 42 15.5cm shells at Armenian and French positions. The latter suffered 25 dead and 70 wounded, whereas Armenian casualties were 11 dead and 41 wounded. This number excluded the casualties caused by the Turkish bombardment of the French convoys. The overall number of French soldiers killed by bombardment and gunfire was 245, of whom 54 were French, 191 Tunisians, Algerians and Senegalese. Around 7-8,000 were wounded.

The overall number of Armenian casualties was 100, including those killed and wounded. We have already provided the list of those who suffered during the 70 day war.

Turkish casualties are not clear. According to a health official working at the Turkish hospital, their casualties totaled 4,000, whereas according to a municipal report, it was 8,282. Some people claimed this number should have been 15,000, including those who suffered in the vicinity of the city.

However, none of these numbers are reasonable since the Turks did not compile any statistics. The number of army deserters is uncertain and there were no reports on the number of people buried under ruins. Although the final number of the wounded, killed or lost is not clear, we believe that it exceeds 8,000. This is the most reasonable number.

The aftermath of the fighting in Aintab.

The triumph of Kazim Karabekir over the Armenian armies compelled the latter to turn towards the communists as a last resort for the physical security of the Armenian people. This political change troubled the French so that when the Armenian National Union met Colonel Abady, the latter gave them a very indifferent reception. The Colonel even cursed the Armenians of Armenia.

After a few weeks, the Colonel invited Father Tavoukjian to his office and expressed anger, stating that the Armenians were thieves, since an Armenian craftsman had built a table for him and demanded 15 Syrian liras as payment. Moreover, he claimed that Armenian jewelers were mixing copper in gold rings and were selling them as pure gold. He concluded that all the Armenian shopkeepers and businesses were profiteers.

Father Tavoukjian replied:

> Dear Colonel, we are not thieves. Do you know the cost of a ball of wool in the city? Nowadays it's worth one mejidiye, whereas before the war, it was 15 kurush. Do you know how much silk we can make from one ball? Four or five, whereas this flannel that I carry on my back is worth 500 kurush. Hence, you are selling one liter for 10,000 kurush that was worth just 10 and we have never called the Europeans thieves. You have no right to attribute the term "crook or thief" to our people. The Armenian craftsman sells

> you art, rather than wood. You have the freedom to buy it or not. What else do you expect an Armenian craftsman to do, when he has a family of five or six members to feed. A bag of flour worth five kurush after the war is bought today for 75. Such developments are natural in times of war, for which we can blame no one. As a military commander, you have structured your organization on obedience and order. You have the right to punish refractory people by death. Why can't you restrict the theft and embezzlement by your soldiers, when each convoy returns to Aintab with a loss of 2,000 Ottoman gold liras? When you can't even restrain your soldiers, how do you expect a population of 15,000 starving people to behave properly?

After hearing this reasonable answer from the priest, the Colonel dismissed him.

Appended by Translator

SAGA OF BEING A REFUGEE (OR DEPORTEE)

İmanım Mennush took part in heroic self-defense of the Armenian of Aintab and fought heroically. Below, you will see one of her folk poetries, *Saga.*

Listen aghas! Let me recite a saga,
Let me describe the way the world turns,
I died, what would I do with this world,
The sun did descend, the world turned into a dungeon,
Mobilization was announced,
It robbed the Armenians, made him naked,
It made him set off dead end track,
Let's go, Havran became home…

They said: there is not danger in Aintab,
If you mention Zeitun, there has been a lot,
Let alone being an immigrant (deportee), if they die, they deserve it,
It left to the wife, marriage,
Wealthy people were rounded up, came to the palace,
Union and Progress intervened,
They negotiated wheat with money,
The final decision was to deport them,
Memorandums were given out at 3:00pm,
Lamentation reigned in the Armenian house,
Many lives separated from their hearts,
Cry, our harkening left to the judgment day…

Every one went to the grave by crying,
Our houses were scattered into the bazaars,
Turkish women always got into them,
Everybody snatched whatever they found,
They had us set off noon,
They did not let us look around,
There was no remedy except for God,
The army stood up, roads became smoky/foggy,
We arrived at Akçakoyun within two days,
We stayed six days in there,
Wife and children, we all were in need of food,

Only God can help us…

We stepped down to Hama plain at 5pm,
Nobody would not look at the face of a deportee,
They had an eye on Armenian's girls,
Each agha captured one,
We pitched tents for three months in the Hama plain,
There was no kindness in the human face,
We did not see cold water for three months in the summer
My lung burned by drinking boiling water…

Many of deportees lied sick in the tents,
They threw death bodies to the wells,
They [Armenian deportees] sold their children because of hunger,
Many sold their children, help was at the mercy of who bought them,
Hundreds of thousands famished in a day,
Survivors were worse than who died,
Lie did appear three hundred times in a day,
Truth was exhausted, lie became the upper hand,
Ringer was baffled to whom he would bury,
Malady was spread from one person to a thousand,
Many died and they were put in a cart,
A piece of burlap and two sticks,
Coffin was shroud, heart could not bear,
Two persons were needed to hold from the end of the coffin,
It was not found either, the coffin was left homeless…

One morning, gendarmes came,
They destroyed tents around us,
Children were forced to take the road,
Our homeland became Salamiyya,
God damn this German,
May god ruin their fame, reputation,
They became the reason, shed Armenian blood,
Bloody tear reaches to the sea,
We set out of hometown, a stick at our hands,
We were needy of a cup to drink water,
Effendis understand, this was the moral of a story,
People's fate was egregious,
We were devastated us in this desert,
We had to leave our homeland, our property (wealth),

We couldn't recover the misery,
Our grind stone was left to the lamentation,
French, Muscovy, British didn't come,
They made the world wreck, without cave,
Mother, father died, kids were orphans,
Innocent babies were left homeless…

All mothers burst into tears in open space,
Numerous people became homeless,
Huge buildings became wreck,
The world became devastated, left to the furnace,
Our braid hair was shaved,
They would not tell us what our fault was,
Our bible, cross was defeated,
They became masquerader outside,
Our schools, church were locked up,
Our million lives were perished,
May god take our revenge,
Our sharia was left to the supreme court,

Imanian Mennush was the author of this saga,
She would groan day and night,
Please my God help us,
Your sinner servants were at your mercy.

[Translated by Ümit Kurt, Jan. 29, 2018]

ABOUT THE AUTHOR

Ümit Kurt received his PhD from Clark University, History Department in 2016. He got his MA degree in European Studies from Sabancı University in 2008 and undergraduate degree in Political Science from Middle East Technical University in 2006. He taught in the Faculty of Arts and Science in Sabancı University, from 2012 to 2014 and Clark University in 2016-17. In 2014, he was the recipient of Armenian Studies Scholarship Award of Calouste Gulbenkian Foundation. He worked as Kazan Research Associate in the Armenian Studies Program at California State University in 2015-16. Subsequently, he was a Postdoctoral Fellow in the Center for Middle Eastern Studies at Harvard University in 2016-17. He has written extensively on the Armenian genocide, the confiscation of Armenian properties, the transfer of wealth, the transformation of space, mass violence, inter-ethnic conflict, local historiography, early modern Turkish nationalism and the Aintab Armenians. He is the author of 'Türk'ün Büyük, Biçare Irkı': *Türk Yurdu'nda Milliyetçiliğin Esasları (1911-1916)*, (İletişim, 2012) and the editor of *Kıyam ve Kıtal: Osmanlı'dan Cumhuriyet'e Devletin İnşası ve Kolektif Şiddet*, (Tarih Vakfı, 2015). He is also the author, with Taner Akçam, of *The Spirit of the Laws: The Plunder of Wealth in the Armenian Genocide*, (New York and Oxford: Berghahn Books, 2015). He translated two books from Armenian to Turkish: *Antep'in Varoluş Mücadelesi* (authored by A. Gesar; Belge, 2016) and *Günlüğümden Sayfalar* (authored by Nerses Babaian; Tarih Vakfı, 2017). His articles have appeared in *Nations and Nationalism*, *Middle Eastern Studies*, *British Journal of Middle Eastern Studies*, *The Journal of Genocide Research*, *Genocide Studies International*, *Patterns of Prejudice*, *Holocaust and Genocide Studies*, *Journal of Armenian Studies* and *Balkan and Near Eastern Studies*. He is currently working as a Polonsky Fellow at the Polonsky Academy for Advanced Study in the Humanities and Social Sciences in the Van Leer Jerusalem Institute.

INDEX

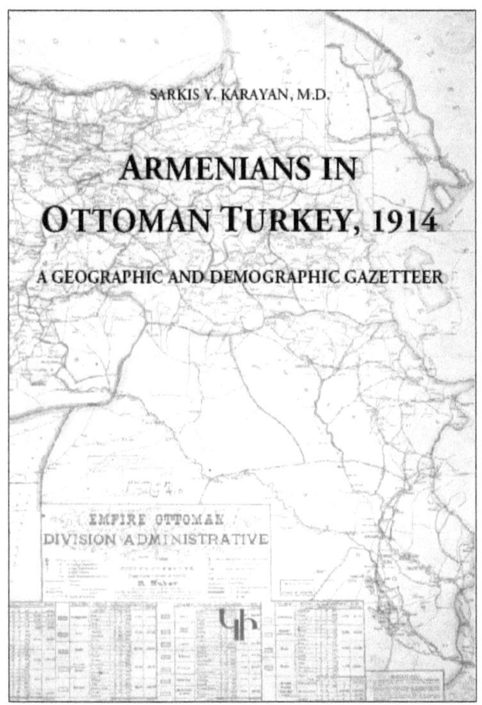

"An authoritative, mammoth work, listing 4,000 Armenian communities in the Ottoman Empire with maps, statistics and further information."

Sarkis Y. Karayan, *Armenians in Ottoman Turkey, 1914: A Geographic and Demographic Gazeteer*, (London: Gomidas Institute, 2018), 640 pp., maps, photos, index, pb., ISBN 978-1-909382-42-8

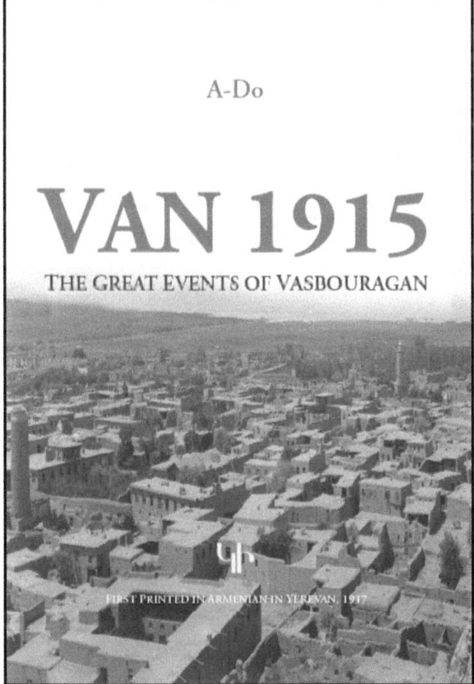

"The single-most important report on the historic events that unfolded in Van 1915. Originally published in 1917."

A-Do, *Van 1915: The Great Events of Vasbouragan*, translated from Armenian by Ara Sarafian with historical introduction by Rouben Gasparyan and Rouben Sahakyan, (London: Gomidas Institute, 2017), 345 pp., maps, photos, index, pb. ISBN 978-1-909382-37-4.

For more information visit *www.gomidas.org* or contact *info@gomidas.org*

"The most important work about the Armenian Genocide by a US diplomat since Henry Morgenthau'sgroundbreaking Ambassador Morgenthau's Story *in 1918."*

John M. Evans, Former US Ambassador to Armenia, *Truth Held Hostage: America and the Armenian Genocide - What Then? What Now?* with a foreword by Dr. Dickran Kouymjian (London: Gomidas Institute, 2016), 200 pp, maps, photos, index, hb. ISBN 978-1-909382-26-8

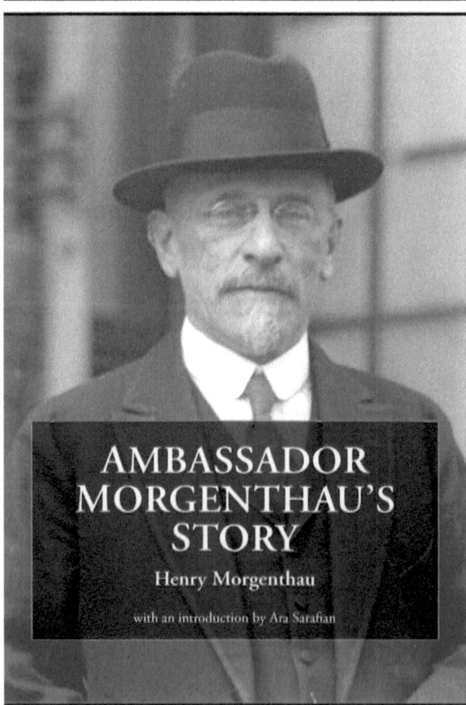

"A classic, authoritative account of the Armenian Genocide originally printed in 1918."

Henry Morgenthau, *Ambassador Morgenthau's Story*, (London: Gomidas Institute, 2016), 310 pp, maps, photos, index, pb. ISBN 978-1-909382-21-3, paperback

For more information visit *www.gomidas.org* or contact *info@gomidas.org*

www.ingramcontent.com/pod-product-compliance
Ingram Content Group UK Ltd.
Pitfield, Milton Keynes, MK11 3LW, UK
UKHW041857190726
13854UKWH00002B/954